BROWN'S NOT FOR TOWN

I don't mind failing in this world

Somebody else's definition isn't going to measure my soul's condition

I don't mind failing in this world, when you are who you are

Every morning, when you wake up, you put on a new disguise

Just how long did you think it would take me to realise?

That the things you were ain't real, you never tell me just how you feel

When you could be so very beautiful, if you are who you are

Yeah, when you are who you are

I don't mind failing in this world, Paul Weller (P. Weller)

BROWN'S NOT FOR TOWN

A PERSONAL JOURNEY THROUGH 40 YEARS IN BANKING

Copyright © 2024 Graham Pannett

First published in Great Britain in 2024 by Bo The Dog Press. All rights reserved. No part of this publication may be reproduced, stored in a retrieval system, or transmitted, in any form or by any means without the prior permission of the publisher, nor be circulated in any form of binding or cover other than that in which it is published and without similar condition being imposed on the subsequent purchaser.

A catalogue record for this book is available from the British Library

ISBN : 9798867149239

graham.pannett@beyoutoday.co.uk

To Dad, Grandpa, Uncle Rod, Dickie & Aunty Audrey

If there's Wi-Fi up there, can one of you let me know

and I'll send you the link to Amazon

Preface

After being made redundant one miserable afternoon in November 2021, not unlike my start in banking, I found myself writing 'Brown's not for Town' before I'd given it too much thought. And, after a lifetime of having a purpose for getting up in the morning, I needed something to do to keep me busy as I started a few months' 'gardening leave'.

Trawling back through so many years of the memory bank has been challenging (I can't remember where I was last Tuesday sometimes) but I've done my absolute best to accurately describe the events, dates, and people although naturally my recollection of some of this has faded over time. Everyone I mention is a real person, albeit I have changed their names in some instances.

In the 18 months it's taken me to complete Brown's Not For Town, I've spent countless hours sitting at home, in coffee shops, in the pub, and even while waiting for my chiropractor appointments, and I'm still not sure whether it's any good, but hey, I've done my best, and that's all I can do. Regardless, I've enjoyed writing about my experiences, and more importantly, I sincerely hope that you enjoy reading about them

Introduction

'Come in Smithers old boy, take a seat, take the weight off your feet, I've some news to tell you, there's no longer a position for you. Sorry Smithers Jones'

'So what do you think of the new structure?' the boss asked as I sat in his pristine but soulless office, devoid of any personalisation by two years of COVID-induced emptiness and prior to that, a lack of any effort.

'Underwhelming, to be honest,' I said, 'it looks very much like the current setup up, and there only seems to be a nominal reduction in the number of Directors across the country.'

As usual, it felt like he'd ignored my response as he proceeded to explain he'd be reading from a pre-prepared script; standard stuff to keep the boys from the Unions and the gals from HR happy. 'Of course, any restructure like this is always done for strong commercial reasons but also to preserve jobs whenever possible' he explained, before going into detail that I'd already heard on the conference call held the previous afternoon to announce the changes; familiar words, same old, same old. In my boredom, I drifted off to thinking about Chelsea's Champions League game against AC Milan that evening, the reason why I'd bothered coming into London for the meeting rather than doing it over Zoom.

'And so, as a result of these changes, you no longer have a position within the organisation.'

BOOM!

'Sorry Robin, could you please repeat that last bit?' I asked, genuinely not believing I'd heard him correctly.

He told me again. I had heard him correctly. Bugger.

Well, I wasn't expecting that. Less than half an hour beforehand, I was travelling from my home in Hampton to the regional office in Oxford Street, planning how I would get to each of my new branches when I was appointed as the new Director of the new West London Area. I'd even enjoyed the journey as, only a short time after the last round of COVID restrictions had been lifted, it had been the first time I'd ventured into London for many months and I'd felt the excitement of a kid going on a big train for his first school trip. But any enthusiasm had now turned into a feeling of shock and my head was fuzzy with news I hadn't expected, although I did manage to work out that I was most likely the only one of my peer group in this predicament.

'So effectively, you're telling me that I'm the most shit Director in your team and that you're sacking me?' I said.

'No, I'm not telling you that you're my most shit Director and no, I'm not sacking you, but I am telling you that you don't have a role in the new structure' he replied, with an air of smug correctness, like someone who'd actually managed to get a question correct on 'Only Connect'. I thought of asking for clarification about the actual difference between his and my definition of the situation, as the outcome of both seemed worryingly similar, but I decided against entering into a futile debate that would no doubt end up, as usual, with me being wrong and him being right.

With my head still spinning, I asked a couple of further pointless questions, neither of which I remember, let alone the answers, and all I could muster in response was 'OK, thanks', as I stood up, put my hand out to shake his, and started to walk out.

'Oh, and by the way, you're not allowed to discuss your situation with anyone else for the time being' he instructed. Again, I thought about seeking clarification, of asking how long 'the time being' might be but knew that he wouldn't be able to tell me, so I just continued for the door.

Numbed by the news I'd just been given, I trudged back into the reception area to collect my coat, literally and now metaphorically. Two of the regional team, Sharon and Simon, noses to their desks, ignored me in an uncomfortable statement of 'We know what's just happened, but we really don't want to talk to you about it'.

'See ya,' I said, punctuating the painful silence, and shuffled off into the November cold of London's West End. As the door closed behind me, I wondered whether they'd already blocked my security pass in anticipation of me never returning.

It was 2 p.m. I decided to head for the warmth and solace of a boozer and ended up in the Red Lion pub in Duke of York Street, far enough away from the office and a familiar haunt from years before. I've always enjoyed my own company, especially when shared with a drink of some description. I sat in the buzzy atmosphere of the old-fashioned, wooden-floored pub, supping on my first pint of Camden Pale Ale, and pondered on the prospect of not having a job in a High Street bank for the first time in over 40 years. As I tucked into my second, the realisation that at the age of 57, I had been tossed onto the 'not wanted' pile became a more painful reality and by the time I was on my third, I found myself wondering how on earth I'd ended up spending a whole life working in High Street banking and questioning whether it had been worth it.

Part 1

The 'Life Before Banking' years

(1964-1981)

1
'Playground kids and creaking swings'

As Frankie Valli and his Four Seasons proclaimed *'Oh, what a night.* Late December back in '63, what a very special time for me, as I remember what a night' Well, whether my Dad did *'feel a rush like a rollin' ball of thunder'*, I neither know nor cared to find out, but nine months later, late September back in '64, I was born in a small cottage hospital on the North bank of the River Thames at Hampton Court. Apart from the obvious significance to me, 1964 was memorable for many reasons — it was the year of Beatlemania, the year in which the American Civil Rights Movement gained significant momentum, and the year that the first episode of *Thunderbirds* was screened; Please, Please Me, I Have a Dream, FAB Virgil.

My parents grew up in Southampton, and met when they were both in the Navy and subsequently married. They moved to the 'big smoke' when Dad was offered the chance to relocate with his job and bought a typically suburban three-bedroom terraced house in Twickenham, not much more than a loud *'Swing-Low, Sweet Chariot'* from the home of England rugby. Soon after, my sister, Sue, was born, and so my appearance three years later completed the stereotypical nuclear family: two kids, a back garden with a swing, a front garden with a fishpond, gnomes, and dahlias, and Dad's mauve Ford Anglia Estate company car parked in our quiet street of other three bedroom terraced houses and Ford Anglias.

Dad was a chocolate salesman for Cadbury's. The Anglia covered several miles as he travelled between sweet shops across West London, helping the local shopkeepers order their chocolate supplies and arranging for them to be delivered in due course. He would carry samples or excess stock that, luckily for

Sue and me, would often end up back at our house. Boxes of the bloody stuff. Although unaware of it then, this availability of copious amounts of *Crunchie* and *Dairy Milk* enhanced my popularity at school and definitely with my mate Vince. He was unashamedly extra keen to come to my house in the lead-up to every Easter, in order to satiate his obsession with *Creme Eggs*. From February to April each year, about 600 of the little blighters were hidden under Mum's well-used Hostess Trolley in our dining room. In truth, they weren't *that* well hidden as I knew where they were, and Vince definitely did. I remember when we challenged each other to eat ten eggs in one session, and, probably for the better, neither he nor I achieved the feat. We did both eat seven once, which was still a stupid thing to do, especially if you were an 11-year-old boy — overindulging and being sick is one thing, but that's nothing compared to the impact this amount of chocolate consumption has on male adolescent skin; the eruption of a creme egg-induced spot is volcano-like in its ferocity and just as messy. Vince had striking ginger hair in an era when being ginger was almost classed as a recognised disability, so despite his love for those sickly little things, April was always a self-induced tough month for him.

Mum held various bookkeeping jobs over the years, and also, for a short time, for a bank. It amazed me that she ever had the time to hold down a position at all, as, in addition to bringing up Sue and me, she was involved in so many other activities, helping so many people, whether that be raising money for our school, running the local floristry club or just generally doing stuff for people who needed stuff doing. As I write this, I expect she is arranging the next race night or charity coffee morning for the folks at her senior living apartments in Weybridge.

My Primary School years were mostly spent during the nineteen-seventies, which, despite *Glam Rock* being one of the prevailing music genres, was a decade anything but glamorous. Memorable for the rise of football hooliganism, worldwide terrorism, three-day working weeks, and constant strikes leading to frequent power cuts and streets full of uncollected, rat-infested rubbish bags, it was a difficult period to feel nostalgic about. Many people who lived through it didn't realise exactly how shit it was until hindsight gave them clarity many years later. Having said that, a decade that spawned the *Ford Capri Mk 2*, *Concorde*, and, most importantly, *The Jam*, can't have been too bad.

In any case, most of the challenges weren't relevant enough to bother a child growing up, and some became just as much fun as they were a problem — a power cut would often mean leaving school early, and Sue and I playing board games by candlelight as Mum cooked dinner using a calor gas stove. And even though my hatred of liver and bacon stemmed from those butane-powered evenings, I remember them being fun, unless I lost at *Mousetrap* or *Ker-Plunk*, in which case I got the right hump, even had a little cry; I never have been a good loser.

We had friends with more money than we did, but we never missed out on anything we really needed or wanted. We were usually allowed to do whatever we wanted and always felt safe and happy. We were loved, and we knew it, and we also knew that we were lucky. Even if Vince's dad did drive a Jag.

We were fortunate to have regular weekends away and long summer holidays. Despite moving to London, my parents had kept the two caravans they had bought some years earlier at a site in New Milton in the New Forest. The park has been significantly developed since the days of basic toilet blocks, decrepit swings, and a really crap clubhouse. Still, I wasn't bothered by the old-school, crude facilities, not even having to wipe my arse with sandpaper. I thought the place was magical. We would go there most weekends, and, as all of my grandparents still lived in nearby Southampton, we would pop in to see them either on the way there or when travelling back home. Being an era of almost no technology whatsoever when compared to today, we had to make our own fun so if ever I dared to suggest to Dad that I was bored, he would merely chuck me out of the van with a football or a bat and ball and tell me to go and find some other boys for a game of something. I invariably did, usually until I wandered home much later in the day, content, knackered, and probably with a re-match arranged for the following day. Unless I'd lost, then I'd have a little cry. (But still be back the next day.)

If we weren't going to the caravan park during the summer, we'd be on holiday at my great aunt's place in Paignton, South Devon. Travelling there involved a nearly five-hour drive throughout the night to miss the holiday traffic and the inevitable, indeed obligatory two-hour queue past Stonehenge. I suffered from travel sickness, so a mauve Ford Anglia parked up on a grass verge on the A303 at 3 a.m. with a skinny eight-year-old kid dribbling sick down his favourite cheesecloth shirt, was a regular sight, despite Mum's blatant lie that marmalade sandwiches would make it better. They never did, but that didn't matter to me. I loved Devon and still do.

Paignton had a massive beach, a couple of crazy golf courses, a steam train, and an ice cream parlour called *The Igloo*, the best I'd ever been to; a young child's heaven. There was also a pier with a theatre to which my sister and I were taken on many evenings to a show, full of the stars of the day; going to your fourth *Bachelor's* concert before your ninth birthday is a strange achievement, but it certainly gave me an insight into the quirky Irish pop-folk music scene as well as that of middle-aged women physically swooning at the presence of two brothers and another bloke with really shit haircuts; a bit like an early version of *Bros*.

We enjoyed many of the big musical names of the time, all of whose vinyl records can still be easily found at any good boot fair. We were also entertained by the some of the comedians of the day, like Ken Dodd and Mike Yarwood, who I'd seen on the tele and whom Dad told me were very funny. We also saw Rolf Harris.

Our holiday accommodation was unconventional. My great aunty Connie was the matron of a retirement home called Fernham. She lived in a flat upstairs with enough spare rooms for all of us, so if I wasn't on the pier enjoying sophisticated and frequently racist seventies humour, I would spend my August evenings watching *Its a Knockout** and playing cards with old age pensioners, many of whom had dementia. When I returned to Fernham each year, I would be confused why only a few residents remembered me and why some had since 'moved out' when they had promised me they would still be there. And while I would never make light of that horrible disease, it was undoubtedly helpful when you're desperate to win a game of gin rummy.

I've seen at close hand the devastation that dementia causes, including my grandfather and my aunt. My mum, my sister, and I watched Dad die of losing his marbles over a four year period, not helped by his incapacity due to a major stroke a few years earlier. He always held back on emotion and often seemed to prefer his own company to anyone else's, but that was OK, we knew what he was like, and there was no reason to let that be a problem. But his dementia took hold of his angry self and his frustration turned into bile, which, unfortunately, Mum was on the receiving end of many times during her daily visits to see him in various hospitals and the care homes that he hadn't been banned from for abusive language. He accused me of many things in his last few months, including never really loving him, trying to kill him, and not being as good a cricketer as I thought I was. That last one really hurt. I'm pleased I didn't take any of it *too* seriously and was able to write most of it off as a symptom of his illness. Mum was less able to ignore his ramblings, not least when he was in Teddington Memorial Hospital for about six weeks. Every afternoon when she would visit him, the conversation would follow the same pattern.' Hi Mike, how are you today?'

'All right, I suppose,' he'd grunt. 'I was seen by Desmond Tutu again.'

'Don't be silly Mike, of course you weren't,' Mum would reply. 'Here, have another *Jaffa Cake*.'

I would often pop in later in the afternoon and see them both, Dad miserable and propped up in his bed, Mum wonderfully caring but outrageously tired for being there so often and for so long. 'How's it going?' I'd ask rhetorically, hoping he hadn't been too caustic during the day.

'Well, your dad has been looked after by Desmond Tutu again,' said Mum, winking at me while Dad lay there nodding in agreement. It's a delicate balance when you're watching a loved one drift away with dementia — do you disagree with them when they talk nonsense in the vain hope that the challenge suddenly makes their thinking clearer, or do you accept what they say, agree, and move on to the next inane conversation? Mum, in her desperation to keep him with us, usually chose the former approach. 'Don't be so stupid, Mike; Desmond is in South Africa, not Teddington.'

I was happier to let him believe it was true, along with a few of his other strange beliefs. I didn't see the point in arguing, as there could never be a winner. Not long before he died, I walked out of the ward with tears in my eyes after a particularly challenging visit. As I made my way along the corridor, I saw a small black man, wearing a brightly coloured 'tribal' shirt and black trousers skipping towards me. I stopped, literally open-mouthed, and pointed at him.

'Desmond Tutu' I mouthed.

'No,' he replied, 'I'm Doctor Olawusu, but many people think I do look like him,' he said as he hopped off towards the ward. I never did get to tell Dad that I had met his Dancing Bishop, but it makes me smile to think that even in his most difficult times, he kept his sense of humour.

*When I said *It's a Knockout*, I refer of course to the more glamorous European version, *Jeux sans Frontieres*, an extravaganza of ludicrous games played in even more ludicrous outfits. I think that even the most die-hard Brexiteer would struggle to argue that ten-foot chefs flipping three-foot pancakes while rotating on a massive greased-up turntable in the middle of a German castle wasn't far more impressive than four fat blokes wearing string vests having a tug-of-war competition in a muddy field in Cleethorpes.

Like my weekends at the caravan, I spent most of my time in Paignton playing sports. Rain was the only thing that could ruin proceedings, as this would usually result in Sue and me being bundled into the Anglia (or any one of the subsequent Cadbury Company cars, including, over the years, several *Ford Escorts*, two *Ford Cortinas*, a *Morris Marina*, a *Hillman Avenger*, and a couple of *Vauxhall Cavaliers*) and taken to some 'interesting place' or another. We visited several interesting places, with a trip to a pottery in the middle of bloody nowhere being a Pannett family favourite —Mum's extensive collection of Devon-blue milk jugs and salt and pepper shakers still reminds me of the countless afternoons spent in middle-of-nowhere places like Bovey Tracey and Cockington Forge with me endlessly staring into the sky, literally begging for the sun to come out.

My hours of practice on beaches, at caravan sites, and at my local park whenever I could, resulted in me graduating to formal local teams in football, table tennis, and cricket, the latter, it turned out, I had a talent for. I became one of the better players at The Heathfield Junior School and got put forward to the Richmond Borough team and, at the age of ten, I got scouted to play for Middlesex County Colts. Playing for Middlesex was special, but going to practice nets was less so, mainly because the cricket school was based in Finchley, meaning Dad would have to drive me up the North Circular Road every Friday night for the best part of five years. If you know the route, you'll fully appreciate the rush-hour joy of Staples Corner and Hangar Lane; it was a weekly experience that meant I would think twice before moaning about my kids asking me to take them somewhere just down the road.

As well as playing sport, I was also lucky to be taken to watch it. When my parents moved, Dad wanted to find a nearby first division football team to support, as travelling back every other week to watch Southampton wasn't logistically doable. On his first Saturday in London, Chelsea were playing at home, Fulham were playing away. Thank goodness. He bought a season ticket for Stamford Bridge and another one a few years later to share between Sue and me; my first game was in 1969, we beat Arsenal 2-1, I was blown away by the whole experience, and I've been going there ever since.

2

'Life is timeless days are long when you're young'

When Mum and Dad were deciding what comprehensive school they wanted me to go to, travel time was clearly not one of their selection criteria, as my journey to 'big school' ended up being either a 40-minute cycle ride or even longer on the ridiculously long-winded 281 bus route. Fortunately, a few old mates from primary school, including Vince, had also been sent there, which helped me get used to the new surroundings, even if both the buildings and the fifth formers were enormous and intimidating. Teddington School for Boys considered itself sports-based, so in between *Great Expectations*, algebraic equations, and dissecting rats in a laboratory, I played plenty of it and managed to get into the school football team and stay in it throughout my time at school. I wasn't the best player, but I wasn't the worst either; that particular accolade was Ed's.

I'd become friendly with Ed, and one Friday, not long into the new term, he asked me if I wanted to go ice skating the following day at Richmond ice rink. I thought it was kind of him and said yes. Call it fate, but that invitation shaped my life and took it in a specific direction, and I don't just mean anti-clockwise, the standard skating route at all UK ice rinks.

Mum had first taken me skating when I was about five. Sue was having ice dancing lessons, and I was made to tag along. Like most people when they first step onto an ice rink, including I'm sure both Jayne Torvill and Christopher Dean, I managed a convincing impression of a newborn giraffe wearing blue plastic boots, falling over, getting back up, falling over again; I quickly learned that freshly compacted ice is hard and wet.

I'm convinced that my sister was laughing at me as Mum, who could at least shuffle around the rink, instructed me to reach up and grab hold of the rubber ledge across the top of the side barrier with one hand and cling to her leather driving glove-clad hand with the other. After about half an hour of dragging myself once around the rink, to put me out of my misery Mum suggested that it might be a better idea if we stopped for a while and had a hot chocolate in the cafeteria while Sue finished off her lesson of pirouettes, triple-salchows, and double toe loops.

Now, seven or so years later, I was trying again with my new mate Ed. The embarrassing and painful memories became more vivid when he turned up holding his own skates, and I realised exactly why he'd invited me. I was still useless, although I did get marginally better as the two hour-long session progressed. At one point, I may have even started to enjoy it but that positivity was overshadowed by my all-consuming envy of Ed and the other boys who skated quickly, elegantly, and arrogantly around the rink. They were permanently surrounded by girls and I desperately wanted to be like them. The fact that Ed was crap at football no longer seemed important. It certainly wasn't to Ed.

Unlike the graceful and pretty figure skating I'd watched my sister learn, these guys were hockey skating. The skates are different, as is the technique — it's more aggressive, dangerous, and, of course, much more macho. Figure skaters come to a stop by pressing a dainty, jagged skate toe into the ice, whereas hockey skaters do it by going as fast as they can and then, at the last minute, violently digging their skates into the ice at a 45-degree angle, creating a massive spray of ice. The bigger the spray, the more impressive it was. Sound familiar?

I started going to the rink every Saturday, sometimes with Ed, sometimes with Vince (who was worse than me), and even sometimes on my own. I went during the school holidays and found out that there were job opportunities available, including sweeping up the rubbish after each session, for which you would get paid with a free skate pass; so began a predictable and regular rhythm — sweep, skate, sweep, skate, sleep.

After months of bashed knees and dented pride, I eventually earned the right to hang around with Ed and the cool guys, so I was now in a position to start impressing the girls, many of whom were hanging on to the barrier like I had years before, although not with their Mums, that would be weird. Attempts to engage with the fairer sex included several techniques, not least the romantic act of spraying them with ice or cutting them up like a Range Rover driver at the end of a dual carriageway on the A303. The most effective manoeuvre of all was the 'removal of the comb from the jeans back pocket' trick. Brightly coloured combs nestling in girls' arse pockets were actually a thing back in the late seventies and early eighties, so if you fancied the girl (or just a new comb), you would skate past the unsuspecting victim, grabbing the comb as you did and then disappearing off into the distance, looking back with a cheeky, spotty-faced grin. Ice Rink etiquette demanded that you return the comb to its owner shortly afterwards, which gave you the opportunity, should you wish to take it, to weave your magic. It might have been more effort than swiping left or right, but it burned more calories. However, unless you were at the rink in Nottingham (not only the home of Torville and Dean but also famous for allegedly having a ratio of four women for every fella), there just weren't enough girls to go around. So, Richmond ice rink became a courting battlefield, forcing otherwise socially inept blokes to learn even more tricks and skate more dangerously in an attempt to look more fabulous than everyone else; *peacocks on blades*.

But, regardless of how impressive your 'barrel-rolls' were or how slick your comb-stealing ability was, constantly lurking at the back of all teenage male, recreational skaters' minds was the spectre of their nemesis, the junior ice hockey player, God-like beings who had no need to steal any hair care products, nor bother doing any skating tricks. They didn't even have to be on the ice; the mere act of sauntering through the rink with their Bauer kit bag on their shoulder looped over their Koho hockey stick would be enough to make most ice rink girls go weak at their wooly leg-warmer-covered knees. I'd been fascinated by ice hockey ever since watching the Soviet 'Red Machine' bulldozing its way to one of many gold medals at the Winter Olympics in Sapporo in 1972. I was also intrigued by the bobsleigh and the luge, so much so that I practiced my own 'sliding' down the stairs on a tray —it may not have been as impressive as the actual olympians, but I became the 9, Gloucester Road, Twickenham champion and, whatever happens, nobody can ever take that away from me.

Occasionally, when sweeping up, I would watch the ice hockey team practicing. It was brutal but breathtaking to watch; football, cricket, and table tennis were suddenly completely dull in comparison. Eventually, after endlessly nagging a guy called Ned who was good mates with Tony, the team coach, I got him to ask whether I could go for a trial. Tony said yes and that it would be the following Saturday night at 11 p.m. after the rink had closed to the public. In what turned out to be a lifetime habit, I arrived about an hour earlier than I needed to, just in case the bus broke down or I got lost going to a place I'd been to hundreds of times before. In the end, I was grateful for the extra time as it took me ages to put on the kit I had borrowed from Ned as I struggled to fathom out where all the protective bits fitted. Eventually, I waddled onto the smooth, fresh ice, looking less like a macho sportsman and more like a pissed Michelin Man. I followed Tony and my new teammates in a skate around the rink, nothing too strenuous until he barked the order to 'hit the ice' as I crouched in amazement as the other 20 guys started doing press-ups. Bugger that, I could hardly do them in normal circumstances, let alone on ice with all this garb on.

After a few further exercises, we moved into a practice *scrimmage*, the ice hockey term for a practice match. We played, I got smashed to pieces, but it was brilliant. 'You're in,' Tony said as we skated off, 'assuming you're still up for it?'

'Of course I am.' I replied, barely able to get the words out due to a lack of breath but also in my total excitement.

'I'll see you next week and we'll get you fully signed up,' he said, as he disappeared into the early morning darkness of the near-empty Richmond Ice Rink car park.

It turned out that getting 'fully' signed up meant agreeing to buy the required kit, that even secondhand would cost around £300, probably the equivalent of a small car in today's money. It also meant paying the annual membership fee of £100 plus the weekly subs of £10. And I had to sign a piece of paper saying that if I got mashed into a pulp, it was no one else's fault but my own. At least that bit didn't cost a fortune. I made an appointment at the Bank of Mum and Dad, submitted an application for a personal loan, which they agreed to, and, without leaving a footprint on my credit history that didn't actually exist at the time.

I played for the *Phoenix Flyers* for about three years, graduating from what was called the 'Pee Wees' up to the 'Junior Team' and loved every scary and adrenaline-fuelled minute until a rather unforgiving goon decided to take me out at the knee one very late Saturday night in Grimsby. From that moment, I could never skate quite as well, and, along with regularly getting home from games at four in the morning, it became difficult to continue playing. It had been brilliant while it lasted and was undoubtedly the coolest thing I'd ever done, or have since. I still love watching ice hockey, always with a hint of regret that I didn't, or couldn't, carry on for longer. I also feel a little guilty that I never repaid Mum and Dad, albeit that doesn't bother me quite as much.

I also wonder whether my life would have taken a different path if I hadn't also given up playing cricket. I was progressing well at Middlesex, including going on a successful tour of the Midlands when I ended up rooming with a 13-year-old Phil 'The Cat' Tufnell. He might not have been as famous or wild back then, but he was still good company. But, despite taking plenty of wickets and occasionally scoring some runs, by age 15, I had started to lose interest, not least because I'd found other pastimes, including spending time with the fairer sex. Dad said nothing when I told him I wanted to stop playing, but I knew he was disappointed —I didn't blame him as he had invested so many hours on the North Circular Road, taking me to training and all over the country to matches. I don't remember Tuffers being much better than me, and *he* became an international cricketer, so who knows what might have been? Having said that, I'm nowhere near as funny as he is, and I certainly wouldn't have made it on to *A Question of Sport*, let alone become *'The King of the Jungle'*. Then again, there's little point in wondering *'what if?'* *If* my aunty Audrey had bollocks, she would have been my uncle Derek, but she didn't, so she wasn't.

Before I stopped skating completely, I nicked a comb from the back pocket of a girl who was wearing a lovely pair of Pepe jeans. When I skated back to talk to her, I found out was called Lisa. We've been married for 31 years.

3

'And when I lie on my pillow at night, I dream I could fight like David Watts'

Maybe I'm an exception, but I enjoyed senior school and was one of the few disappointed people when it came to an end; it wasn't such a hardship being around your mates, spending large chunks of the day playing sports and picking on the smaller kids, and it required very little thought from one day to the next. But now the real world was beckoning, and as much as I liked the idea of spending the rest of my life playing and going to football and listening to The Jam and Bob Marley, I was rapidly reaching the point when I needed to make some decisions about what I was going to do with my life. Or, at least, how I was going to start.

Although taking 'A' levels was an option, that felt like it was delaying the inevitable unless I was aiming to go to university, which I definitely wasn't. Uni wasn't for people like me —in the early eighties, going there still seemed to be an entitlement of the super-intelligent, which I wasn't, or the super-wealthy, which my parents definitely weren't. Besides, the lure of earning money and becoming more independent was too strong so I decided that I wanted to leave the world of education and join the world of work. But to do what? I loved the idea of being a musician but, as cool as that might have been, any attempt to learn an instrument had failed miserably, primarily due to having a lack of any real talent and also a music teacher called Mr. Tickle whose ill-fitting toupee and propensity to spit made concentrating, and therefore learning, impossible. The best I could ever muster was a crap rendition of *Go and Tell Aunt Nancy* on the recorder and I didn't think that would be sufficient to secure a lucrative recording contract with Island Records.

Despite my old man's incredible practical ability (I reckon he could have made a football out of a plank of wood), doing a trade was equally out of the question for me as I was hopeless with my hands, confirmed by less-than-impressive school performances when I attempted to make a pair of salad servers in woodwork which ended up looking more like a baby's knife and fork and in metalwork, a weather vain which didn't actually move, even on the windiest of days. I never spoke to him about what I should do for work as we didn't have that kind of relationship. I wish we had, not necessarily to get any specific direction from him but to understand why he didn't enjoy his seemingly straightforward and stress-free life selling chocolate. Maybe he would have advised me to do something I was fundamentally interested in, or that paid serious money. I ended up doing neither.

I'm not sure why I thought Mum would be qualified to provide sound career advice. Still, I asked her what she thought I should do, and she suggested I join a bank, mainly because she had previously worked for one and so it seemed like a good idea. And when subsequently, Mr Neal, my PE teacher who doubled-hatted as the school Careers Adviser, wholeheartedly supported her recommendation, my fate was sealed. In retrospect, that this careers lesson took place in the school sports hall and he spent more time talking about the following Tuesday's cricket match, I probably should have heard the warning bell telling me I was blindly stumbling into something I had no idea about. But I didn't, and again, it's far too late now.

To Mum's amazement, and to mine, I managed ten 'O' level passes (none of this easy GCSE nonsense), proof that listening to John Peel and David Rodigan playing New Wave, Punk, and Reggae until the early hours of most mornings isn't necessarily a bad thing for one's education. In fact, I can categorically say that passing my English Language exam was entirely because I *had* done that, gambling that the person who marked my essay wasn't familiar with the catalogue of work by Paul Weller: '*Write a story about being afraid,*' it said on the front of the exam paper, which I proceeded to do by weaving in the full lyrics of '*Down in the Tube Station at Midnight*' by *The Jam* into an otherwise bland few pages.

'*The smell of brown leather, it blended in with the weather, it filled my eyes, ears nose and mouth, it blocked all my senses, couldn't see, hear, speak any longer*' must have sent the bloke marking it absolutely *Garrity*. I'll have an 'A' grade, thank you very much.

'So, Mum, how do I get a job in a bank?' I asked.

'Well, maybe you should write to a few of them to find out whether they're interested in employing you,' she replied.

Good point, I thought, as I realised that I'd not, until that point, considered I would actually have to do anything to get a job; Mr Neal certainly hadn't mentioned it, although he did blame me for losing the post-career-lesson cricket match for bowling too short.

Without using any Paul Weller lyrics whatsoever, I hand-wrote four standard 'Please may I have an interview with you as I'm a good bloke' letters and sent them off, first class of course, to the Big Four banks as they were known at a time when the UK financial system was worryingly uncluttered with any healthy competition. It wasn't long afterwards that a couple of them replied, including Mum's previous employer, and before I had the chance to think for one last time about what I was doing, I was heading towards somewhere called Cannon Street for my very first job interview. A few days before the big day, I had panicked when I realised that I didn't have the faintest idea what an interview was nor what I was supposed to do or say at one. I had my biggest meltdown when I started to think about what I was supposed to wear. Still finding its own identity following the outrageous fashion cock-up of the seventies, the early eighties was experimenting with pastel colours, double-breasted suits, shoulder pads, and leisure wear, in some cases all at the same time. It was genuinely awful in retrospect but, at the time, believing itself to be the dog's bollocks, as I thought were my new pride and joys, my brown leather tasselled loafers that I'd bought in Richmond the previous week. They were the coolest and most expensive item of clothing I'd ever bought and were almost identical to the pair I'd seen Paul Weller wearing on the front cover of a recent copy of the NME. I also chose a fine fawn three-piece suit that, again, purely in my opinion, looked the absolute 'nadgers'.

Venturing into the big wide world as a 16-year-old is an exciting but also daunting experience, one that many kids today don't face now that mandatory education has been extended until they reach their mid-thirties. On the one hand, I was full of confidence from recently being the 'biggest' at school (except for Mad Twat Coxy, who was fully bearded and ripped just before his 13th birthday) and from some decent qualifications (something which I don't think Mad Twat Coxy got many of). On the other hand, I was a sack of nerves and full of trepidation about stepping into a completely new, unchartered, grown-up world. Only a few weeks beforehand, I'd only had to worry about what was for dinner, whether my jeans had been washed, and what time the match kicked off, but now my head was cluttered by grown-up stuff like salaries, learning to drive a car, holidays abroad, and opening a bank account. Cocky but still not too proud to ask Mum for help. So as I sat on the 10:36 am train from Whitton to Waterloo, I was quietly grateful that Mum and Lisa, my girlfriend from the ice rink were travelling up to town with me.

Much of the interview was a blur, but I think I answered most questions OK, even if I found some of them pointless. 'What frustrates you the most?' asked the pompous personnel guy. I was tempted to reply with 'My sister's mates or when Chelsea lose to Arsenal,' instead defaulting to the more obvious cliche of 'When others don't share the same high standards as I do'. Total bullshit that Mr Leyton would no doubt have heard multiple times before, and no doubt since. In truth, if his disinterested expression throughout was any indication, I'm not sure he was even listening to most of what I said. When the interview had finished and as I was leaving, he said, 'Young man, whatever the outcome of this interview, please be advised that *brown is not for town*'. Initially shocked that this was an insight into the bank's approach to diversity and inclusion, I quickly realised that he was, in fact, referring to my new loafers. 'Fuck,' I thought, 'these little puppies cost me sixty-five quid'.

'And also,' he followed up with, 'beards are frowned upon,' a random comment bearing in mind that I was clean-shaven and would have needed about six months to grow anything resembling one.

'Even if I could grow one, it would be ginger, so I don't think I'll bother.' I joked and then scuttled out the door as Mr. Leyton glared at me, the first example of many at work when I wished I had resisted the temptation to try and be funny and kept my big mouth shut.

My now offended brown shoes took me from the building across Cannon Street to a cafe in Walbrook where Mum and Lisa were waiting. In the days when a Costa Coffee was something only for those who enjoyed cheap package holidays to Spain, ordering a hot drink was simple —tea or coffee, black or white, sugar or no sugar. No barista degree needed. Mum ordered three white coffees, and I told them how the interview had gone, omitting the bit about my inappropriate shoe colour and my poor attempt at a joke. We finished our drinks, headed home, and I waited to hear my fate.

The letter confirming I had successfully secured a position with the bank arrived one Saturday morning in mid-August; my brown shoes were no longer ordinary brown shoes, they'd become my *lucky* brown shoes. The letter contained lots of important information, some that I read, some that I didn't, and some that I didn't understand. I *did* note the start date (22 September 1981), the salary (£3,695 + bonus and profit sharing), and something about an old people's savings scheme called a pension. Additionally, it told me that my job would be something called a '*Waste Clerk'* and that I would be a *'Waste Clerk'* at somewhere called Walham Green. What on earth is a *Waste Clerk*? I wondered, realising I hadn't really considered what working in a bank would involve. I'd presumed it would be dealing, in some way, with money, but '*Waste Clerk'* didn't sound even loosely close to what I had in mind.

'Where the hell is Walham Green, Dad ?', who, after many years of driving around the sweet shops of West London, had a pre-Sat Nav, cabbie-like knowledge of the capital. His response was the best news of all. 'When we go to Chelsea and spend ten minutes squashed against the window of a bank outside Fulham Broadway tube station, well, it's there' he said, looking quite pleased with himself for knowing where it was but nowhere near as pleased as I was for finding out that I'd be working only yards away from one of my favourite places on the planet. I only needed to be told that Paul Weller was the branch manager and my life would have been complete before I'd even had my 17th birthday.

Self-assessment: The 'Life Before Banking' years

'Well, that showed them, didn't it? I know that Mum and Dad didn't expect me to pass all my O levels, but I proved that I could listen to music and learn boring stuff at the same time. Having to quit hockey was tough as I loved playing, and although I wasn't brilliant, I probably could have made it to the senior team. I may live to regret giving up cricket and I totally understand why the old man has secretly got the right hump with me, but I just couldn't spend another weekend standing on that bloody green at Twickenham watching the busses go by, often with my mates sitting on the top deck going somewhere fun.

I'm pleased, if a little surprised, that I have been accepted by the bank. I'm really looking forward to earning some decent money, however, I'm still not sure whether it's what I want to do or if I will be any good at it — then again, I don't really have a clue what it will be like, so let's wait and see and if it doesn't work out, I can blame Mum. She said that it will be fun, but then again she also told me that marmalade sandwiches do help to reduce car sickness, so I don't know what to believe. Either way, I am shitting myself and I keep thinking that I probably should have given a bit more thought to how I want to spend my life, but it's too late now anyway — my brown shoes and I start next week'

Part 2

The 'Starting Out' years

(1981-1985)

4

'Pin stripe suit, clean shirt and tie, stops off at the corner shop, to buy The Times'

The country wasn't in tremendous shape when I started my working life. VAT had doubled to 15%, interest rates were sky-high, the UK manufacturing industry was in steep decline, and the recession was the deepest since the 1930s. Three million people were unemployed, representing one in ten of the adult population, a depressing reality brilliantly captured in UB40's song of the same name. It was indeed *a statistical reminder of a world that didn't care*.

Thatcherism had been encouraging free markets and entrepreneurialism that had venerated an increasingly individual over community mindset. Not even the temporary national coming-together to celebrate the wedding of Charles and Di was sufficient to make the country a contented one, brutally evidenced by the summer riots in many cities across the country. The problems in Northern Ireland spilled onto the English mainland, and, with tensions also running high between Russia and the West, the folk at Greenham Common constantly reminded us that we were all only four minutes away from evaporating in a nuclear cloud. It didn't bother me though, as I'd watched the Protect & Survive public information film that had assured me that in the event of a potential armageddon, I'd be OK if I hid under the stairs.

As frustrating as life was for many, nothing compared to the level of disappointment and upset that Midge Ure of Ultravox was experiencing every Thursday morning. After the quick application of some eyeliner, he would rush downstairs in his New Romantic tartan dressing gown, frantically open his post only to find that yet again, his masterpiece, *Vienna*, one of the finest musical compositions of the era that included a viola solo influenced by German composer *Max Reger* and supported by a video that drew inspiration from *Orson Welles'* epic 1949 film *The Third Man*, was still stuck at number two in the music charts. To make the pain even more excruciating, for about the 50th week, he'd been outsold by *Joe Dolce's Shaddap You Face*, a novelty song by an American bloke pretending to be Italian, playing a toy guitar and wearing a dreadful straw hat. Hey Midge, 'Whats-a-matter-you? Why-you-look-a-so-sad?

The one shining light of optimism during the summer was provided by the England cricket team, who, against all the odds, retained the Ashes in the final match of the Test Series despite being bowled out in the first innings 227 runs behind Australia. As well as some incredible pace bowling by the shaggy-haired, James May look-a-like, Bob Willis, England's 'St George' was the legendary Ian Botham who took several wickets and scored 199 runs across the two innings. 'Beefy,' as he was affectionately known, became a national hero and someone who I and many others idolised. He was super talented, a maverick, and even occasionally a bad boy and I loved his rebellious approach to life; I bet he wore brown shoes whenever he wanted to.

At 9:45 on Tuesday 15 September 1981, I reported for duty at Walham Green branch. Although the day and time seemed random, I subsequently learned that both were for good reasons — Tuesday because Monday was too busy for the other staff to be fannying around with a new entrant, and 9:45 because the branch didn't open until 9:30 and the staff needed 15 minutes to deal with the immediate first-thing rush. I guess we all remember those 'first days at' whether it be work, school, cub scouts, prison, or wherever, often because we're scared shitless about the new, the unknown, and the overwhelming feeling of being on your own, which is how I felt as I entered the branch and followed my instructions, which were to go to the enquiries window and ask for Janet. Oh well, here goes.

The enquiries window wasn't difficult to find in the small banking hall, not least because of the word 'ENQUIRIES' illuminated above a small window which opened onto a countertop. Despite the bank being only open for a short time, there were already four people queuing at it with their 'enquiries', which, by the tone of voice of the guy at the front, were all very important. After a nervous ten-minute wait, I was at the front of the queue and facing somebody I assumed wasn't Janet, as he had a beard (really, how unacceptable) and bore a remarkable resemblance to Marvin Gaye. He looked friendly and kind, and I immediately thought I would like him. 'I have been told to ask for Janet,' I said. 'I'm Graham, and I start here today.'

'I know who you are,' he replied. 'I've been expecting you. Do you have your letter and your ID, pal?' he asked, 'You were told to bring them with you.' I had them both. My ID was my birth certificate, pretty much the only acceptable document that I had — too young for a driving licence, no need for a credit card, and too soon for a passport as, at the time, they weren't required for Devon or Cornwall. I handed them over, and Edwin, as I later found out he was called, smiled at me some more. 'Wait there mate, I'll be back in a tick' he said, still with an air of excitement in his voice.

Although he was only gone for a few minutes, it felt like an eternity. I was convinced that everyone from inside the branch was watching me, the new boy, anxiously staring into nowhere. Maybe they were admiring my shoes as, in a show of rebelliousness, I'd ignored my recruiter's advice and had gambled on wearing my lovely brown loafers. After all, if Edwin could have a beard, I could wear brown, and I was sure his beard hadn't cost him about a week's salary. Maybe I could prove that brown was for town? Edwin finally returned, gave me back my documents, and directed me to the door at the far end of the banking hall. I shuffled over and waited, realising that this was more than just a door, it was a portal into the rest of my working life. I readied myself to go through, into the unknown, and into my future.

The door was solid, dark brown oak with a large round glass porthole in it, presumably positioned at the average person's head height, and staring at me through it was a big pair of eyes framed by massive black plastic glasses. The owner reminded me of Velma from Scooby Doo, and I wondered whether everyone here looked like someone else. I realised that the door opened outward as it thumped into the side of one of my tasselled beauties, and a short lady of indeterminate age came out. 'Hello,' she said in a broad Belfast accent, I'm Janet, nice to meet you, come in'

She led me through the cluttered office past several politely nodding heads, as I gripped my birth certificate like an innocent man clutching his blanket as he was being shown to his prison cell for the first night. The first thing I noticed about the inside of an early nineteen-eighties bank was that it had dreadful wallpaper, in places barely hanging on to the walls, the stripes of mauve and beige being strangely reminiscent in both style and quality to some of the shirts that Dad wore to work during the seventies. I was also struck by just how many people there were, all older than me, some considerably so, as they busied themselves about the surprisingly scruffy office. The gents were suited and booted in their black shoes and, although the ladies were more mixed in their appearance, the outfit of choice appeared to be a pastel-coloured 'leisure suit' made of a material that I have since learned is velour and was inspired by the Jane Fonda workout fitness craze of the time. The other surprising thing was that most people were either eating, drinking or smoking, or in some instances, all three. And, apart from Edwin, who was still smiling at me, everyone was white.

Janet led me down some narrow stairs to the 'restroom' where we were to have our introductory chat. As the name suggested, the restroom was where people actually retired for a rest, something I had never considered I might need as I'd not thought about whether I'd be working hard enough to get tired in the first place. In the restroom were several rickety chairs with worn brown covers and well-used cushions that looked exhausted through lots of use but clearly well-appreciated for the same reason. Sat in the middle of the worn, grey stained carpet tiles was a low-slung coffee table cluttered with yesterday's copy of *The Sun* (including the obligatory mindless headline), an even older copy of the *Radio Times*, and a martial arts magazine, *Fighter*. I couldn't see a copy of the *Financial Times* anywhere. Hung at the wrong height on the back wall was a very well-pricked dartboard, with two darts sticking out and a third one with a broken flight lying on the floor underneath. In the far corner was a sink area with a beige-brown Formica cupboard above it for cups, saucers, and plates, and sitting on the smeared stainless steel draining board were some recently 'washed' mugs next to some used tea bags, which oozed brown liquid back along the grooves and into the sink. There was a massive, industrial-size coffee jar from *Key Markets* with a dessert spoon sticking out and a bowl of brown encrusted sugar standing alongside. It looked and smelled like I assumed a student flat at a Uni would.

Janet told me what I needed to know for my first day, including that I would be allowed to leave early, at 4:30, rather than the usual 5 p.m. Already, the days were feeling a lot longer than they used to and I realised that I was unlikely to ever see another episode of *John Craven's Newsround* again. My basic induction over, it was time to be formally paraded around the office and introduced to my new colleagues, most of whose names I instantly forgot. After I'd mumbled 'Hello' to about 30 people (it was actually 15, but you try and remember that many names when you're still shitting yourself), I was shown to an area at the back of the office: *The Waste Room*. It was finally time to learn what 'Waste' was and what a 'Waste Clerk' did.

The Waste Room wasn't a room but a separate open-plan area of about 15ft by 12ft with long wooden desks at the back and whirring machines sat on either side. In front of the desks were five bright-red 'pleather' covered swivel chairs, four occupied and the other waiting expectantly for my new-boy arse. A still-grinning Edwin was sitting in the one next to mine, Janet sat in another, and I just about recognised through the dense smog of cigarette smoke the other 2 guys, introduced to me as Brian and Warren.

My first day and the rest of my four-day week were a blur as I slowly got to grips with my new daily tasks and the basic concept of simply being at work. I learned that doing waste was the collective term for a variety of back office processes that ensured people's hard-earned money ended up in the right place at the right time, and that the most mundane of all these tasks was 'sorting up' which meant putting a massive pile of cheques into alphabetical order by the name of the customer. To make this incredibly dull task more exciting, Brian explained that whoever finished last sorting up their pile had to go and buy the coffee and bacon rolls; forget any clever motivation theories, this was simple — lose and it will cost you money. 'The good news', Brian told me, was that I was excluded from the competition in my first week, meaning I had three days left to get as quick as they were, highly unlikely on the basis that Edwin had been practicing for a year, Brian and Warren for even longer. Naively, I had assumed when I started working for a living that I would be better off, but after two solid weeks of buying weak coffee and bloody bacon rolls, I realised that might not immediately be the case. And, I knew now why that smug bastard Edwin was so pleased to see me when I first arrived.

5

'You can't wait to be grown up, acceptance into the capital world'

The UK was in a period of significant social change, desperate to shake off the misery of the late seventies. It was almost no longer OK to be working class, yet the number of people living in poverty was increasing, while those that *could* afford to live were rushing towards a new world of fast food, exotic holidays, outrageous clothes, and gleaming new Commodore 64 computers. In parts of the country, it was Ataris and Vauxhall Cavaliers everywhere while, elsewhere, the suicide and crime rate was rapidly increasing. For many young people, especially those living outside of London, the dystopian view of life showcased by the Specials' track *'Ghost Town'* perfectly summed up their disillusionment.

Unaffected by these issues and therefore blind to them, I was full of optimism as I embraced the excitement of my new job, even if I had spent a large part of my first few weeks becoming friendly with Joe at the Bridge Cafe during my daily visits to buy the bacon rolls. But, like most things, eventually, I started to get the hang of sorting up as I began to recognise the names on the cheques and remember where they would fit in relation to each other, muscle memory kicking in; either that or the simple fear of spending my salary before I'd even got it forced me to do it quickly. A few weeks after I'd taken so long that Warren had gone to lunch by the time I'd finished, I was now completing the daily task in less than 20 minutes. On October 13 1981, I finished third, and Edwin had to make the morning walk of shame to the cafe. That wiped the smile off his face.

I became more familiar with the other waste room tasks too, moving into the state of 'conscious competence' like a learner driver who still had to think about what they were doing but no longer had to say, 'mirror, signal, manoeuvre' out loud every time they pulled away from the kerb. Unfortunately, I'd not progressed quite as well with my actual driving lessons and was still saying, 'mirror, signal, manoeuvre' out loud every time I pulled away from the kerb.

Janet confirmed that I was doing OK (at work, not with my driving), whatever that meant. I'd not really considered before I'd started what 'being good at banking' would be, but I certainly hadn't thought it would be how quickly I could sort a load of bits of paper into alphabetical order while smoking a fag, drinking lukewarm coffee and chasing the prize of a greasy bacon roll. But that is how it was, and that was fine by me.

The boys in the waste room were of a similar age to me, albeit slightly older, due to them joining in a previous September as the new school-leaver entrant. They were all decent blokes in their different ways, and quickly helped me realise that work could be a laugh, as well as something you got paid for. I learned I could take my job seriously but didn't need to take myself too seriously and that having fun didn't have to be a negative, juvenile thing, as some people I've subsequently worked with believe.

A fundamental benefit of working in a bank is meeting many new people, some of whom become friends, especially those who show you kindness in vulnerable moments. The first person who did that for me was the oldest of the waste room team, Brian Phillips. It was only my second day in a strange new world, and Brian showed me that kindness through the medium of steak and kidney, and lager. 'C'mon Chap,' he said, 'let's go and get a pie and a pint,' as he led me across the busy junction of Fulham Broadway and into The White Hart pub. Long since replaced by a Thai restaurant, The White Hart was an incredibly long and narrow boozer whose clientele was mainly Irish, totally smashed, and usually both. To get to the lounge bar, you had to navigate through the saloon bar, aptly named given the number of old Western-style fights that broke out. If it wasn't a fight, it was just an aggressive argument; if it wasn't either, it was just someone falling off a stool. It may have been many things, but The White Hart was never dull.

My trip there with Brian was the first of many. I did the right thing and mentioned to him that I wasn't old enough to legally be drinking, but he told me 'not to worry about that old bollocks', so I didn't, and neither, seemingly did the pub landlord. It says something about the metabolic rate of a 16-year-old when you can regularly eat a bacon roll, a steak and kidney pie, and drink two pints of Carling Black Label before1 p.m. and not be the size of a house. Those were the days. . .

Brian and I became good friends despite his allegiance to Fulham Football Club, a barely known team apparently based a couple of miles away from the branch and therefore also from the real Pride of London. In work, Brian was competent and efficient, however, his other interests were financially more important to him, not least his sideline of selling football scarves and badges at Fulham matches and he also had a string of mates who seemingly could 'get stuff' at very reasonable prices. When I look back now, I realise that, in a new phase of your life, especially when you move away from family, you often look for substitute role models, for people to look up to, and in my case Brian was that person.

The star of the team was Warren. Clearly ambitious and with both of his deep brown eyes on promotion as quickly as possible, he was bright, quick at everything, and oozed confidence. In truth, I was slightly envious of him, including, bizarrely, his green Triumph Dolomite. I don't know why I lusted after a family car that should only be driven by men over fifty wearing leather gloves and smoking a pipe, but every time he gave me a lift to Putney Station, I liked it more.

Edwin seemed less ambitious than Warren and content to stay in the waste room, in fact if they hadn't turned the branch into a Lloyds Bar about 25 years ago, I reckon he'd still be there now sorting up cheques and occasionally finishing last. Like Brian, Edwin's real interests lay outside work, competing at a high-level in a couple of martial arts disciplines. Despite his ever-smiling face and all-around good nature, he was not someone to mess with. But while Brian was a top geezer, Warren a super-smart cookie, and Edwin a smiling assassin, none of them had shoes as brown or as cool as mine.

Not long after Janet had told me that things were going well, I came back down to earth with a bump when I had my first career setback. It involved the daddy of all the waste room machines, the mighty *Encoder*. Like all of our technology, it had been given a name, in this case, Colin, after Brian's Grandad, who apparently always sat in the corner of the room and smelled of smoke. This absolute beast (the *Encoder*, not Brian's Grandad) resembled something out of Space 1999 (but not as shit) and processed all the cheques and dockets that came across the branch counter. On this occasion, I was busily punching Colin's keys when Edwin said something that made me turn around and, in the process, knock over my cup of coffee. The blood rushed to my face as I sat helplessly, watching the milky brown fluid seep into the gaps between the blue buttons on the keypad and beyond. A faint smell of burning caffeine started to waft out, and very quickly, Colin just gave up the ghost, sighed, and turned himself off. 'Janet,' I shouted 'Colin's stopped working.' She hurried over with a concerned expression, immediately realising that, at the very least, a sick Colin would make us all a couple of hours late home that evening, as we would need to wait for someone to come and fix it and wouldn't be able to process any cheques in the meantime. She called the helpline, and an engineer arrived about an hour and a half later.

The nineteen-eighties bank machine engineer was a curious animal, like a really moody plumber, but not as pleasant. He spent about half an hour underneath Colin, lying on his back, obviously wishing he was somewhere else, huffing and puffing away until he eventually surfaced with a look of accomplishment on his otherwise miserable face. He turned to Janet and told her that he'd managed to get him up and running but that as the machine was so old, many of its parts were badly worn and it really needed to be replaced, or else it was going to keep going wrong 'and I really don't want to have to come back to this shit hole again'.

Janet thanked him and said she would get onto Head Office whilst I breathed a sigh of relief that the impact of my faux pas had been significantly reduced by the decrepit state of the ten-year-old E300B model. Poor old Colin was set for the knacker's yard. As the engineer hurried out of the waste room, as a parting gift, he muttered, 'It's also a shame that some twat has spilled coffee all over it' before disappearing into the banking hall and off to his next job. Janet turned, looked at me, and with a near-perfect impression of my mother, just shook her head disapprovingly. Whoops. Why the boys thought it was so funny I don't know, and them pissing themselves with laughter didn't help me feel any better. But it was just banter, and despite my embarrassment at buggering up poor old Colin, I realised that banter was cool, that I now belonged to something, to a team, to a gang, and I liked that. This work lark wasn't so bad after all . . .

6
'We'll see kidney machines replaced by rockets and guns'

Although inflation had reduced to single digits, Thatcher's harsh economic policies meant that unemployment had increased to a new record level of three million. Discontent was running through the NHS, resulting in nurses striking for a 12% pay increase, and like the previous year, not even a major royal event could lighten the general mood, on this occasion, the birth of an already balding Prince William. The TV of the time was an excellent barometer of the changing attitudes — it was still possible to watch nineteen-seventies staples like *The Goodies* or the ridiculously misogynistic *Benny Hill Show*, but on the same evening also tune in to anti-establishment programmes such as *The Comic Strip Presents* or *The Young Ones*. Saturday night 'entertainment' was still more mainstream, albeit that the old guard of *Morecambe and Wise* and my old mate *Mike Yarwood* had been replaced by the total shite of *Little and Large*, the biggest over-promise of all time, *The Les Dennis Laughter Show* and most worryingly of all, *The Krankies*.

Little did I know that I was about to be given the opportunity to watch much more TV than I had expected. I was sitting at Alan, our new encoder (named after Brian's dad, the son of Colin), and furiously punching in account numbers when I felt a nagging pain in my back, which didn't subside even when I stretched or changed my sitting position. As the morning progressed, so did the intensity of the pain, and by about 1 p.m. I was struggling and told Janet that I wasn't feeling too chipper. She suggested that I go and lay down in the restroom, which sounded sensible other than Brian was still at lunch practicing his darts, relentlessly trying for a top score of 120. I admired his dedication. He told me that I would need to get practicing, too, because the annual Beehive Darts tournament at Lombard Street was only a couple months away, and I was in the team. 'I'm not very good at darts, Brian.' I said apologetically.

'I know you're not' he replied, 'I've seen you play, but it's either you or Edwin, and he's seriously fucking hopeless.' I tried not to get in his way as I stretched across a couple of the rickety brown chairs, albeit I was less worried about a stray dart stabbing me in the eye than I was by the relentless stabbing pain in my back. And I was sweating, big time.

'You all right, Chap?' asked Brian, 'You look like crap, even for a Chelsea fan.'

'No, I'm not all right.' I both thought and said.

'You need to get home, mate. Wait there,' he said, disappearing upstairs. To be honest, I wasn't planning on doing anything else. He returned five minutes later and told me there was a black taxi upstairs waiting to take me home. 'Thanks, mate.' I muttered, wincing through the now almost unbearable throbbing in my back.

I don't remember much about the 40-minute taxi ride home, other than it was absolute hell as every bump in the road sent a jolt of extreme pain through my whole body. Mum was home when I got there and, in a slightly more polite way than Brian had put it an hour or so earlier, pointed out that I didn't look my best. I lasted ten minutes before Mum called an ambulance, and it wasn't long afterwards that I was being unceremoniously dumped onto a trolley in the casualty department of the West Middlesex Hospital. After an hour or so of endless prodding with the pain continuing to intensify, I was advised by a reassuringly confident but clearly knackered doctor that I was most likely suffering from kidney stones and that at least one of them was blocking the entrance to my ureter. Oh good, I thought.

Although I didn't realise the significance at the time, he told me he had prescribed pethidine to help relieve the pain. Until that point, the occasional bit of puff behind the bike sheds with Mad Twat Coxy was my only experience of any drug other than alcohol and paracetamol, but almost immediately after I felt the sharp prick in my arse-cheek, I learned that pethidine is genuinely remarkable, removing, almost within seconds, the extreme pain that had been with me for the best part of eight hours. It was relief of the highest quality, even more than earlier that week when I found out that I hadn't actually run over our next-door neighbour's cat during my driving lesson, instead merely scuffing up their new wheelie bin.

Pethidine and I became good friends over the years. As well as the almost instant relief that it provides, 100 milligrams of this opioid could create euphoric feelings and even be hallucinogenic. On one holiday in Spain, I had an attack of renal colic and was kindly given a supply of it by the local hospital; I must have taken a couple of tablets too many one morning and I ended up believing I had spent an entire afternoon smoking weed with a group of Rastafarians whilst playing Cluedo on massive lily pads floating in the middle of a giant pond; Colonel Mustard, in the garden, with the spliff.

I was eventually taken from casualty to a ward that was to be my home for the next three weeks. The Doc's diagnosis that I had kidney stones was correct — three of them. To make me feel like a brave little soldier, I was informed that the pain of kidney stones is considered to be right up there in 'the list of very painful things', only marginally behind childbirth. At least, usually, you get a child at the end of that, whereas kidney stone removal leaves you with little more than a commemorative jar containing some things looking like crusty Subbuteo footballs. Having said that, you don't have to worry about calcium deposits coming home late from parties or not paying attention in maths classes.

The root cause of my stones was a mis-shaped kidney that didn't drain properly, which was troublesome. The only course of action at the time was full-on surgery, which happened within a couple of days and left me bedridden for another 15. To remind me of the fun I'd had, I ended up with a lovely eight-inch scar across my left side, which, for a few years, I successfully passed off as a shark bite that I had got in Cornwall to anyone who seemed interested. I stopped spinning that yarn after some clever David Attenborough wannabe pointed out in front of a large group of girls who I was impressing that, at the time, there were only basking sharks in Cornwall, and they don't have teeth. No one likes a smart-arse.

But if I thought I would get bored in the hospital, I was wrong. The daily insertion and removal of drains and tubes in places that shouldn't have drains and tubes inserted into and removed kept the mind focused, as did the TV that was full of the news that Mrs. Thatcher had decided to send a fleet of warships to reclaim the Falkland Islands from the invading Argentinians. I thought they must have gone a long way around as it couldn't have taken as long as it did to get to North West Scotland, where I assumed the Falkland Islands were. I was even convinced that my Uncle Derek had bought a jumper there during a holiday that he and my Aunty Audrey had been on the year before so I was shocked to find out they were actually 8,000 miles away; I don't know where that sweater came from because there's no way that Auntie Audrey and Uncle Derek would have gone that far. It seemed like one hell of a trek to stand up for about 600 ex-pats, who, having buggered off halfway around the world to a desolate island, presumably hated England anyway. But Maggie was determined to give it a proper go. It got particularly feisty when the British forces managed to sink a retreating Argentinian warship, The General Belgrano, killing, with it, 400 'Argies', as they affectionately became known. This act of barbarism was celebrated in true, *The Sun* stupidity with the headline *'Gotcha'*. I thought about a copy of it lying on the coffee table in the restroom at Walham Green and Brian ignoring it and going straight to look at the tits on Page 3.

Watching a war play out live on TV was both scary and gripping, especially as the alternative was listening to Fred in the next bed from me continually banging on about the stabbing pain up his arse or Jim opposite constantly calling out for Ethel, who I found out was indeed his wife, albeit she'd been dead for four years. Being in a geriatric ward at 17 is about as much fun as being poked in the eye by one of Brian's darts, although I am looking forward to the inevitable day when things go full circle, and I can get my revenge by regaling some poor kid with the extent of my piles, the dangers on hips and knees of drinking too much Pale Ale, and showing him my scar from when I was viciously sucked by a basking shark.

Edwin, Brian, and Warren came to see me in hospital, which was kind of them as they didn't live nearby and had quite a journey in Warren's Dolomite. I don't advocate letting your workmates see you in your pyjamas, but I was pleased to see them, even if they did take the piss out of me, not that I needed help with that as I had a catheter doing a decent job already. I got my own back when I made them look at the drain going into my kidney; if Edwin could have gone green, he would have.

Over the next ten years or so, I had a further eight kidney operations, my visits to hospital becoming as frequent as Oliver Reed getting pissed on a TV chat show. Fortunately, I started to benefit from advancements in medical technology, so not every operation was as intrusive as the first one. After that, apart from having to go to St Bartholomew's Hospital for regular check-ups (having been transferred to the care of the specialist renal unit there) and being told to go on a low-calcium, non-dairy diet, it wasn't too bad. Being ill can catch you unaware, especially as a teenager, still, it gave me a renewed perspective on what was important and prompted me to think more about living in the present. I'm pleased that I didn't feel *too* sorry for myself and managed to remember that there were many people far worse off than me, not least the families of the Argies that had been blasted out of the water, all in the name of preserving a Sunday lamb roast dinner for a few retired British civil servants.

I wasn't sure what Janet honestly thought when I had to take 5 weeks off work after only having been in the bank for a few months, but she said nothing other than 'Good to have you back' when I finally did return. I finished last sorting the cheques up that first Monday morning, but Edwin took pity on me and said he'd get the rolls and drinks in. 'Coffee, no milk, please.' I said.

7
'Sup up your beer and collect your fags'

The spoils of war are not limited to the battleground, and this was certainly true for Mrs Thatcher. Before the Falklands conflict, she had been way behind in the opinion polls, but her so-called victory in 'Las Malvinas' had created a wave of national pride that allowed her to cruise towards a general election landslide. The Tory machine plundered on, crushing the weak beneath it like the home fans at a QPR versus Chelsea football match, in part because it seemed like nobody could deal with her — whether because none of the party had ever had any experience of dealing with a superior female, or because they were all just weak. Maybe a bit of both, but she could seemingly do whatever she wanted.

Now back in the swing of things after my kidney-related fun, I'd graduated to some more senior (well, less junior) tasks, including dealing with customers' queries at the famous enquiries window. It was my first exposure to dealing with the unpredictable general public. There were other exciting 'development opportunities' afforded to me, or to give them their more accurate description, 'the shite jobs that nobody else wanted'. Of all of these, the most unpleasant was 'junior on post'. This end-of-day task involved putting customer statements and other letters into envelopes, sealing them, and then running them through a piece of high-tech eighties machinery called a 'franking' machine. We named ours after one of the more famous 'Franks' of the time, 'Frank Bough'. He was one of the consummate professional presenters of the day, having spent much of his time fronting sports programmes such as the Saturday afternoon classic *Grandstand* as well as becoming one of the first modern-day morning TV anchors when he presented *Breakfast Time* along with Selina Scott and Nick

Ross. A few years after I'd left Walham Green, 'Uncle' Frank got himself the sack for allegedly getting caught taking cocaine, dressing up in ladies' lingerie, and frequently using prostitutes. I never did check, but I wonder whether they changed the machine's name after that.

After carefully ensuring that you had 'franked' (in retrospect, an interesting verb) all the envelopes at the right price for their size, weight and destination, they would be placed into a massive canvas sack, known as an 'end of day bag' which would be collected later that evening by a head office messenger who would take them to an enormous central 'clearing' building somewhere near Waterloo where everything would get emptied, sorted, processed and sent to wherever it needed to go. But the scourge of the junior on post was the dreaded 'registered envelope' which, due to its importance, needed to be taken to the Post Office to obtain proof of posting. It was a pain in the arse because this invariably meant getting to the post office just before it closed at 5:30 and then bringing the receipt back to the branch, often resulting in leaving work well after 6 p.m. A trip to the Post Office was never fun, mainly because it was run by the rudest people on the planet. Admittedly, this was not the golden age of customer experience, including at banks, which relied on the low propensity of customers to move their accounts to a competitor. At the time, people were more likely to leave their other halves than they were their bank, mainly because it was easier to work out a Dusty Bin riddle on 3-2-1 than it was to successfully navigate through the process of closing an account and opening another somewhere else. But the guys at the Post Office took 'not giving a shit' to a whole new level.

Often adorned in frayed, multi-coloured woollen tank tops, the 'gentlemen' that worked there oozed every discrimination out of every pore they had, and most of them had lots of pores. For the customer, queuing inside the airport-style barrier system was an anxious experience, the fear of verbal abuse by one of the slobs preying on their mind as they edged slowly forward to the front of the queue and then waiting for one of the odious creatures behind the glass to grunt in their general direction, signifying that it was their turn. It was unpleasant most days, but Thursday was the worst. Thursday was Pension day; the counters were at their busiest, the queues at their longest, and the woolly jumper-clad twats at their rudest. I remember one chap, probably in his nineties, if not older, shuffling to the counter after being made to stand and wait for about half an hour. 'Good afternoon,' said the pensioner. No words in reply, just a snort from the greasy, overweight, middle-aged bloke behind the screen. 'Shall I sign this in front of you now?', he asked, holding up his hard-earned pension cheque in his shaky hand, trying to be helpful as well as seeking some reassurance that he was doing the right thing,

'You can sign it in the fucking toilets, for all I care,' replied Mr. Rude-Bastard. Really? Shame on you, Mr. Post Office man of 1982 at Old Farm Road Fulham. May all your tank tops have unravelled and your greasy hair caused you much itching.

In the same month that I started in the bank, so had Postman Pat; not, in the bank, of course, but at the sorting office in Greendale. Little did I know then, his and my careers would last for similar lengths. Pat was abruptly made redundant in 2017, but at least he still gets re-runs on CBeebies at weekends, so arguably, he lasted longer and is still going. Even with my considerable pension contributions over the years, I suspect his royalties will provide him a far more impressive retirement income than mine. But, as much as I admired his work, even Pat could not make me feel better about the Post Office and its dreadfully shit service; I can't help feeling that the Post Office didn't deserve someone as good and loyal as Pat Clifton.

Fortunately, the regular pain of being junior on post was, like a slow release of pethidine, being numbed by an impending event — as September approached, it would only be a few more sleeps before my life would change for the better — Darren Stokes, this year's new entrant, would be starting; on Tuesday, at 9:45. Having played the role of Janet's bitch for the last 12 months, I felt I had earned my place one small notch up the hierarchy. And, as well as massaging my ego that I would no longer be the whipping boy, there was another benefit from his arrival — the improved chance of booking a summer holiday. Long before anyone had even heard of, let alone understood, Global Warming, summers in the UK used to happen between June and September. It never occurred to me before I joined the bank that booking a holiday during this period would be a problem, so it was a shock when, in October, I was asked to indicate my holiday date preferences for the whole of the following year. But this came with the caveat that only two people could be away simultaneously, and I could only choose the still available dates after everyone else had chosen theirs. All the staff were ranked, firstly by grade, then by the length of time in that grade. The Branch Manager, Sir John Fidley, was at the top, the whipping boy, Graham Pannett, was at the bottom. Everyone else was in between. Welcome to the hierarchy.

When Edwin finally handed me the very well annotated, cloth-eared paper calendar that had taken about three weeks to be circulated to every other member of the branch staff, I realised why he had been wearing his permasmile since the minute I arrived as he was now able to look forward to his next summer holiday in Clacton when it wouldn't be dark by lunchtime. So, while George Michael and his mate Andy enjoyed free drinks at *Club Tropicana*, I spent my first 'work' summer holiday freezing my nuts off in Devon in mid-October. Whether I enjoyed it, I can't remember, but I did manage to capture a fantastic video on Dad's new Camcorder of our windbreak flying, like an enormous multi-coloured kite over the back of our beach hut.

Shortly after 9:45, on the 21 September 1982, the enquiries bell rang, and I ran to the window to see, on the other side of the glass, a nervous young lad who looked about 12 years old. 'Hello, I'm Darren.' he announced, 'I've been told to ask for Janet.'

'Of course, pal,' I said, 'I've been waiting for you. Have you got your ID?'

As the retiring new boy, it was my job to show Darren the ropes, which made me realise how much I had learned myself over the year and how consciously competent I had become. No need to even think about changing gear, let alone say, 'mirror, signal, manoeuvre'. Darren was as confused and daunted as I had been 12 months earlier, so I tried to be patient when he didn't quite get stuff, even if I didn't feel too guilty about the number of bacon rolls he was going to have to buy over the next few weeks. And, on his second day, I took him to The White Hart for a pie and a pint.

As the year progressed, not much happened. 'Daz' became confident and quickly got to grips with Alan, Frank, and seeing customers at enquiries. The following September, another new entrant, Stephen Harris started; Daz was delighted and I got pushed further up the pecking order. Stephen was a small lad, conveniently small enough to fit into the old lift which was used to take cash-laden wooden trollies to and from the safe in the basement. It was wrong of us to tell him that, as part of his induction, he needed to check the mechanism at the back of the lift, and as he dutifully did, to slam the metal door shut and press the big green button to send it and him creaking and shuddering down to the basement. Although we never heard him scream as he endured the 30-second descent, when Daz let him out, he looked very pale as he muttered some less-than-complimentary words that seemed inappropriate from the mouth of one so young.

Shortly after Stephen had recovered, I was put forward by Janet to train for the dizzy heights of 'the till'; because I knew my alphabet, they assumed I could count too. My initial training involved sitting next to someone else and observing them in action, a common way of learning a new skill and referred to by an old industrial term as 'Sitting with Nellie'. The person I was sitting with was called Nora, not Nellie, and she neither looked nor smelled like an elephant (the only Nellie I had heard of). Nora did, however, have an aroma which I later learned to be that of vodka. She was an angry-looking woman with a ruddy complexion (yes, I know why now) and a propensity to shriek at people if she was unhappy with them, whether that was a colleague, manager, or customer. *Nobody* wanted to get on Nora's wrong side. I never asked her why she frequently went missing for long periods; in fact, I said very little in the two weeks that I sat and observed her, watching closely and with genuine admiration for how she did everything so intuitively and quickly.

Nora cared little about customer experience and had mastered pulling down her 'closed' counter blind at inappropriate moments, clearly signifying that the customer would need to go to another till, even if they had been waiting at hers for 15 minutes. Sometimes she'd do it purely because she didn't like the look of the customer, other times because she just couldn't be arsed to serve them, either way I assumed that she must have picked up some tips from her visits to the Post Office, back when she would have been junior on post. Or maybe they learned from her?

As a cashier, the most important thing was ensuring your till was balanced at the end of the day. Simple maths — what you had started with, plus what you had taken in, less what you had paid out. The prospect of being wrong, having what was known as a *'difference'* scared the crap out of all of us, not least because that would incur the wrath of Nora, who treated the cash on the counter as if it were her own and therefore any potential difference as a personal slight against her. Whilst I admired her sense of pride in her work, there was no need to call me a stupid twat every time I did get it a bit wrong.

A 'difference' could be either *under (*meaning we were missing cash, potentially to the benefit of a customer) or *over (*meaning we had too much cash, potentially to the detriment of a customer). Minor differences of a few quid were, with Nora's permission, allowed to be written off by crediting or debiting an internal 'ledger' account, known by the acronym *I, C & D*, which stood for *Internal Credits and Debits*. Brian told me that this ledger account had the colloquial, arguably more relevant name of *'Ice Cream and Doughnuts'* as it would frequently be used to purchase small food items, often to cheer everyone up when it had been particularly busy. It sounds morally wrong, but it was only a small change, and we did always *try* to locate which customer it belonged to before investing it into sweets, cakes, or ice cream.

Nora controlled how the account was distributed, and Brian decided to pitch a new idea to her. He suggested that instead of spending it all on sugary food, we could use it to fund a new football kit for the branch five-a-side team, urgently needed due to the impending mini-tournament against two rival banks. Even when Brian pointed out that the pride of the branch was at stake and also the irony of an account used for *'shorts'* being spent on a football kit, Nora remained unconvinced and declined his application, in fact I think she told him to 'just fuck off.'

But Brian was made of strong stuff and was not about to let her push-back put him off course. It was time to implement Plan B, which was clever, if a little more *risqué* than Plan A, and which took advantage of the lack of bank technology at the time. Although new 'corporate' technology *had* started to emerge, it was much more prevalent in the domestic market, not least the growth of the home computer, led by IBM and Apple, the latter having just released its latest PC called *Lisa*. Not many were sold, and as a result Steve Jobs lost credibility, while ZX Spectrums and Commodore 64s were selling like hotcakes. Of course, the World Wide Web would not be available for another eight years, so unless you wanted to play PacMan all day, there was little point in having one anyway.

The lack of connectivity in banking meant that bank accounts were still 'domiciled' at the branch where they had been originally opened, so if someone had opened their account at Walham Green Branch, they would need to go there to do anything other than basic transactions. If they chose to go to another branch, a phone call would need to be made to their branch in order to obtain the necessary authorisation, and the customer was charged to cover the cost of this manual process. I have no idea how it was calculated, but the going rate was £1, so we spent much of our day saying, 'I am very sorry, Sir, but I have to charge you £1 for the phone call' and 'as you know Mrs Perkins, as we did exactly the same thing at exactly the same time last week, it will cost you £1.' The beauty of Brian's plan was that the process to collect the £1 (taken in the form of the brand new £1 coin) lacked a robust audit trail, meaning that coins were not always paid into the IC&D (Phone Calls) account, instead, they ended up in the WGFK (Walham Green Football Kit) account. It wasn't an actual internal ledger account, in fact it was a tattered yellow coin bag that Brian kept beneath his till, but that is just a technicality. I would wince every time I had to tell old Mr. Sullivan that it would cost *him* a pound to get *his* 70 quid out of *his* account at Hammersmith, knowing damn well that some of it would be buying a pair of football socks. Ironically, Mr. Sullivan said he would come to watch us play, but I never had the heart to tell him that he had sponsored a decent portion of my left leg.

8
'Thick as thieves us, we'll stick together for all time'

A busy summer on the counter meant we 'raised' enough for a football kit. As the treasurer of the fund, we left the purchase of it in the capable hands of Brian who had said that he knew a bloke who could do us a good deal. It *was* cheap but also purple, allowing our local rivals to relentlessly rip the piss out of us. We finished third in a three-team competition, but we rationalised our awful performance on the fact that, way before being aware that ladies could actually play football, we had the fewest blokes to choose from. In truth, we were awful, especially Edwin, who may have been able to kick someone to death in a dark alley, but he certainly had no idea how to kick a ball to a teammate on a very well-lit football pitch on Eelbrook Common. Mr. Sullivan came in the following day and seemed amused about our performance; I apologised that we were crap but he explained that he didn't give a toss as he had an account at all three banks. I immediately stopped feeling sorry for him and took great pleasure about charging him a quid for a phone call to Hammersmith branch.

It is weird there should be genuine animosity between staff of different banks but it shows how easily we can become tribal— it's that basic human need to be part of, to identify with, and to be proud of belonging to something. I've seen (no, been in) a fight in a Greek restaurant in Kensington between two 'rival' groups of clearing bankers at a Christmas party. Hardly *Gangs of New York*, but hey, they pushed us too far when they suggested that our share price was artificially inflated versus our future earnings potential. Fortunately, we had Ninja Edwin with us, so neither Warren nor I needed to do anything, whilst Brian spent most of the evening telling the guys from the other bank that he knew where they lived. This was at a time when 'Who Do You Think You Are?' was a confrontational taunt, not a celebrity genealogy programme. 'My bank's better than your bank'; how bizarre.

Whilst there was competition between different banks, the intra-bank rivalry between branches was, and still is, even fiercer. Senior leaders cleverly used this 'competition' as a powerful motivational tool. To an extent, I get that it is OK to engender a trench mentality in order to drive incremental performance, but it becomes unhealthy if that's leveraged too much; to me, it's the corporate equivalent of the 'Bear in the Woods' story, in which two guys go camping in the Rockies and, before they leave base camp, the local guide gives them some essential safety advice.'If you see a bear, stand still and, whatever you do, don't run as you'll never outrun a bear.' The nervous yet excited lads set off on their adventure and, sure enough, on the second night, as they're sitting around their campfire, exhausted after a day's wild water rafting, they hear rustling in the nearby forest, and then, in the distance, see the alarmingly giant and unmistakable silhouette of a male grizzly bear, slowly thudding towards them. One of the guys does what he was told to and freezes on the spot, whilst his mate slowly and purposefully reaches into his rucksack, pulls out a pair of sparkling new Nike trainers, and quietly slips them on.

'What are you doing?' whispers the first guy, 'The fella told you that you can't outrun a bear'.

'I know,' replied the second guy, smiling as he tightened his laces, 'it's not the *bear* that I'm trying to outrun, it's you. It's been good knowing you.'

Our bears were, and always will be, the external competition, so it seems ridiculous to be more bothered about what the branch and the guys down the road are doing rather than what the other banks are doing. And, there's a fundamental flaw in the strategy of pitting branches against each other as it assumes that they, and therefore all the colleagues within them, have equal opportunity to succeed, but that isn't always the case, regardless of how much 'targets' are adjusted. The term 'being on a level playing field' is clichéd, but it is appropriate here— originating from a sporting context, it refers to when a pitch has a slope one way, giving one team an unfair advantage and so to mitigate that advantage, the teams swap ends at half-time. But, in branch banking, there is no half-time, so you don't get to swap ends and so at a small branch like Walham Green, you were constantly kicking uphill. I'm not saying that there shouldn't be competition, far from it —my sons will tell you that from when I scored an unbeaten 176 on Woolacombe Beach in 2003; even though they were only six and four years old, they should have known better than to bowl short and down my leg-side.

The one occasion when there *was* more of a level playing field was at the annual Beehive Darts Tournament. One dartboard, three darts, the same distance of 7ft 9+1/4 inches for everyone. After a year of finishing last in most things, we finally got an equal opportunity. Well, kind of. It was played in the basement of our Head Office in Lombard Street and dozens of branches entered. The atmosphere started pleasantly enough, with beers from the bar flowing well. Yes, the Head Office had a full-sized bar, at least five times longer than the one at The White Hart. Before the tournament started, one of the head office messengers explained the format and the rules — there were group matches, then a knock-out and in each game, three players out of the squad of four would play.

Our leader was Brian, a regular at his local social club and a frequenter of many boozers in the Hammersmith and Fulham area. He was our best player by a country mile. Warren, Roy (our branch sub-manager), and I made up the rest of the team. Warren was decent because he was good at everything but despite being northern, Roy was surprisingly useless. I was OK, having practiced with Brian in the restroom at the branch after we'd spent some of our Ice Cream and Donuts money on two new sets of darts, reluctantly agreed to by Nora. Brian had a mate who got us a good deal, including some Union Jack flights, left over from the post-Falklands wave of national pride that had washed over the country. I wondered whether the nine retired Ministry of Defence civil servants played darts in the one pub on the Falklands Islands, possibly before downing ten large Gin and Tonics and then going out to shoot some sheep.

Somehow, we got through the group stage, beating branches that were similar in size to us. Consequently, we were drawn in the quarter-finals against local giants and fierce rivals Hammersmith. Our team for this grudge match was Brian, Warren, and me, as Roy had already left because his wife wanted him back in time for dinner. Each game was 501, straight-in, double to finish, best of three legs. I was chosen to play first and got beaten, two-nil, by a pretty handy guy, who finished the second game with an impressive '114 outshot'. I tried my best not to cry. Warren was next and narrowly won (of course he did) two-one, even though he nearly blew it by taking five attempts to finish on a double one. All square. Down to Brian, our very own Crafty Cockney. He clearly knew the guy he was playing against, presumably adversaries over many years, as rather than shaking hands at the start of the game, Brian called the bloke a knob, and the knob called Brian a fat twat. Brian, fuelled by John Smiths and hatred, the enemy fuelled by Fosters and complacency, locked horns. Brian won the first leg, and then the geezer from Hammersmith won the second; it had all come down to a one-game shootout.

The Hammersmith boys visibly sunk into the beers as I threw most of mine over Warren when I ran to hug the fat twat after his winning dart had sailed gracefully into the double 18. Against all the odds, we had gone and done it — the perennial underdogs had pulled off a giant-killing; little Walham Green had stuffed the mighty Hammersmith. The bragging rights would last forever, or at least until next year's tournament, but that was long enough. I was already looking forward to the next time Mr Sullivan came in, and I would have to make a phone call to Hammersmith, even if I might feel slightly guilty knowing that he funded part of the winning dart.

We got absolutely smashed in the semi-final by Pall Mall Branch, which had about 800 staff at the time and whose team, made up entirely of messengers who seemingly did little else all day other than play darts, went on to win the tournament for the 43rd year running. Or something like that. So again, it wasn't really a level playing field, but that didn't matter. More significantly, it didn't matter that I had been the only one to lose in our overall victory against Hammersmith. It was fair enough; I had got beaten by a better guy on a level playing field. But I still won as part of my team, with my mates. Happy days.

9

'And I think of what you might have been, a man of such great promise, oh but you forgot the dream'

Although it was a turbulent time in the UK with the IRA terrorising the English mainland and many still fearing some kind of apocalyptic event as nuclear missiles owned by Russia and America began arriving in Europe, I was far more bothered by the truly shocking news that Paul Weller had announced that The Jam would be breaking up; I wasn't sure whether there was much left worth living for. In retrospect, I needn't have worried as it wasn't long before we were blessed with the arrival of The Style Council and later his ongoing solo career, but I wasn't to know that at the time.

To help pretend that it wasn't happening, I focused on work, including asking people for their spare change to pay for phone calls to their branch. I got to grips with cashiering and even grew to enjoy it, except for Mondays and Fridays when it was so busy that the relentless queue of moaning and demanding customers seemed never-ending. Dealing with the general public is never dull, and I learned how diverse and quirky people are. I got to know and like some of the more regular customers, including a few of the more 'colourful' ones. Tom Cross was one of those. He was a chirpy fella but unable to read or write, which understandably made it difficult for him to manage his finances and meant that we had to help him. This would involve checking how much he had in his account (usually not very much), writing out the cheque for the maximum that he could withdraw in cash, and getting him to sign the cheque, which ironically consisted of not much more than an X. This procedure could take about five minutes, arguably not that long except Tom was a conductor on the Number 14 bus which stopped directly in front of the branch — it's off-putting enough when faced with a long queue of customers staring at you, but even more distracting when about twenty people are gazing at you impatiently from the top deck of a stationary London Routemaster.

Mr. Galal was another memorable regular. My first experience of him was when I was hiding behind my 'closed counter' blind having a sneaky fag and I saw him go up to Brian's till, dressed in pyjamas, a dressing gown, and slippers. He handed Brian a TDK C90 cassette tape, the type that you tighten with a bank pen, and he explained he was releasing a single soon and that he had recorded a copy for us to listen to. After we'd closed, we played the tape on Edwin's new Sony Walkman. There was no singing, no music, simply a recording of Mr. Galal talking through his real-time process of cooking a steak pie. Unfortunately, as detailed and exciting as this was, it had little chance of breaking into the Top 40. Then again, if Shakin' Stevens could get to number one with Green Door, anything was possible.

His banking behaviour was no more conventional. (I am talking about Mr. Galal as I have no idea how well Shaky ran his account, although based on the number of shite records he sold, I doubt he ever had to pay a £1 charge for a phone call to the Cardiff Branch.) Mr Galal banked at Earls Court Branch (two stops away on the District Line) and would withdraw £4 from his savings account, which meant we would need to make a phone call, which would cost him £1, meaning he only ever got £3. We subsequently learned that as soon as we had given him his £3, he would pay 50p to get on the tube to go to Earls Court and pay the remaining £2.50 back into his account. This process repeated every couple of days, and you didn't need to be Carol Vorderman to work out that this was not a profitable endeavour. After a flurry of withdrawals from his account, we didn't see Mr. Galal for about six months.

We were all genuinely delighted when he returned to the branch, dressed impeccably in a suit, shirt, and tie and, to my total joy, a fine pair of brown shoes. He was coherent, in control, clearly feeling better, as he confidently asked to withdraw £50. It was only later that afternoon when Nora opened the night safe, a letter box for Business customers to leave wallets of cash, that she found around 20 defaced marketing brochures from all of the other banks and an extensive set of written instructions on 'How to cook the perfect steak pie'. Two days later, Mr. Galal came back in wearing his pyjamas. It was my first conscious experience of dealing with vulnerable people and, to my shame, I did little to seek to understand the challenges that other people had, in truth thinking of Tom as just being a 'bit thick' and Mr. Galal as just being a 'bit of a nutter' and, even if we didn't use his telephone charges for our football kit, that was no excuse. Banking never was, or is now, designed for vulnerable people.

I served hundreds of customers, some lovely, some not, some patient, some not, some interesting, some boring, some easy, some demanding. The *most* demanding were often the local business customers, understandably, as they paid more for the privilege of running their accounts. One regular local business, SW6 Tours, was a travel agent from the North End Road who specialised in cheap package holidays to all the usual destinations as well as some of the emerging ones and they were doing well as it was the heyday of the cheap foreign trip. Like many businesses, they had an office boy who would do all the menial tasks, including the banking. Chris Shanks was theirs, and apart from occasionally getting a bit cocky, he was all right. Whenever he did get a bit lairy, we ignored him anyway because we knew he was like us. The hierarchy existed in the big wide world, not just in banking.

We got to know Chris and learned about his love for darts, Manchester United, and Ford Escorts. I was okay about two of those things, especially the

Escort, less so about the one that involved supporting a football team 200 miles away that now often plays on a Thursday night. However, I was prepared to overlook this fundamental flaw in his character when he offered us all a 20% discount on any holiday booked at the shop. I needed a holiday.

I trotted down to North End Road the following lunchtime and met his boss, Jeff, who took me through the (very) manual process of booking a package holiday. Before long, I was staring at a load of brochures strewn across the desk, turned over at the appropriate pages and with hotels and prices ringed in pen. Everywhere looked exciting, everywhere looked sunny. Up until this point, my only view on what a European holiday was about had been based on watching four episodes of 'Duty-Free' on ITV, a seriously awful sit-com in which a middle-aged couple go to Spain only for the bored wife to spend most of her time trying to get off with a waiter. In the end, I chose Tunisia, firstly because Jeff told me it was guaranteed to be hot in June, confirmed by the corresponding sun and rain charts in the brochure, and also because I was running out of time and had to get back to the branch. I was so excited, not least because I was going to get a summer holiday actually in the summer and because this was my first trip abroad, to another continent, to a completely different culture. I was also hopeful that, like the first adopters of Apple's new computer in Silicon Valley, I, too, would get the opportunity to put my floppy disc into Lisa.

Meanwhile, Mrs. Thatcher's policies had driven unemployment to a record high of over 3.2 million. The old industrial Britain, where the men worked at the local factory and spent their evenings down the pub while the women spent their days cooking, cleaning, and looking after the kids, collapsed in ruins. Not necessarily a bad thing, but it did have a massive economic impact for many while also creating a much wider north/south divide. The rich got richer, and the poor got poorer, and the guys in the middle would soon feel guilty as they stepped over the homeless on their way to selling their BT shares. Like branch banking, the country was not on a level playing field; losers *and* winners. She wasn't getting it all her own way when Arthur Scargill crossed her off his Christmas card list as the miners began striking and TV images of donkey-jacket-clad northerners setting light to dustbins to keep warm became common as they angrily waved their placards pleading for *Coal, not Dole*. Unfortunately, this brilliant slogan ultimately proved fruitless, ending up very much as *Dole, not Coal*.

Although ice skating was no longer consuming much of my spare time, I, along with 24 million others, stayed up late to watch Torvill and Dean win Gold at the 1984 Winter Olympics with their now-famous *Ravel's Bolero* routine. I had no idea what a Ravel or a Bolero was, but that didn't matter; they were brilliant and their success paved their way for a lifetime of TV appearances with Philip Schofield, which, after recent news, may not have been such a good reward for all their efforts.

The new girl, Tina, started in September, and I took another mighty step up the branch ladder. In reality, it was more a case of another rung being added below me. Regardless, it felt good as I had become obsessed with the hierarchy. The hierarchy in large organisations was, and still is, how staff get sorted into their level of 'importance' and, in a branch, the most important person was the branch manager. Other than the occasional cursory nod, it was only after I had returned from my kidney expedition that I had any dealings with the top man at Walham Green when I was summoned into the office of Sir John Fidley. He wasn't technically a Sir, but that's what we addressed him as, a title I'd not used since I'd been sent to the headmaster's study at school for laughing out loud at 'Mad Twat Coxy' when he'd set light to a dead sparrow, stuck it on the end of a stick and made it 'fly' past the window of our French class. In truth, there was no such thing as a headmaster's study at Teddington Boys School, just a shit room in the pre-fab hut next to the football pitch. Still, it's nice to occasionally pretend to be posh. Incidentally, I do blame Mad Twat Coxy for my poor grasp of French, as he never stopped mucking about, and as I sat next to him, I just couldn't concentrate. As a result, I took the decision when it came to my options in year three to drop it and take German instead, as my French vocabulary was limited to very few words, similar to a dear friend of mine, Jimmy, who, told me that the only words he knew were *Le Singe est dans l'arbre*, which translates into *the monkey is in the tree*, taken from an Eddie Izzard sketch. Neither of us could be described as fluent.

Compared to the ragged decor of the rest of the branch, Sir John's office was verging on palatial with velvety wallpaper (all on the wall) and a massive walnut desk topped with green leather. Sitting on the desk was the stereotypical-of-the-time brass reading lamp, pen holder, and wooden in-tray; the trappings of success. Paradoxically, despite the opulent feel, it was the brass ashtray stuffed to overflowing with fag-butts that was most noticeable; Sir John was clearly no ordinary smoker but a super-smoker. His large frame was covered in a really expensive-looking three-piece suit, with a pocket watch and solid, shiny *black* shoes. He oozed authority and power, and he was very scary.

'How are you, young man?' he rasped, probably not even knowing my name.
'Fine, thank you, Sir.' I said, trembling as my loafers sank into his creamy shag pile carpet. 'I hear you've had a bit of a tough time over the last few weeks, but good to have you back'. I apologised for being off work for so long so soon after joining. He said nothing, just nodded at me, effectively validating my belief that he thought I was a pain in the arse and that head office had clearly stitched him

up with a 'sicky' new entrant. And that was it, no more than that, and he sent back to sort some cheques.

Despite my woefully inaccurate teenager's estimate of his age (I'd assumed he was about 80 when he was actually only 65), he'd clearly been around for a long time, so it was no surprise when, late in autumn 1983, he announced he would be retiring. There wouldn't be any leaving do, but we were welcome to share a glass of brandy in his office on his last day. Unfortunately, I was away, shivering in a beach hut in Devon at the time, so I couldn't make it, but I heard the brandy was top quality and that he made a pleasant, if rather formal, speech.

I brought back the customary holiday present, which, according to tradition, had to be edible. There was a rumour that Derek, the foreign clerk, had once returned from his trip to Naples with a miniature replica statue of the Venus de Milo, which Nora had told him to 'Stick it up your arse'. Fearing similar repercussions, I opted for the easily shareable selection of cream fudge, which everyone gratefully tucked into after the bacon roll run. But, neither my sugary gift nor my description of how cool snow on a caravan can look was enough to overshadow the excitement of the impending arrival of the new branch manager, Clive Sanders.

Having wrongly assumed that all branch managers were equally as important as each other, I learned there was even a hierarchy within the manager population, ranging from junior (but still very important) up to very senior (God-like) level of importance. Having only recently become important, Clive Sanders was one grade below Sir John as the bank had taken the opportunity to downgrade the branch based on its current commercial importance and complexity. It was a further blow for the underdog and far from my last experience of branch downsizing.

When he arrived on his first day, everyone was struck by how young Clive looked, especially compared to Sir John. He seemed significantly more friendly too, and almost in deference to his lower managerial rank, and maybe even representing a change in the bank's culture, he told us that we could call him Mr. Sanders rather than Sir, which we did, albeit behind his back he was known as *The Colonel*. He was a quiet guy with a gentle and polite manner. Although he would spend most of his time sitting in his office, either with or without customers, he'd come to my till most days just before going out for lunch and withdraw cash from his account. The amount varied, but it was often about £100, which did seem a lot on such a regular basis, however, it wasn't for me to reason why; he was the branch manager, even a relatively junior one, so he could afford it.

A couple of months later, Gina, one of the other cashiers, was leaving to go on maternity leave, and on her last day, she had a 'bit of a do' at The White Hart. Clive was more sociable than Sir John and announced that he would be coming, and that so would his wife, Jane. These occasions usually involved a table of, at best, average quality sandwiches, often curled up because they'd been prepared and put out about six hours earlier, sausage rolls often without the sausage, crisps that definitely weren't Golden Wonder, and, only if the person leaving was exceptionally generous, prawn and chicken vol-au-vents. Gina wasn't that generous, but the (sausage) rolls were OK, and to be fair to her, she did stick a couple of quid behind the bar. Brian, Warren, Daz, and I got stuck into Gina's tab, as did Nora, who had clearly started on the sauce sometime before we'd got to the pub, possibly even before lunch. It was only about 6 p.m., but she already had her trademark ruddy face and was laughing increasingly louder at everything, even if it wasn't funny, including all of Edwin's jokes, some of which weren't even jokes.

Mrs. Jane Sanders arrived at about 7p.m., and in a scene reminiscent of Lord Delfont introducing the Queen to a line of artists after the Royal Variety Performance, politely nodded as Clive told her who each of us was, no doubt forgetting the name of the first person by the time she had got to the last, and probably like the Queen, not giving a toss either. She was pleasant and friendly and suited Clive. At one point in the evening, we chatted, and she seemed genuinely interested in whether I enjoyed work and what it was like to work with her old man. She even asked about my kidneys, and I told her they seemed to be holding up, despite the six pints I'd drunk. I didn't lift my shirt and show her my scar. In fact, I didn't mention sharks of any kind.

She told me that she didn't work but that she really enjoyed reading, belonging to a book club, which, at the time, I didn't even know was a thing. She mentioned that the coming weekend would be taken up by looking for a new shower unit, as their existing one had broken and needed replacing. She seemed genuinely concerned about whether they could afford it as apparently one of these was expensive. Despite my minimal knowledge of the cost of DIY, her level of anxiety still felt out of kilter with someone whose husband was a bank manager and a bank manager who spent about £500 a week on lunch.

It was a fortnight later when the shit really hit the fan. The branch doorbell rang at about 8:50, and I strolled to the door, looked through the spy hole, and saw four stern-looking gentlemen standing outside. Not knowing who they were, I opened the door slightly, still connected to the safety chain. 'Hello, may I help you? I'm afraid we haven't opened yet?'
'Let us in, young man. My name is Mr. Evans, these are my colleagues, and we are from the Internal Investigations team.'
Shit! The *narks* had arrived. Thankfully I remembered to ask them for ID and told them to wait as I scuttled away to ask Janet what the hell I should do. She

checked their ID and let them in. I had heard about these guys, or Inspectors as they were called. They were the internal police and acted in line with their remit. Nigel Evans, their leader, was a short bloke in his mid-fifties and was a mean (little) bastard. Like a scene from an episode of The Sweeney, Nigel and his minders almost burst into the waste room and told us all to 'touch nothing and go down to the restroom,' and I assumed they weren't planning on a game of darts.

Within five minutes, we were all nervously waiting downstairs, wondering what the fuck was going on and what the fuck we had done. Maybe they knew about the Ice Cream and Donuts? I felt sick. Evans marched in and explained 'Sanders' had been suspended and removed from the premises and that we would all be interviewed during the day. We were put under strict instructions not to talk to anyone else. What the fuck had *he* done?

At various times during the day, we all disappeared into Mr Sanders' (old) office to be interviewed. As we each returned from the grilling, the penny started to drop. I had no idea there even was a local casino, let alone that Clive was having fun in one every lunchtime using the cash that I had been giving him. But surely, if that was what he fancied spending his money on, then that was up to him? Well, I guess it would have been if the money he was gambling with had been his own rather than taken from a few dormant customer accounts, which he had found a simple way to access and an even more straightforward way of covering up.

'Did you not ever think it strange that he took out so much cash every day?' Evans asked me.

'Well, no, Mr. Evans, he is, I mean was, the branch manager, so I never thought anything was wrong with that.'

'Did you ever check the account number on the withdrawal docket he gave you?'

'No, I didn't. I wish I had now, but, as I said, he *was* my Manager, so I never thought I would need to.'

I felt stupid. I felt guilty, even if I had been completely oblivious to what Clive had been up to. As much as I hated Evans for being a horrible (little) bastard, I had to agree with the sentiment of what he was saying. Yes, in hindsight, of course, it was odd, and yes, with hindsight, I should have checked the account number, but it simply never occurred to me that someone as important and respectable as a bank manager, my boss, would be on the fiddle. I didn't even know that being on the fiddle was a thing.

It was my first experience of the *either/or* scenario. *Either* I knew what Clive was doing (in which case I was complicit), or I didn't know what he was doing, but I *should* have (in which case I was negligent). *Did* you know, or *should* you have known? Either way, you look and feel like a twat. I'd not been as confused as this since I had seen Boy George when he first appeared on Top of The Pops the previous month.

It was scant consolation when Roy told me I'd been partly responsible for Clive getting caught. When I had mentioned to him that I had found my conversation with Jane about the shower strange, he did some digging, found out what was going on, and called in the Gestapo. Within a couple of weeks, we were told that Clive Sanders would not be returning to the branch, and a few months later, we heard that he wouldn't be returning to Jane for about three years either. I never did find out whether she got her new shower.

10

'Saturday's boys live life with insults, drink lots of beer and wait for half time results'

Although it was the decade in which I first had money, first had independence, and first officially became a grown-up, I still think of the nineteen-eighties as, without doubt, the most naff ten years in history — especially in fashion. Some people still describe the eighties as iconic, and if that means a cultural disaster, then I absolutely agree. As I'd learned from my experience with Mr Sanders, hindsight is a wonderful thing, so despite my views now, at the time, I was more than prepared to get involved, not least my occasional dalliance with a curly perm and salt and pepper highlights. However, my most significant contribution was to be a regular and proud wearer of the white fluffy sock, readily available at all good Sunday morning markets, including Wembley, at £3 for about 20 pairs. The fluffier and the whiter, the better, and when worn with a brown loafer, they looked marvellous. Well, they did to me.

Following Clive's sudden departure, we were due to get our third Manager within just a few months, not unlike Fulham Football Club. We didn't know what to expect, but whatever we had, none of us expected the whirlwind that was Reg Groot. We were allowed to call him Mr Groot, which was about the only thing he had in common with Clive, and he wore a three-piece suit, which was about the only thing he had in common with Sir John. He'd clearly been chosen for his no-nonsense style, venerating our paranoia that head office had blamed us all for his predecessor's wrongdoings. And, as is often the case, a new leader feels that they have to make an immediate impact, and Reg was intent on making a significant, immediate impact. One of his first actions involved me, Brian, Daz, and Derek being summoned into his office and lined up like soldiers about to be inspected by a Sergeant Major. One by one, he stared us up and down and commented on our appearance. 'You need to learn to iron a shirt and could do with losing a few pounds', he said to a speechless Brian. 'I'm not quite sure what's going on with your hair, but you look like a girl,' he told Daz, who reeled from the criticism of his fresh new highlights. 'You need to get some dark socks, lad, this is a bank, not a gymnasium' he barked as he turned his attention to me. 'And you can take those fucking monstrosities off, brown is not for town.' I don't remember what he said to Derek exactly, but it was something about 'trying not to be so ginger' and that his beard 'looked like a 'fucking bush'

Whether he was under instruction to be tough or just super-keen to flex his leadership muscles, we never knew, but regardless, he was terrifying. But, over time, he seemed to warm to most of us, and most of us warmed to him; a sheep in wolf's clothing and another lesson for me to not always judge someone on first impressions, even if they do behave like a total twat. Unfortunately, Derek never managed to warm in any way to Reg. Admittedly, Derek was *very* ginger, even more so than my old creme egg-eating mate Vince, and he was also so nervous that you could almost see his knees knocking whenever Reg was nearby. Sensing this weakness, Reg, who had a playful streak underneath his impressive mahogany tan (his kind of brown, *was* for town), never missed an opportunity to embarrass Derek. I recall one afternoon when Brian and I were sitting in what was colloquially known as the *securities box*, the area of the office where the 'grown-ups' who did important stuff worked, when a buoyant Reg came bounding out of his office, his chirpy demeanour fuelled by his impending holiday in Spain. He made a B-line for Derek, who, as the 'does-what-it says-on-the-tin' foreign clerk, was in charge of all things foreign, including ordering and giving out currency, to staff as well as customers.

'Where are they then?' Reg demanded.

'Err, where are what, Mr. Groot?' replied a clearly confused and petrified Derek, like a ginger cat caught in the headlights.

'Pesetas, Derek, you know, Pesetas, for Spain. Not potatoes, like the ones that are probably growing in your beard.'

I've sat through many uncomfortable silences over the years, but this will go down as one of the more painful ones, as Derek, cheeks brighter red than his hair, shuffled off and proceeded to unlock and then search through an actual (tin) box where all the foreign currency was safely stored, After what seemed like hours of us all sitting there watching Derek, clearly unable to focus, fumbling through loads of envelopes in the box, he eventually pulled out the one containing Reg's holiday loot and handed them over to him. 'Thank you, Derek,' said Reg. 'I only hope the Spanish blokes at the hotel bar are a lot bloody quicker than you' as he skipped back into his office, winking at Brian and me as he trotted past. It was wrong to find it enjoyable watching a grown man squirm, but I was immature enough to believe that if the boss was doing it, then it must be OK and that it was funny. Reg disappeared on his holiday and no doubt enjoyed spending his Pesetas on San Miguel, Sangria, and Ambre Solaire. Derek left the bank shortly afterwards.

Fortunately, Reg was still parading around the pool in Torremolinos in his yellow and green budgie-smugglers when I had my second awkward career moment. Typically for a Tuesday, it had been quiet, so I had used the last part of the afternoon before we closed to do the checking and counting that I needed to and had already balanced my till by 3:30 when the final customer had left, and Brian had shut the front door. I was ready to load the notes and coins from my till onto one of the industrial wooden trolleys, which would then be wheeled into 'Stephen's' lift. The tattered grey leatherette stools we perched on behind the counter had big, heavy bases, such that they needed a good shove to move. As I grabbed hold of my countertop to give me extra leverage to move my stool back, I felt the blood rushing to my head again as I realised I had accidentally pushed one of the personal attack buttons underneath the desk. These buttons, situated at multiple points across the branch, were a primary safety control in the event of duress, for example, during a raid, which, when pressed, would be silent at the branch but ring loudly at the nearby Nick. Had I, hadn't I? It was a rhetorical question and, any lingering hope that I hadn't, was quickly erased when, at 3:50, the doorbell rang and I saw the two uniformed police officers waiting outside. I opened the door on the chain.

'There has been an emergency alert from your personal attack system. Is everything OK?' asked the male officer.

'Well, you took your bloody time,' I was tempted to say, but instead, feigned confusion and told him that we were all fine and that it must have been the ultimate false alarm.

'We still have to check,' the female officer asserted. While that was the last thing I wanted, I knew they had no choice other than to check that everything *was* OK, as someone could have been behind the door pointing a gun at my head. As much as I wanted them to just go away, I knew that wasn't going to happen. I let them in, showed them to the back office, and introduced them to Roy, explaining why they had arrived. Roy confirmed that everything was OK and that nobody was under any duress before checking with all the staff if any of them had pressed a panic alarm. No one had. No shit.

I'm not proud I didn't own up there and then, but by this stage, I was in far too deep to dig myself out. 'Just go with it,' I kept telling myself. Unaware of the irony, Roy asked me to take the police officers around the branch to check each of the 20 or so buttons. I could have suggested starting at my counter first, but that felt too obvious. Instead, I took them to the other side of the office so it was about 35 minutes before, eventually and inevitably, in the words of Cilla Black on her new TV show *Surprise, Surprise* we found that my panic button had been pressed. Well, bugger me, how on earth did that happen?

'Do you have any idea why your alarm has been pressed, Graham? ' Roy asked me, 'Either deliberately or by mistake?'

'No, Roy, I don't, other than I did drop a bag of 50p pieces onto the counter, and I wonder whether that may have triggered it,' I said, almost blushing at how ridiculous the suggestion was.

'Well, yes, that has happened once before, so it is possible' Roy agreed.

I did a mental celebratory fist pump as he explained that given this 'obvious' fault, we would need an engineer to fully service the system. Even now, I didn't muster the decency to 'fess up and save the bank the time and expense. I showed the two coppers to the door, apologised that we'd troubled them unnecessarily, and thanked them for their speedy response. 'It's good to know you guys have got us covered'.

I didn't get out early that day, but I wasn't bothered, more relieved that I'd gotten away with it. I left the branch with Brian, and we headed towards my battered but well-loved MG Midget parked on Old Farm Road as I'd promised to drop him off at his place on Dawes Road. 'I need to let you into a secret,' Brian said as I turned into North End Road. 'I know Roy thinks that a bag of coins triggered an alarm before, but that's not strictly true. I pressed the button by mistake as I pushed my stool back, but didn't have the bollocks to admit to it.'

I smiled as I pulled up outside his flat. 'See you tomorrow, mate,' I said. 'Don't worry, I won't tell anyone . . .'

Just when I thought my sense of shame couldn't get any worse, the following day, Roy asked whether anyone could do overtime at the weekend to let the engineers come and service the alarms. I volunteered and got the gig. Triple time, both days. To Reg's delight, I spent most of my hard-earned cash on a pair of very *black* brogues, which may have pleased him, but I felt like I'd sold myself out — better to conform and keep the boss happy than be myself; winning *and* losing.

I also gave some money to my Mum towards the purchase of a video cassette recorder. In today's world of streaming, Smart TVs, and everything on demand, it's easy to take for granted the capability to pause, fast forward, and rewind content, but when the VCR arrived, being able to do these things was like wizardry; to stay up the pub for an extra couple of pints on a Friday night knowing that I wouldn't miss the start of *Vic and Bob's Big Night Out* was life-changing, even if, in the early days, my poor grasp of the pre-record function meant that I often taped episodes of *The Sky at Night* and *Question Time* by mistake. It wasn't long before we were introduced to the ubiquitous blue and yellow of *Blockbusters* and the frequent ritual of driving three miles to a video shop, pretending not to look at the porn films on the top shelf and ending up with a copy of *Blazing Saddles* for the fifth time and then, two days later, getting fined £2 for returning it three hours late.

Despite barely being out of the worst recession in post-war history, with unemployment at almost four million, the Tories continued encouraging us to indulge in a lifestyle of excess, so a common challenge for people was finding the money, not least to embrace the stream of emerging new technology, The solution for many, and excellent news for the banks, was to borrow it. People felt entitled to the good life, so new video recorders, microwaves, and computers invariably got put on *Access* or *Barclaycard* or *Visa*, or, if they were going for it big time, a loan. To support this increase in demand for borrowing, banks invested in their own technology, including a new concept called credit scoring. Until this point, lending money had been very much a dark art, only known to and practiced by the sorcerers of the securities box — in our case, Steve Collins and Steve Russell. These boys were 'proper' bankers, doing all manner of important stuff, while the rest of us were pissing about eating bacon rolls and nicking money for a football kit. Lending money had to be done carefully, skilfully, and evidently by a grown-up named Steve.

Reg announced that we would shortly be given a new-fangled credit scoring machine, meaning that now anyone could lend money, including Brian, Warren, Daz, and me. Even Edwin. The Steves were understandably unhappy and skeptical about the capability of this technology. 'There's no way that a machine can replicate what we do with the same level of accuracy,' said Steve R, and Steve C agreed wholeheartedly. Of course, they were right — there was a disparity between human decision-making and the use of algorithms and data, just different from the way round that the Steves wanted to believe. It was the first time that I saw the realisation that technology could replace people and put jobs at risk. 'If I refuse to believe it, it might go away' — a fear that still rages on 40 years down the line.

I was intrigued by this machine and its capabilities, even with its dependency upon a stable telephone connection, which in Fulham Broadway in 1984 wasn't easy to get, meant it frequently stopped working. And of course, we needed to give it a name. Brian suggested we call it Nora ('probably won't work after lunchtime'), but eventually, we settled on Reg's suggestion, Steve. For some reason, Messrs Collins and Russell didn't see the funny side.

Roy explained that also, the branch would soon be opening on Saturday mornings to see more customers who wanted to give the new Steve a try and borrow some money. Initially, I was a little defensive about it because that was when I would usually watch Sarah Green on Saturday Superstore until I remembered that I could record her on Mum's new VHS recorder and watch her (much) later in the day. Once Roy had explained that we would get paid double time and I realised that I would finish work two hours before kick-off at Stamford Bridge every other week with only The White Hart in between, it started to sound like a brilliant gig. Not only that, Saturday mornings, according to Roy, were going to be different from weekdays — we wouldn't be opening the tills (so we couldn't give anyone any cash), but we could talk about anything else the customer wanted to talk about, mainly of course lending them more money than they needed. It was the start of Personal Banking.

So, for the 1984-1985 football season, I got to wander up to watch Chelsea after getting paid what to me at the time was an obscene amount of money to do nothing all morning except repeatedly say to customers, 'I'm very sorry, we're not offering a counter service today, but you can have a loan if you want one, as long as the phone line doesn't get cut off.' Another benefit of Personal Banking was that I was allowed to have my very first business card — a moment of seismic importance and I didn't even let the fact that they were printed in blank and that I had to write my name in pen across the middle of them to ruin the moment. I couldn't wait to fill one in and give it to Mum so that she could proudly stick it to the fridge. 'My boy's really doing well you know, look, he's even got his own business card, he's a Personal Bonker'; apparently, my handwriting wasn't very good and this wasn't the last time that I would get told that.

At the end of the summer, Roy was advised by Head Office that it was time for me to leave Walham Green and move to Hanover Square Branch, another place I had yet to learn where it was. I immediately popped over to the White Hart and reserved the far corner of the lounge bar for my leaving do. There had been times during my first few years at work when it had been dull, occasionally a slog, but overall, I'd had a wonderful time there. I met some fabulous people, and I learned so much. Whatever else I did or wherever else I ended up, Walham Green would always be my first place of work, my first proper job, and that would always stay with me.

My leaving do wasn't a lavish affair. There were no odd moments, such as the incumbent Manager's other half giving away that their husband was on the fiddle, but I did order some vol au vents. In truth, it was a reasonably uneventful Friday night — Nora was pissed, Edwin was sober, Brian had a row, with some idiot and Warren was his usual competent self, and Daz was just being a good mate. I was sad to be leaving, but I knew I was ready to move on and was looking forward to Monday morning and starting the next chapter of my journey.

Self assessment: The 'Starting Out' years

'Although initially I found work scary, it surprised me how quickly I got used to it. 'Waste' wasn't as bad as it sounded even if sorting up and going to the bloody post office became tedious after a while. I'm pleased I was able to learn other jobs, including the counter where I had a good laugh with Brian.

I still can't believe that I used to give Clive all that cash at lunchtimes but I'm going try and forget that happened, as well as the fact that I ruined Colin and set off the alarms. Hey, everyone makes mistakes. I shouldn't have locked Stephen Harris in the lift either, but I couldn't resist it and despite the traumatised look on his face when we let him out, he got over it, eventually.

I've enjoyed being at Walham Green, especially being part of a team, but I'm still not entirely sure whether a career in banking is what I want— I seem to be doing OK and Roy keeps telling me that I should believe in myself more but I know that I'll never be as good as Warren, he's far brighter than me and seems to do everything much better and quicker too. But, I do like having my own money, even if I have spent a big chunk of it on bloody bacon rolls and now I have to give my Mum loads too. (Well, not loads, but it is a few beers worth.)

I finally had to get rid of my brown shoes after Reg shouted at me, which I'm not happy about as I now look like everyone else, especially as I've got the same highlights as Daz. Maybe I can find another way of being a bit different to the others now that I'm off to a new branch'

Part 3

The 'West End' years

(1985-1990)

11

'The more we get, the more we lose, when all is more it's more we choose, there's always something else in store'

My new adventure at Hanover Square started at a time when the continued focus on wealth creation and the implication from the Government that *greed is good* helped venerate the belief that flaunting money was socially acceptable. And, coupled with the further decline of manufacturing, the country became increasingly polarised. Labour had surged ahead in the opinion polls, driven in part by the racial unrest across the country that had fuelled riots at Handsworth, Brixton, and Tottenham, the latter marked by the death of PC Keith Blakelock at Broadwater Farm. Outbreaks of football hooliganism were increasing, including the tragedy at Heysel, where 39 football fans died and hundreds were injured at a Liverpool game when a wall collapsed. As a result, all English football clubs were banned from playing in Europe until further notice. It wasn't really a big issue for Chelsea.

Having become unconsciously competent at driving and passed my test a couple of years earlier, my journeys to Walham Green had been in the comfort of my new pride and joy, my super-slick Ford Escort Popular Plus, listening to Mike Reid on the Radio One Breakfast show not playing Relax by Frankie Goes To Hollywood. (I'd long-since sold the MG after my sister, who I'd started dropping off at Charing Cross hospital where she worked, had kept complaining that whenever it rained she had to sit with her lunchbox on her lap to stop the rain from ruining her clothes) But now, I faced the new challenges of getting on a train and a tube as I entered the world of proper commuting.

Something as simple as catching a train is not meant to be stressful, but merely waiting on the packed platform for the 7:06 train at Whitton station on my first morning was exactly that. I had no idea where to stand or, more accurately, where I was *allowed* to stand. The front of the platform was by far the most crowded because the train terminated at London Waterloo, where 95% of the people got off. The other 5% were the poor bastards who worked in Euston and had to get onto the Victoria line at Vauxhall, so they stood towards the rear end. I plumped for somewhere between the two. As the old slam-door style train growled and clunked its way along the platform, even before it had stopped, the seasoned commuters, knowing exactly where the door would be, started to make their move, surging forward using their significant shoulder pads to jostle for position and then piling in. I followed at the rear, the new boy in his rightful place. Even in commuting, there's a hierarchy.

As I struggled to hold my newspaper with both hands and not fall over while I stood for the entire 30-minute journey, I quickly understood the importance of getting a seat, envious of the seated guys who looked comfortable whilst reading theirs, as well as there being a few lucky buggers having a quiet nap. As a new boy, I was also one of the few passengers who was listening, indeed remotely interested in the frequent announcements from the rush hour train guard, albeit by the second week, the relentless and inane interruptions had become boring, and in more recent years, a genuine source of irritation. I already *know* that there are other passengers who 'need a seat more than I do' and I am also aware that all bikes should be folded, even if that must be confusing for people with non-folding bikes. I know where the next stop is because I've done the same journey a million times, and I'm fully aware that Waterloo is 'where this train terminates'. I honestly couldn't care less that I could change at Clapham Junction, and cross to platform 11 for a train to Three Bridges; I mean, where on earth is Three Bridges, and who has ever made that journey at 7:25 a.m. or gone to a children's attraction like

Chessington World of Adventures in a double-breasted suit? I can personally guarantee that nobody ever will.

Back on my first journey to Hanover Square, I managed to make it to Waterloo and then on the tube to Oxford Circus, where I arrived not long after 8 a.m. Despite nearly 5 years of experience in the bank, I was still as anxious as a young boy starting at a new school, so I found a place between the branch and Regent Street to grab a few coffees to calm my nerves. I think that's the point of caffeine. The cafe I'd discovered was extraordinary. Whereas the Bridge Cafe in Fulham Broadway had (extremely) tattered pictures of the Chelsea FA Cup-winning side from 1970, this place had a long tapestry of the Amalfi Coast running along one wall. Hanging from the ceiling in SW6 were cobwebs and loose wires, here were dried flowers and terracotta jugs. One had a framed five-star hygiene certificate, clearly displayed on the counter, the other had a two-year, out-of-date, 3-star certificate blue-tacked to the grimy fridge. The two places could not have been more different and nor could the staff. Judging by his exaggerated 'Gino de Campo' type accent, I assumed the guy behind the counter was Italian, or Joe Dolce. 'Whatta d'ya want?' he asked.
'I'll have a coffee, please'
'Whatta exacta coffee d'ya wanta?' he asked impatiently
'Just coffee, black, please,' I replied.
'You meana an Americano,' he clarified.
'Whatever,' I thought.

At this point, I should have realised that if buying a drink was so complicated and intimidating, ordering food was going to be a real challenge. I stared at the immaculately handwritten menu on the chalkboards behind the counter, a long list of exotic sandwiches and other items. Cheese and pickle had been replaced by egg Florentine (What actually is a florentine?), and sausage and red sauce on white had given way for chorizo and sun-dried tomatoes on ciabatta. I could hear the experienced customer behind me tutting at my incompetence and for keeping him waiting. 'Do you do bacon rolls?' I enquired, realising as soon as the words came out of my mouth that it was a ridiculous question. 'Guiseppe' looked at me like I had asked him to warm up a hamster in the microwave. 'Noa, we do notta do those,' he laughed.

'How silly of me,' I thought, as I started to get irritated by the pretentiousness of the whole charade. After being advised of the alternative options, I eventually scuttled off to the furthest corner of the restaurant with my extra hot Americano and a Brie and crispy bacon sandwich on sourdough. It might be a long way to Fulham Broadway, but my heart was (still) right there.

45 minutes later and filled once more with the new-boy jitters, I took longer than I needed to get the very short distance from *Bar Remo* to my new branch. I rang the front doorbell feeling horribly on my own, waiting for an eternity until the door was finally opened. 'Hello, can I help you?' asked a scruffy-looking bearded guy, 'I'm afraid we don't open until 9:30'.

'Hi, I'm Graham, I start work here today.'

'Oh, OK, I didn't think we had any new starters today, wait here a minute,' he said as he shut the door and left me standing there, feeling about as welcome as Jimmy Saville at the BBC's Christmas party. Maybe I'd got the wrong day, or even worse, I'd got the wrong branch, but either way, there was a stark contrast between the high anticipation of my arrival at Walham Green and the total indifference this time. I wasn't expecting a red carpet, but I at least thought they would know I was coming.

The guy returned and, to my relief, confirmed I *was* in the right place at the right time. He introduced himself as Robert Dexter and, following the now-familiar-to-me protocol, asked for my ID. I showed him my paper driving licence, and after a brief check, he let me in. It immediately struck me how much bigger this place was, how much tidier it was, how much newer it looked — there were even two enquiries windows in the long, spacious banking hall. Robert took me into an enormous open-plan back office where the wallpaper was stuck to the walls, and the carpet tiles were relatively free of tea and coffee stains. Most noticeably, there were people everywhere, and unlike Robert, they all looked well turned out; Reg would have been impressed at how smart they were.

Rather worryingly, considering he didn't know I was coming, Robert was to be my 'buddy' for the first few days, so he took me on a tour of the office, starting upstairs. 'This is the restroom,' he told me, by which I realised he meant the toilets rather than somewhere to play darts or eat saveloy and chips. I never really understood why khazis are called restrooms; that's not what people tend to do in them. I got introduced to loads of people whose names I instantly forgot before being shown the actual restroom, which like the rest of the branch was impressive. In it was a free-vend drinks machine, which not only dispensed tea and coffee, it also had hot chocolate. And soup! As exciting as that was (and strangely, it was), I couldn't stop staring at the pool table, standing proudly in the middle of the room, almost as a symbol of the elevated status of the branch. Salaries for staff were broadly the same, regardless of which branch you worked at, but the working environments could differ significantly. Not a level playing field; winners *and* losers.

Before being shown to the separate office where I would be working as a 'Lending Officer,' I was told that I was to attend a 'What's On Your Mind' meeting. I'd only been working there for about an hour, so I wouldn't have endeared myself to my new colleagues if I'd raised any concerns, so other than being curious about the name of the blond girl with the long legs and who was going to take me to the pub at lunchtime, I treated it as an early opportunity to listen and learn from, rather than contribute to.

I did listen, and I did learn. The sessions were in groups of about eight, each with a facilitator whose job was to keep the discussions on track, and my group was led by Steve Mac. I liked Steve Mac. I hadn't formally met him at this point, but he seemed intelligent and I assumed he was ambitious based on a solid pair of black brogues. We'd held similar sessions at Walham Green that tended to be generally positive, maybe with the occasional gripe about having to mop up the tramps' piss and shit from the banking hall or that the shared toilet kept getting blocked. But here, evidently, the issues were far worse and far more deep-rooted. Tracy raised the first point and it seemed reasonable enough. 'We still don't get sufficient training,' she said, to nods of approval all around, 'and we always get dropped in at the deep-end without any time to learn the job.'

Judging by his expression, Steve Mac had heard this before. 'Personal development is by its very nature personal, Tracy, and so is therefore very much your responsibility, but thanks for raising it.' I'm sure he wanted to say, 'Thank you Tracy, well done for speaking, but do fuck off,' but he was far more professional than that.

Unfortunately, that was the high point of the session, and the mood deteriorated from there. Andrew raised his concern that the tea and coffee dispenser was slow and that the soup was watery, but Steve managed to overcome this major breach of human rights (everyone should have access to a decent broth) by reminding us that Len, the messenger, would make soup to order and would bring it around to your desk if the translucent nature of the free-vend offering was a problem. OMG wasn't an acronym then, but OMFG.

Just when I thought we couldn't get any more trivial, we really got down to brass tacks when an irate Stuart, a red-faced guy in his forties, almost spat at Steve. 'I keep mentioning this, but again, nothing has been done about it.' Worried that he was about to provide evidence of a fundamental problem with the bank pension scheme or that some emerging technology was about to make us all redundant, I braced myself for the worst. 'So, when will the baize on the pool table be re-covered? It is so worn at the baulk end, and I'm sick of it.' My desire to slap him was only tempered by the assumption that someone else would do it for me, but to my amazement, his moan was met with almost unanimous support from all the blokes in the room. They clearly played a lot of pool at Hanover Square. I regretted saying nothing, but my expression of complete bemusement must have given away what I was thinking. Walham Green may have been rough around the edges, even occasionally depressing, but it wasn't full of entitled twats. In fact, we were grateful for having a job at a time when millions of others didn't and I immediately wanted Stuart and a few others to be sentenced to two years of hard labour in Fulham Broadway to give them something worth moaning about. After the meeting, Stuart introduced himself to me as the branch union representative, the point at which I decided not to join the union.

I did get the answers to the two questions I had before the meeting; Debs, and nobody. And so, as I headed for the chaos of Oxford Circus tube at the end of my first day, I reflected that Brian might have been a Fulham fan, even a fat twat, but he still took me out for a pie and a pint. Salt of the earth.

12

'The distant echo of faraway voices boarding faraway trains'

I was quickly learning about the art of commuting to and from the West End. Navigating the four stops to Oxford Circus in the mornings was reasonably straightforward, especially as I would get there early, however, the return journey in the evening, with the rush-hour condensed into a shorter period and numerous camera-clad, apologetic Japanese jaywalkers wandering around, was far more exciting. As an 'official' commuter, I did of course have a legal right of way over tourists—'I live and work here, so I have priority, you are just on bloody holiday.'

The real fun would begin when, after telling all the tourists to 'Stand on the bloody right' of the escalator, I would arrive at the platform, and, based on how many people deep the mob was, I would discover how high my blood pressure was likely to rise during the rest of the journey. Today, we are lucky to have the commuter's best friend, the 'next train dot-matrix indicator board,' a simple invention but, when introduced, significantly reduced the stress levels of thousands of commuters; simply knowing when the next train is coming, even if it's not for eight minutes, reduces anxiety massively because it removes the guessing— I'm informed, and I now have choices; I can huff and puff, I can moan, I can get my phone out and play a game, I can read a book, I can get a bus, go to the pub, walk, run, cycle, whatever I want to. But I have a choice. And I know that if I'm going to be waiting for eight minutes, I have about seven minutes to get over myself. It really is a brilliant way of managing customer expectation.

In 1985, we had no idea how long it would be until the next train. In 1985, if there was a major incident somewhere on the network, we'd only hear about it when we got home three hours late. In 1985, you had no choice but to stare down the tunnel in hope; in the hope that you would soon hear the distant rumble of a metal can rattling along some tracks, followed by the faint gust of wind, and finally, you'd fist-pump the air in celebration at the glimmer of light at the end of the tunnel that confirmed that it was all true and that a tube train really was about to arrive at the platform. And for eight minutes, that's all you could do; staring, hoping, praying. No wonder it was stressful.

In my new role, Steve Mac would be my immediate boss, which was good news as he seemed like a guy I could learn from, and I was to work alongside a bloke called Simon Ravel, who would teach me about lending money to customers and even more about getting it back from them. Under Simon's guidance, my job was to monitor customers who were, or were about to go overdrawn or to exceed their overdraft limit and, when necessary, politely ask them to stop being silly, stop using their accounts, and pay-in some money, or else we'd have to bounce their cheques and charge them a ridiculous amount of money for the pleasure. In extreme cases, we would confiscate their cheque or credit card, the ultimate sanction, the ultimate embarrassment, but often the only way to stop their out-of-control spending.

Not only did this *help the customers to help themselves*, but it also gave us the raw material for the plastic card horse mural on our office wall. Spanning about 10' x 8' Simon calculated that we would need approximately 750 cut-up cards to complete it, and, with an average daily haul of three cards, we reckoned on a year-long project. I did try not to smile when taking out the scissors to cut the customer's card up in front of them, as it was such a humiliating experience, but the desire to create our plastic masterpiece became all-consuming. In the end, helped by Thatcher's continued encouragement to relentlessly keep buying stuff, and another recession, our daily recovery rate increased substantially, and we only needed 8 months to complete it. The estimated value of the unauthorised borrowing spent on the cards was somewhere in the region of a million quid, so this was not just a load of plastic stuck on a wall, it was a valuable work of art. Well, sort of.

Months passed, and, like travelling on the tube, I got used to the daily routine and even started to enjoy it. I thought less and less about Walham Green and Brian and Warren and Edwin. I even started agreeing with Stuart that the pool table should have been repaired by now; you become a product of your environment for sure. I even sampled some of Len's soup, but it took ages to arrive, so I never bothered again, although I didn't complain to him because he was such a lovely old guy. As well as Len, there were many other characters working at the branch, some I became friendly with, others I didn't, and a few who were just a pain in the arse. One particular pain in my arse was the operational sub-manager, Chris Harper. In his late forties, he always seemed tense and, most of the time, was either angry or really angry; I assumed his other half gave him such a tough time at home that he only came to work in order to let out his frustration on us. He was intelligent, articulate, and well-turned out, always wearing trousers with a sewn-in adjustable waistband, which impressed me because that made his suit bespoke and expensive. His shoes were solid, black brogues.

Unfortunately for anyone who got on his wrong side, which wasn't difficult, Chris tended to throw things at people. Once, while I was doing 'senior on post*, (look at me!) I didn't notice that Jason, the junior on post, had committed the most heinous of crimes and left a registered parcel unattended. But old eagle-eye Harper spotted it, sending him into a spin and prompting him to hurl a stapler at Jason and me from about ten yards. It missed us both, but we never left a registered envelope unattended again.

*I later found out a guy called Mark Hansen had actually been '*doing the junior on post*'; lucky Debs.

As dangerous as it was to have a metal object thrown in my direction, the primary recipient of Chris's irritable outbursts was Robert. I got to know Robert well and liked him as he was funny and quirky. He always looked untidy, wearing the same scuffed, soft-soled shoes and a bland grey and maroon pinstripe suit, which, like Chris Harper's, was made to measure, unfortunately not for him.

He would always give the impression that his potential was unfulfilled, epitomising many High Street bankers of the eighties — desperate to do well, to get on, but never quite succeeding and, in the process, convincing themselves that it was never *their* fault; a victim mentality that, like others, Richard could never find a way to cut through.

Robert could be self-destructive, lapsing into total stupidity, no less than on the day of the 'blue spot' incident. It was summer, Chris was on holiday, so Robert was in charge. But he was also bored. As hard as it is to believe with the technology we have today, putting a sticky blue spot onto a piece of paper was still a crucial part of the UK bank clearing system, so we had an abundant supply. They came in sheets, and you just peeled them off, which Robert decided to do that afternoon and then stick them to his face. I remember him putting the first one on his nose, then one on either cheek, and it escalated from there. After two minutes of frenzied spot-sticking, he was completely covered. It was funny, and he looked ridiculous, but, like when you go to a fancy dress party, the novelty quickly wore off. I think even Robert forgot they were there.

At about 5:15, the doorbell rang, and Robert plodded out to the banking hall to let in Debs, who was bringing back the registered envelope receipt from the post office. Unfortunately for Robert, there were no registered envelopes that day and it wasn't Debs, she was upstairs having a quiet chat with Mark in the restroom. Instead, standing at the door was George Baxter, the grumpiest, nastiest Chief Inspector of them all, who made Nigel Evans, the nark who interrogated us at Walham Green, seem as soft and cuddly as John Craven. And there was Robert, covered hair to chin, in sticky blue spots. As he trudged back to his desk, I could tell that Robert was distraught as he watched any remaining chance of career progression going down the pan. To make it worse, Robert knew that George and his team of Stormtroopers were due to visit as part of the bi-annual audit as Chris had even tasked him with making sure it passed smoothly. If Chris hadn't been on holiday, he would have probably thrown the franking machine at Robert. It wasn't his fault, of course, just bad luck.

Way before he spent his time knocking around with child sex traffickers, Prince Andrew gave us another royal event when he married Sarah Ferguson although unfortunately, he wasn't high enough up the Royal family hierarchy for us to get even a sniff of a bank holiday. The BBC debuted its new hospital drama, *Casualty*, attracting controversy because it highlighted the underfunding of the NHS and also condemning us to a lifetime of watching Robson Green going fishing. Sadly, ITV ended its long-running Saturday afternoon *World of Sport*, the arch-rival of Frank Bough's *Grandstand* and a fundamental part of growing up during the seventies; no longer would we be able to enjoy the danger of ice speedway from Oslo or the stupidity of caravan racing from Ipswich when the weather was too shite for horse racing.

Although nobody at Hanover Square had taken me to the pub on my first day, several guys were clearly up for a regular beer, either at lunchtime, after work, or both. Daytime drinking, now long extinct in banking apart from by closet alcoholics, was still almost considered an expected part of the culture rather than just a nice-to-do every now and then. Having only known The White Hart as a work local, I was delighted to discover two new concepts — the West End pub and the West End wine bar. Both were further examples of the contrast between these two very different parts of London. In Fulham, the boozers were predominantly full of old drunk men, shouting and swearing at each other over their pint of Light Ale. In the West End, the pubs and bars were busy, buzzy, and even had people in them under the age of 60; men *and* women. The only females that ventured into The White Hart were those who were coming to drag their pissed other halves out. Or Nora.

I was enjoying the social scene; going out was exciting, and I felt I belonged to something. However, one of the downsides of drinking at lunchtime was the risk of occasionally having a little more than was advisable, with the resulting loss of inhibition making me a tad more playful than I probably should have been. Although I liked most of the guys at Hanover Square, one person who I didn't get on with was Charlie Tonks, even worse, I didn't try, instead choosing to judge this book by its rather greasy-looking cover. He wore Reactolite glasses and for some reason I've just never trusted anyone who wears dark glasses when it's not sunny. Why I thought it would be funny or clever to put a cloth coin sack over my head and stumble around the office pretending to be John Merrick, the *Elephant Man*, saying, 'I'm not an animal, I'm Charlie Tonks', suggesting that he looked like a disfigured victorian freak, I don't know, but I did. As I couldn't see where I was going, it was inevitable that I would start bumping into things, and people and eventually into Charlie, an awkward moment for us both. My embarrassed apology of 'Don't take it personally, Charlie, I was only mucking about' didn't cut it then, nor does it thinking about it now.

While a few beers could sometimes give me a dose of Dutch courage, it didn't always work, and definitely not when it came to one of my lifetime phobias, the office Christmas party. I know they're supposed to be something to look forward to; plenty of drink, often free food, and the chance to have a boogie sounds like a good night out. My problem was I hated dancing. I was, and am, shit at it, and fewer things put me more in a spin (or not as the case may be) than the 'come and dance' insistence of someone who thinks it's fun. I would rather have a kidney stone stuck in my ureter than be forced onto a bloody dance floor, and a decent dose of pethidine wouldn't be enough to help me willingly strut my stuff.

I regret never having learned, and I still carry the fear with me, albeit these days, occasions when it's a problem, are far fewer and further between. Lisa is a brilliant, effortless dancer, so perhaps she'll teach me one day, however, I suspect she already considers me a lost cause. Indeed, her lack of belief in my rhythmic ability was confirmed recently when I announced to her and the kids that I fancied a new hobby and that I had reduced it to two options: lawn bowls or learning to play the drums. I know what you're thinking, and I agree that these are at the opposite ends of the rock and roll spectrum. There was a nostalgic logic in the bowls option, having enjoyed playing it with my grandpa as a kid. The idea of the drums came from a raw desire to do something cool, exciting, and well out of my skill set. The kids didn't vote for bowls, recognising a soft-souled, brown shoe step closer to a life of pipe and slippers, so the drums it was to be. In a loving show of support, Lisa kindly pointed out I have 'no sense of rhythm, beat or timing, and you can't read music, but, fortunately, your grandpa's old bowls are still in the shed'.

Well, that was like a red rag to a bull in a music shop, and within a week, I was at a reconditioned drum warehouse in Cambridge.

'Take your time and try as many as you want to,' the owner said. 'I'll be back in about 20 minutes'.

'How long have you been playing for?' he asked when he returned.

'About 20 minutes,' I said, although I think he had already worked that out and I saw the glint in his eyes when he realised that he could have sold me a load of plastic buckets and some saucers, and I wouldn't have known any better. Four hours later, I was unloading my £550 worth of nearly new drums from the car. I had forgotten to mention to Lisa that I was going, but even so, I didn't expect to be called an 'absolute dickhead' when I told her how much they cost. When I said I was planning on spending more to rebuild and soundproof the shed, she disappeared, muttering something about being more responsible at my age, and 'I'll have that bloody necklace if you've got so much money to waste.'

Four years later, I have achieved my drumming ambition of being capable, if ever called upon, to stand in should the drummer from a band get stuck in traffic or be sick at the last minute. The only proviso is that I can only cover them for one song, that one song must be *Cruel to be kind* by Nick Lowe and it also has to be played slightly slower than the original.

I don't know why I feel so self-conscious in certain environments, but it's an issue that has been with me for as long as I can remember. Even as a young child, I would crap myself at the thought of getting picked by the magician at a birthday party, when everyone else seemed very keen to volunteer to have milk poured down their backs and be turned into a teapot. Maybe it comes from a deep-rooted lack of confidence and the fear of looking foolish, stemming from Dad's own lack of self-belief. My increasing self-awareness and the fear of being 'shown up' in front of others had manifested itself in other environments, not least at the corporate conference. I hated them. Spending a day, or even worse two days, at some shit venue, listening to a load of shit speakers blowing smoke up each others' arses was usually painful. Worse, was being forced to have pointless table discussions with a bunch of similarly bored people and for one of the group to 'playback' to the whole room the shit you had been talking about, which unsurprisingly, was the same shit as every one of the other 56 tables. I didn't ever volunteer to be the table spokesperson.

These events often included external speakers, who admittedly were always much better than the internal ones. Often, these were ex-military or ex-sporting heroes, extraordinary human beings with breathtakingly compelling stories to tell. But when you're already lacking confidence in your own ability, it can become tiresome to constantly get reminded how pathetic your life's been as you compare yourself to an SAS bloke who single-handedly freed 200 prisoners of war from a high-security Iraqi jail or a young para-olympian who managed to do the 100 meters in under 11 seconds despite having previously had both of her legs amputated. Whilst I would be super-impressed by their feats, I would always go home struggling to translate their brilliance into the dangerous and demanding world of clearing banking and reflecting on what a loser I was in comparison.

The silver lining in the conference and seminar cloud was that I occasionally met some famous people. I was in the car park of the Hilton Hotel in Swindon one morning when a Jaguar XK8 pulled up next to my red Astra GTE. Looking like she'd been out all of the previous night, the knackered-looking driver smiled at me, and I smiled back. Only when the conference started, and Carol Vorderman came bouncing (literally) onto the stage, did I realise who I'd met only minutes earlier. She looked remarkably well-scrubbed up, and this was way before she'd (allegedly) had any work done.

Like most of them, I have minimal recollection of what that conference was about, but I do remember thinking how good Ms. Vorderman was. I'd learned from watching the occasional episode of *Countdown* that she was no fool, still, her ability to control the day and understand the banking issues being discussed made me realise why these guys get paid the big bucks. I've been equally impressed by the likes of Jonathan Ross, Eamon Holmes, and even that bloke off *Good Morning* and *Crimewatch*, Nick Ross, who had just started telling us all not to have nightmares about murderers breaking into our houses at night, something which I hadn't been until he bloody mentioned it. But all of them were highly skilled, professional, and often funny. I've also been to a conference hosted by Anthea Turner.

Things worked out OK at the 1985 Hanover Square Christmas party. Nobody forced me to dance, although I did discover why the toilets were called restrooms, as after devouring the best part of a bottle of Southern Comfort, I was grateful for somewhere to have a little lie-down and a snooze for a couple of hours. Take my word for it, once you have vomited that fruit-infused 'smooth, satisfying touch of sweetness' through your nose, you will never be tempted to drink it again; ever.

13

'What chance have you got against a tie and a crest?'

The world was still ostensibly analogue, but the pace of technological change was rapid, including how we bought and listened to music. I loved vinyl (and still do), and so I wasn't a massive fan of the new and much-lauded CD, despite being told that I could put one in the dishwasher, which was highly unlikely in my case, as Mum and Dad didn't own a dishwasher and even if they had, I would probably forget to put dishes in it, let alone my music. This indestructible media meant that cassette tapes started to disappear, and Mr. Galal would struggle to continue to record his domestic chores; winners *and* losers.

I and many others quickly realised that we would have to replace our entire music collection from scratch, which would be horribly expensive, but fortunately, we were saved by the Britannia Music Club, which, for a very reasonable monthly subscription, allowed us to buy discounted CDs. The available selection in the early days was limited, so I ended up with a dreadful Kenny G album and an even worse Sheena Easton one. I drew the line at wasting £7.99 on Shakin' Stevens' dreadful *The Bop Won't Stop*, although if ever there was a CD worth risking in the dishwasher, this was it. Also, like many lads my age, I got to splash out on a Blondie CD.

Despite still having horribly clunky, manual processes, breakthrough technology was now being regularly introduced to the branch, including when we received our shiny new fax machine. In a pre-email world, it revolutionised communications and was an early example of technology that enabled things to be done more quickly and accurately as well as fundamentally changing *what* could be done. Creating the ability to instantly share documents, including signatures, it removed the need for phone calls between the branches and any opportunity to get an even newer football kit; winners *and* losers.

Staff reaction to this new sorcery was mixed. Early adopters loved it, but the laggards resisted it, fearing, with some foundation, that it could ultimately take their jobs away. Those most unprepared to adapt to it were, ironically, the ones most at risk as they became slower at tasks than those who embraced it; just because something has been done in a certain way for a long time doesn't mean it should be done that way forever.

In their own attempt to make a change with tradition, the Tories continued to push their Council House Purchase Scheme, which allowed millions to own at least part of their home. It was unfortunate that I no longer drove to work as, with such vague qualifying criteria, I think I would only have needed to get stuck in traffic in the Hammersmith one-way system to be given the right to purchase a cheap property there. Instead, Lisa and I chose to buy a flat in Sunbury-on-Thames, having just about managed to scrimp and save a deposit. I lived in it, and Lisa kept a few pairs of shoes there. It was only small but was conveniently situated near the station. It also had a lovely view of the tyre repair centre next door. On the day we were due to move in, the concrete stairs to the first floor were still not set, taking the term new build to a whole new level, even if we couldn't get access to a whole new level. Fortunately, Gorbachev and Reagan had started to get on famously, reducing the threat of being wiped out by a nuclear missile strike, so it was unlikely I would have to shelter under those stairs; I doubt there are many more unpleasant things than suffering a slow and painful death from radiation while having cement drip onto your Sergio Tacchini tracksuit, to the backdrop of the sound of wheelie guns.

We did manage to get up the stairs a week later, however, it would be a further week before we had any electricity. I spent the first few days with an extension cable connected to an external generator coming in through the letter box. This was not how it had been shown in the sales brochure, nor did the Estate Agent tell us that the walls were so thin we would hear the explicit detail of every argument and shag the couple next door would have. Then again, even before the days of Estate Agents wearing ridiculously skinny suits and suede slippers, did any of them ever tell the truth? At least I no longer had to phone Mum and tell her if I wasn't going to be in for dinner or was staying out for the night. Which, at the age of 22, felt about time.

At work, I continued cutting up credit cards and although I was more interested in how they would help shape our horse's right fetlock, I realise now that I was doing the right thing for my customers. The world of Yuppies and 'Loadsamoney' meant that the image of a customer crawling on the floor in front of the miserly bank manager to increase his overdraft seemed horribly old-fashioned and pompous, yet arguably, it was more responsible than allowing a generation of people to run up debts they often couldn't afford.

My branch manager was called Kevin Hewson. He was young, intelligent, and humble, especially for someone who had progressed so quickly through the managerial ranks. He took me under his wing and helped me think more clearly about what I wanted from a career, including what I enjoyed doing and what I was good at. He warned me against falling into the trap of chasing promotion for the sake of it or, even worse, allowing myself to become something I didn't want to be. He also explained that if I wanted to progress, I would need to get onto the internal fast-track leadership programme. In fact, *unless* I was on the 'Management Development Scheme,' it was unlikely that I would make it much beyond 'Robert' level and I had seen too much of his anxiety to know I didn't want to end up there. Kevin was prepared to sponsor my application, but only if I committed to work hard, do my best, and not let him down. He introduced me to the concept of 'the personal brand' and made it clear that if I didn't take this opportunity seriously then I would not only ruin my own but damage his too. Make your mind up time Graham — commit to a career or carry on *just* doing a job. Take work seriously, or treat it as just something to do in between mucking about with your life. Go for it, or go home (at 5 p.m. every day).

I convinced Kevin he could trust me, so he submitted my application. A few weeks later, he was pleased to tell me that I had been accepted for the first stage, an assessment centre at the regional head office at Pall Mall, which would decide whether I had the *right stuff* for a career in banking. Even though Pall Mall was only a 20-minute jaunt down Regent Street, I allowed an hour for my journey as being late for something this important was simply not an option. I found a small Italian coffee shop nearby, and, after a quick Americano with a splash of milk (I was still watching the calcium intake but couldn't hack just black coffee), I found my way to the Regional Office, based above the Pall Mall branch. It was an extraordinarily grand Regency building, spread over several floors, each with deep carpets over white and grey marbled floors. In its heyday, the branch had nearly 1000 staff, so I can only begin to imagine the frustration of being bottom of that holiday list. As I stood outside the fourth-floor door marked *Regional Personnel*, I took a couple of deep breaths and stepped into the next phase of my working life, whatever that was going to turn out to be.

The wood-panelled walls of the reception area were filled with oil-painted portraits of bank dignitaries from many years before. These gentlemen (obviously) were the top dogs of their day, and I doubted that any of them ever did senior on post, let alone junior. Sitting behind a large and plush desk was a lady who, according to the brass nameplate, was called Pat Whelan and I told her who I was. 'Wait over there,' said Ms. Whelan, looking down her nose at me and pointing towards a seating area dominated by an elegant, worn green leather Chesterfield sofa, 'You are *too* early.'

'Bollocks to you, misery drawers, is that really such a bad thing?' I thought, but fortunately, discretion grabbed hold of me, and I just thanked her for her help. Over the next half an hour, seven other people arrived, all male, all of a similar age to me, and all given the same instruction, but without being chastised for over-eager punctuality. I knew that most people accepted into the scheme were graduates, and at the time, my narrow, comprehensive school view on life meant that I didn't like them, believing that whilst these guys might have academic ability, they lacked common sense, having all been born with silver spoons in their mouths and having had privileged upbringings, some even having gone to schools with a proper headmaster's study. It wasn't a level playing field for us commoners; winners *and* losers. I looked around at the other lads, unsure whether to consider them friend or foe, as teammates or the opposition. I decided they were the latter and wished I'd brought my *Adidas Gazelles* with me just in case there were any bears about.

Eventually, we were ushered into a large boardroom dominated by an enormous, brightly polished walnut table, which dwarfed everything else. We sat there for ages, silence other than the sound of eight anxious young men shitting themselves. The other occasion I sat in a room for so long with so many people saying so little was when I did jury service at Kingston Crown Court. After listening to 13 days of graphic evidence for a drug smuggling case, I, along with 11 other *good men and true*, were despatched to a room and sat round a table (nowhere near as shiny or expensive as the one at Pall Mall) and told to take whatever time we needed to agree a verdict. Initially, nobody did or said anything so eventually, more from embarrassment than anything else, I spoke and, for my sins, got voted in as the foreman.

I'm not claiming I was Henry Fonda in 12 Angry Men, but I did my best to keep the discussion balanced and the decision-making objective. At about 5p.m., after a couple of hours of debate, we reached a position where 11 people believed the lady was innocent, and one person thought she was guilty. The Court Clerk explained that we had until 7 p.m. to reach a unanimous decision but if we didn't, we would need to return to continue our deliberations the following morning.

'I've changed my verdict to *not guilty*,' announced the large red-faced gentleman, who had spent most of the afternoon telling us why the defendant was 'Obviously guilty, they're all the same.'

'OK, what has made you change your mind?' I asked him.

Remarkably, he was totally OK about telling everyone the truth. 'I've got an important darts match this evening which I can't miss, and I don't want to come back tomorrow as I spend Fridays at my local boozer.'

It would be an understatement to say that my faith in the British justice system, not to mention humanity, took a knock at that moment, as I saw, first-hand, someone prepared to make a decision about whether another human being should spend their next 15 years in prison, not on whether they were guilty beyond a reasonable doubt, but because they had a commitment to the Molesey and District Darts League (Division 2) and a Wetherspoons full English breakfast.

Back at Pall Mall, unable to wait any longer, a fella with bright blond hair piped up. 'Perhaps the assessment has already begun' he suggested, 'and we're being watched to see whether anyone takes the lead?' Nobody agreed or disagreed with him, but it was an interesting suggestion, and even if I did think that he sounded like a dickhead, I wished I had spoken first rather than him. A few of the others also considered that he could actually be right and started talking, trying to take the lead and the noisy chaos was only interrupted when the door opened, and an incredibly tall, thin man with an immaculate blue, chalk pinstripe suit entered. He introduced himself as Roger Barnett, the Deputy Head of Regional Personnel. He looked and sounded important, and I was curious about how impressive the *actual* Head Of Personnel must be if this imposing fella was just the deputy. Reg would have loved his Hermes tie and the subtle but distinctive aroma of his Givenchy Gentleman aftershave. Roger Barnett explained that the assessment day would last for about six hours; bloody hell, I was due to meet Robert in the pub at five, although thankfully, I didn't have a darts match to get to. I was given a timetable for *my* day and told that we were 'running to a strict schedule' and 'punctuality is an important leadership competency'. Not having heard the term competency before, I assumed it meant 'something you need to be good at to do a job'. Roger proceeded to confirm that my assumption was correct and that it would be competencies that were being assessed today.

The day would involve a range of exercises, including a meeting scenario in which the blond twat simply couldn't shut up, a team exercise in which we were instructed to make the tallest structure we could out of a load of bendy straws, a psychometric test, designed to reveal my character traits and in particular how I coped under pressure, and, the final activity, an hour-long interview with Colin Leyton, the guy from Cannon Street who had first interviewed me for a job nearly six years earlier. I assumed he must have liked me, so I gave him a look of 'Hi, you must remember me?' He didn't. Being his eighth interview of the day, he was clearly bored. 'Tell me a bit about yourself,' he asked, without the accompanying look of someone who gave a toss about hearing the answer. I'm not sure what kind of information he was after, but I mentioned going to football as being a favourite activity and socialising as a primary interest. Maybe not the most cultured of pastimes, but at least I was being honest. I also spoke about Mum and Dad and how I had only recently left home but was grateful to them for how they had brought me up. I also told him that my Dad was *only* a sales 'rep' for Cadbury's; I don't know why I felt the need to be almost apologetic about what he did, not to mention use the word *only*, but I was, and I did. Shame on me.

Eventually, the interview and the whole assessment day ended. I headed back up Regent Street to The Bunch of Grapes in Dering Street, where Robert had been waiting for me. He asked me how it had gone, almost from a sense of duty rather than genuine interest, so I told him it had gone OK, but it was difficult to really judge. I spent more time telling him about Mr. Dickhead (who I'd found out worked at the Piccadilly branch) and his massive gob. 'He'll probably be our boss soon,' said Robert, with his usual air of despondency. 'No doubt he's got rich parents and a degree in something irrelevant,' he muttered as I cracked on with my first pint after a very stressful day, wondering whether I had a future in banking, and whether Robert would ever find his own happiness.

14
'To be someone must be a wonderful thing'

1987 had been an eventful year. In January, I had arranged a ski-ing trip for 20 people, mates and mates of mates, which was remarkable as somehow I had also managed to get seven people to be away from the branch, at the same time, playing havoc with the holiday list. Daz from Walham Green came, and also to Agios Theodoros in Greece with Lisa and me that summer. I remember the three of us eagerly rushing down to the lovely sandy beach only to find that the lovely sandy beach wasn't a beach at all, just a strip of concrete. 'Hi,' I said to the Thomson holiday rep as I collared her in the hotel foyer. 'I don't suppose you could tell me where the beach is? It seems to not be where I expected it to be, which is between the hotel and the sea?'

'I'm afraid it blew away last week' she said, apologetically, 'We had a big storm and it's no longer where it should be.'

I've heard some excuses over the years, but this one was up with the best. Nonetheless, we had a fun two weeks, although the beach volleyball was far more painful than it should have been.

This wasn't the only time that the wind had been inconvenient. Kevin had told me I would hear the outcome of my assessment by the end of the week, that was until Michael Fish had assured some old lady 'there wasn't going to be a hurricane, so don't worry, just some gusty winds', hours before the UK was hit by the most destructive weather in about 300 years. 'The Great Storm' wreaked total havoc across the UK because it caught everyone off guard. The Met Office was still reliant upon very primitive technology, including, bizarrely, observations from shipping in the area, who, because of the conditions at sea, were told to come into shore, cutting off a valuable supply of intelligence.

Fortunately, it was during the night when the winds hit 120 miles per hour, meaning that only 18 people died — still tragic, but the death toll could have been so much worse had it hit earlier or later in the day. 15 million trees were also lost, including six in Sevenoaks, making it technically Oneoak, although I'm not aware that they ever officially re-named it. As devastating as the storm was, I slept through the whole thing, unsurprising, bearing in mind I also didn't wake up when the fire brigade came round our house in 1971 to extinguish our garden shed that Mum had accidentally set fire to.

Somehow, I managed to get to the branch despite much of the power in London being cut off. The few curious commuters who managed to make it in emerged from the steps of Oxford Circus tube, like families coming out from their air raid shelter during the blitz, nervously assessing the damage of the onslaught. The signs of the ferocity of the storm were everywhere, but none as dramatic as at the branch where the main front window had been completely blown out and was now being protected by a security guard. Although the cash is kept in the safe, a gaping hole in the building is not the ideal setup for a bank, and the vulnerability that this created caused a good deal of head office anxiety. Fortunately, not many would-be bank robbers wandered around the West End in a hurricane, and the guys who boarded up windows soon arrived and did their business. They, the glazers, and the roof tilers had a few lucrative weeks as one in six households claimed on their insurance. Over £2 billion was paid out in claims, which insurance companies struggled to cope with.

This was my first experience of attempting to get into work during extreme conditions, a pursuit that became an irresistible challenge over the years. Before email, working from home meant doing absolutely no work and watching a stream of talentless people making thousands of pounds by doing up crap northern houses 'to a high standard.' And although he hadn't yet started on *Homes Under The Hammer*, I can't be the only person who wonders what the fuck Dion Dublin knows about buying and renovating property.

As pointless as it was to spend six hours getting to work, arriving at lunchtime, and leaving an hour later to get home before midnight, a few of us did. When we've had heavy snow, I've been known to do a decent impersonation of Captain Oates after a long day in the Antarctic. 'I'm just going out, and I may be some time,' I'd tell the missus as I headed off towards the station, knowing full well that the UK's ability to deal with any adverse weather meant there would be no trains and that I would end up walking at least the first leg of the journey. But usually, the hardcore of us would find ways and means to get wherever we needed to. It was totally pointless but a convenient excuse to be self-righteous for a few days.

In 1987, our Weathermen got a beating when it emerged that the French had successfully predicted the Great Storm. To make things worse, many stockbrokers didn't make it in, forcing the historic decision to close the Sock Market. When it re-opened three days later, chaos ensued, shares tumbled, and tens of millions of pounds were lost in just a few hours on what became known as Black Monday. On Tuesday, Kev called me into his office. 'Well, it seems like you did OK,' he said, looking like a proud father whose son had been selected for the school football team. 'They reckon you might have what it takes.' Wow. Not bad for a comprehensive schoolboy, I reflected; maybe this banking lark really does have a future for me.

If social media had existed then, I would have told everyone how humbled and proud I was to have gotten onto the programme. But, contrary to what some people would say, I've never been comfortable with self-publicity, even though (whether I like it or not) it's now become such a seemingly important survival technique within large organisations. Maybe it's a generational issue, too, as in today's world, telling everyone else how bloody wonderful you are seems to be the norm, to the point where not doing it makes you the weird one. I do use *Twitter (or 'X')* occasionally, it does a decent job of feeding me with sports news, but unfortunately, it also allows total twats to talk absolute bollocks. Ironically, we have more technology in our mobile phones than they used to send a man to the moon, yet some people just use it to spew bile while sitting on their toilet.

I understand that *Facebook* is now officially for old people, so maybe I should give that a proper go, but then again, I'm not overly desperate to let everyone know what my dinner looked like before, during, and after I ate it, or announce that it's possibly my dog's birthday. *Instagram* and other popular platforms seem full of pictures of cakes and people from *Love Island*, so I don't think I'll bother with those either.

A relatively new kid on the social media block (for me anyway) is the so-called 'community' site *NextDoor*. Its intention to connect local people with each other is admirable and could have obvious benefits, especially for the more vulnerable people in society, however, it has descended into yet another opportunity for sad, presumably bored people to moan relentlessly about the local, first world issues of 20 mile-per-hour speed limits, the ULEZ extension or government conspiracies about global warming. On the positive side, you can use the classified section and pick up a bargain second-hand mattress (soiled but only £4).

In the corporate world, the daddy of all social media is, of course, *LinkedIn*. Launched in 2003, it was designed and offered to *'connect the world's professionals to make them more productive and successful.'* For all I know it may well have achieved that, but it's also become a vehicle for pointless self-publicity, often driven by the toxic culture of organisations forcing employees to try and look good. This is especially true in banks, where the current trend is for meaningless posts (tagging in anyone senior and important) that are clearly only done because the boss has decided 'we need to up our visibility on *LinkedIn*'. This is quite often a photograph of a staff member standing in a library somewhere saying what a fantastic event they'd held, and here's the evidence to show how amazing it was. Wait a minute, aren't they all staff? I can't actually see any customers? But that doesn't matter; nobody cares, and it also allows the boss and a few others to follow up with, 'Wow, Jenny, that looks brilliant.' No, it doesn't, it looks shite, and Jenny looks sad and lonely whilst I'm getting frustrated trying to get through on the telephone to discuss my overdraft.

LinkedIn also gives people with nothing to say for themselves the ability to vicariously take credit for someone else's thinking by re-posting a poignant quote by one of the great philosophers of the past or a current management guru, providing the opportunity for other dullards to follow up with 'So true' or 'Great share'. What is the point of that? I'm not asking everyone to be Confucius or Simon Sinek, but at least try and say something original or worthwhile.

To publicise my achievement back in 1987, I would have needed to use one of the self-congratulatory type posts, of which there are plenty about; some are genuinely for outstanding achievements, but some are less so: 'I don't normally post on here, but well done to me for the 30th anniversary of passing my Cycling Proficiency test; I'm so proud of what I've achieved — only 25 years ago, I would never have had the courage to cycle on the road at all, and now I occasionally stray onto the A316 dual carriageway.'

Before I'd had the chance to congratulate myself too much for getting onto the Management Development scheme, Kevin reminded me that every silver lining has a cloud and that I would need to do the banking exams. The cloud in the silver lining was that I would be allowed to apply for day release to attend college to study, although that privilege needed to be agreed by personnel, and only after a three-month progress review, presumably required to make sure they'd not made a terrible mistake in putting me on the scheme in the first place. As I left his office, my head spinning with the significance of what he had told me, I could see Robert waiting. His fake smile barely concealed that my good news had added to his misery, to his ongoing feeling of being hard done by. I felt for him, but the evils of comparison are as old as time; we are the way we are because of what has happened to us, so it wasn't my fault. Robert was responsible for his destiny; I now knew I was responsible for mine.

Three months later, on a bitterly cold January morning, even my latest pride and joy, my new long, black wool and cashmere overcoat struggled to do its job effectively as I headed down a freezing cold Regent Street to Pall Mall for my first quarterly review. When I had walked this route before, I had spent most of the journey worrying about whether I would find the office and whether I had a career in banking. This time, I had a much better idea where I was going in both respects.

Not wanting to give old snooty drawers Pat any opportunity for a condescending dig, I arrived dead on time. 'I have a meeting with Roger Barnett,' I told her. 'I know,' said Pat, still keen to maintain the upper hand, 'Take a seat.'
Not long after, Roger emerged from his office, his suave demeanour enhanced by his slicked-back hair, greying temples, and statement waistbanded trousers. The interview started well enough. 'How have things been?' he asked, like a doctor with a well-developed bedside manner.
'Really good,' I said, as I told him what I'd been doing, without mentioning the plastic card horse. I talked about how excited I was for the development

opportunities I would be getting, not to mention the day off per week to study, although I didn't say the last bit out loud.

He explained the purpose of the meeting was to give me feedback on any specific development areas that I needed to work on based on my performance at the assessment panel and also from a separate review that Kevin had done. 'It seems as though things have gone quite well,' he said, 'apart from a few areas, for example, this issue of not always working collaboratively with other colleagues.' Feedback is, apparently, a gift, so I resisted telling Roger he was talking bollocks and kept listening. He then questioned me about my 'restless curiosity' — bank-speak for not accepting things at face value but seeking to understand them — again, not something I'd considered a weakness, if anything, I probably had too much, meaning I could sometimes come over as a pain in the arse. This was not going well, and I started wondering how much longer I had on the leadership scheme and worrying that I was totally oblivious to my own personality.

When Roger questioned my lack of attention to detail (probably fairly), I thought about getting my (new) coat and buggering off. Roger could tell from my bemused expression that I was struggling to process what he was telling me. 'Try not to worry, Adam,' he said, 'these are all competencies that can be developed.'

Adam? Did he just say, Adam? 'Mr. Barnett, I'm not Adam; I'm Graham,' I said, nervous at having to correct someone so senior.

'Oh my Goodness, that's not good at all; I thought you were Adam Packham. I must have been given the wrong file'. His reddening cheeks were either a sign of his embarrassment or a symptom of him getting angry, probably both, and he politely excused himself and marched outside to talk with Pat. I couldn't hear his exact words, but from the muffled tone of his voice, it was evident he was blaming her entirely for the mistake. He was not happy with Pat.

I was disappointed that Roger literally didn't know me from Adam, but I was relieved that I wasn't quite as flawed as I'd just been told I was. It also amused me that snotty Pat was getting her 'comeuppance'. *What goes around, comes around.* Roger eventually returned with another file and rattled quickly through *my* feedback, most of it ringing true and making sense.

'You'll get a detailed report through in the next few days', he said, 'and as everything seems to be going well, I'm pleased to agree to your request for day release.' What started badly had ended well.

A few days later, Kevin called me into his office 'I heard about the mistaken identity issue,' he said, 'old Barnett must have looked like a right dick!' 'Yeah, it was a bit embarrassing'. I said and also explained I'd found out that Adam Packham was actually the ″Twat from Piccadilly' but Kev seemed distracted.

'I'm leaving' he announced.

'Bugger' I thought.

He explained that he'd been promoted and would be moving the following week. Of course I was pleased for him but I was gutted at losing my first sponsor, and Kev knew that. 'You'll be fine,' he said, and I knew I would be, but that didn't mean that I wouldn't miss his help, and his friendship. Oh well, shit happens and I'm sure that the new boss will be OK . . .

15

***And in my mind I saw the place, as each memory returned to trace,
dear reminders of who I am, the very roots upon which I stand***

1988 was a year marked by postal workers walking out over bonuses, nurses still striking for higher pay and the Health Secretary being forced to resign after making a ridiculous comment. It all sounds horribly familiar. At least the politicians back then had the good sense to agree new licensing laws allowing pubs to stay open all day; as a team player and an upright citizen, I was more than prepared to undertake extensive consumer research into the impact of this new legislation.

As a parting gift, Kev had given me my feedback. It was his opinion, and that of the assessment panel, that I learned new things quickly, I worked well in a team and on my own, and that I was good at using my initiative to get things done. However, I *did* need to pay more attention to detail, be less defensive about criticism, hide my feelings better, and not get so frustrated when things didn't go to plan. And there it was— a 24-year-old me, laid bare on a page. I was what I was, except, of course, when I was being Adam Packham.

Kev's replacement was called Guy Rook. He had fingers like bananas and a massive, puffed-out barrel chest, which provided ample space to pin his many military medals on, mainly awarded for running around Dartmoor on a weekend with the Territorial Army; hardly what I'd consider active service in the Falklands. He was clearly wealthy, evidenced by his Saville Row suits (with adjustable waistbands), his massive and super-shiny black Church's brogues and his always visible Rolex Submariner watch, apparently waterproof to 3000 metres, very useful I'm sure although if I'm ever that far underwater, I don't think I'll give a toss what time it is. He couldn't have been less like Kev and certainly had no interest whatsoever in my development, preferring instead to get me to make him his special Turkish coffee or to go down Regent Street to get refills for his Mont Blanc fountain pen. The only thing that Guy developed in me was *twat spotting* which unfortunately wasn't on the bank's competency framework.

Fortunately, as I was now on the fast track scheme, I spent less time in the same role and so both the disappointment of Kevin's departure and the frustration of working for Guy was softened by being told that I was moving on to do 'Securities'. I had no idea what that really involved, as the *Steves* at Walham Green and the guys here had always kept their work shrouded in mystery, but any concerns were short-lived when the boss of the Securities team, Ray, a small, bearded chap from Kent who reminded me of the PE teacher out of Grange Hill, told me that I would soon be going on my securities course and that this would teach me everything I needed to know.

I hadn't been on many courses until that point, other than a few day events, oddly known as workshops, despite a definite absence of any wood, metal, or any tools that I would be useless at using. The securities course was different, not just because it was over two weeks but also because it was residential, held in the opulent Surrey countryside at the bank's training centre at Hindhead; go down there on a Sunday evening, stay until Friday lunchtime, get back home for the weekend, and repeat the following week.

The Ford Escort was Britain's best-selling car for the sixth year in a row, but none was as cool as my white 1.1-litre Popular Plus. As its white wheels, black boot spoiler, and go-faster stripes sped me down the A3 past Guildford and towards the Devil's Punchbowl, my mind was working overtime, wondering what would happen over the next two weeks. In truth, I was shitting myself. It wasn't the being away that bothered me, I was worried about the sleeping arrangements. A week earlier, I'd received a brochure about the training centre and what to expect. The front cover showed a grand old country house surrounded by luscious green fields edged with tall pine trees and conifers; it looked like the kind of place where someone might get killed in an Agatha Christie novel. It explained that the enormous property was formerly owned by a member of the local gentry before the bank bought it and converted it into a residential venue with sophisticated training facilities and participant accommodations ranging from small dormitories to single and twin rooms. Sleeping in a dormitory would be a nightmare for me— the mere thought of it took me back to the traumatic time when, at Cub camp in 1972, I'd wet myself in my sleeping bag, and whatever piss was left in me when they woke up was ripped out of me by my young yet ruthless campmates. If there had been a cub badge for severe embarrassment, I would have been given it. Then again, if there had been one for having a dodgy kidney, I would have had that one too.

Being forced to share a twin room and having to become more familiar than I would want to be with a complete stranger would be nearly as bad, so I became obsessed with the need to get a single room and, with it, the opportunity for the occasional 24-year-old private moment, which was possible even before the internet and the mobile phone had been invented.

I pulled into the tree-lined entrance to the training centre and into a car park full of much bigger and more expensive cars than mine, my pimped-up sex machine suddenly feeling totally naff, so much so that I drove past loads of empty spaces and parked under a tree at the very far end, hoping that nobody would see me getting out of it. I slowly crunched my way back across the gravel, praying to the 'God of Room Allocation' before arriving at the grand, arched reception entrance and waited at the back of a small queue of equally nervous-looking blokes. In a time when the '2 metre rule' had only ever been used in sport, I was standing close enough to the guy in front of me to hear that his name was Peter and that he would be sharing a room on the second floor with a guy called Sam. Dinner was at 7p.m. in the dining room and Ron would be there to tell us everything we needed to know about our stay. Whether Peter had suffered his own embarrassing scouting incident, I didn't know, but he looked visibly traumatised as he sulked off up the wide, heavily carpeted winding staircase, not looking that keen to meet Sam.

My turn; I introduced myself, and Kim at the reception desk welcomed me to the Training Centre. She checked a few personal details, including my 'emergency contact' (blimey, maybe people do get murdered here) before asking me whether I had a car in the car park. 'Err, yes I do,' I admitted as she asked for my registration number, make, and model. 'Oh, so yours is the white one with the painted wheels parked in the trees at the back,' she said, looking up at the CCTV monitor. 'I was curious whose that was'. I don't think Kim thought it was as cool as I used to think it was. 'You'll be staying in one of the single rooms on the third floor,' she said. 'I'm sorry, it's a bit of a trek because the lift isn't working currently.' Like I bloody cared. For the sake of a single room, I would have run to Guildford every night. I thanked Kim, probably more enthusiastically than necessary, and skipped upstairs, got to my room, lay on my bed, and breathed a long and contented sigh of relief.

At about 7 p.m., along with my fellow inmates, including Peter, who looked like he'd been waiting downstairs for a while, we shuffled into the restaurant area to be met by Ron. A short bloke with bulging eyes like a pumped-up Billy Joel, he had the confidence of a man who knew everything, about to talk to a room full of people who knew nothing. As well as the usual health and safety stuff, he explained the 'House Rules' — swearing and laddish behaviour would not be tolerated, but, apart from that, it seemed that pretty much everything else was OK. Outside of study time, we had full use of the games room, which had three full-size snooker tables (one of which allegedly one of the trainers was caught shagging one of the students on), two pool tables, and a couple of table tennis tables. Nestled in the extensive gardens was a tennis court, two five-a-side football pitches, and a sloping, full-sized football pitch. Not a level playing field.

Ron then led us along the main corridor of the building, the walls adorned by A4-size portrait photos of the trainers, all looking successful and happy. They reminded me of the portraits of the Tracey brothers on the wall of the lounge on Tracey Island, albeit I doubted that any of the trainers' eyes lit up when there was an impending disaster on the other side of the world, or even Haslemere. We ended up in the bar, which Ron explained would be open until ten that evening — even with the new licensing hours, that still seemed reasonable. Finally, we were given our individual timetable, which in my case, told me that after breakfast the following morning, I would be expected to report to Room Six at 8:45. I'd almost forgotten I was here to work.

Quite a few of the gents stayed in the bar for a while, drinking cheap beer and chatting about nothing very much in particular. Presumably, at a Legal Firm's Training centre, everyone would talk about the gory details of a big murder case that they'd worked on, or if at an Estate Agent's Training Centre, everyone would talk about all the people they'd ripped off by talking bollocks, but at a clearing bank's Training Centre, there's really very little to boast about, other than how many times you'd taken a registered envelope to the post office or how many plastic cards you'd cut up. So, instead, we talked about football and cars and that it was starting to look like the next couple of weeks might not be as bad as we had all first feared. Especially if you had a single room.

The following morning, and as usual, I built contingency time into my journey, entirely unnecessary as the likelihood of encountering any travel difficulties on the three flights of stairs from my room to the restaurant was minimal, so I arrived for breakfast way earlier than I needed to. While I was 'enjoying' some dry scrambled eggs, marvelling at a new experience of eating something without actually being able to taste anything, somebody slumped into the chair next to me. 'Hello, I thought I recognised you, mind if I join you?'

'You already have' I thought, as Adam Packham proceeded to sit next to me and shovel a plate of sausages and beans into his massive gob. 'It's good to see you again,' I lied, surprised that I'd not heard him in the bar the previous evening, which he later explained was due to him attending a family party and only having travelled down that morning. I was tempted to ask him whether he had 'got on well' with the people there but I decided that wouldn't have helped, especially as he told me he was in the same syndicate as I was and that I'd therefore be spending a lot of the next two weeks with him.

After Adam had finished filling his face, we strolled along the photo-covered corridor and to room six, to find out what this Securities lark was all about. We were met by our trainer, Malcolm, who seemed really friendly and laid back, suggestive that we were going to have an enjoyable two weeks. That was until he broke the news that as well as learning how to take a legal charge over residential property and how to lend money against an endowment policy, at the end of the course we'd be taking a test, in exam conditions, which we would need to pass to be allowed to undertake the securities role when we got back to the branch. Well, that upped the ante a bit. I hadn't taken an exam since leaving school, and, although quoting *'Days of speed and slow time Mondays, pissing down with rain on a boring Wednesday, I say That's Entertainment'* might be a stark and insightful observation of the struggles of the lower class in a harsh financial environment, Mr Weller's genius wasn't likely to prove to Malcolm that I understood fully why a freehold property was better security than a leasehold.

By the end of the first day, everyone (apart from Peter who apparently hadn't slept particularly well) was settling in and had taken advantage of the 'much cheaper than down my local' bar. Many of the colleagues were away on their own for the first time, whether that be from parents or their 'other halves', and with that came the realisation that they could let their hair down a bit, albeit they would need to 'report in' occasionally to whoever they needed to report in to.

Although mobile phone networks had started to grow, owning a phone was still rare, not least because you needed about five grand to buy one and, because they were so big, to hire someone to carry it around for you. The prohibitive cost of these 'brick' phones limited ownership to the wealthy, including solicitors and estate agents, but eliminated every single one of us at the training centre, meaning the only way to 'touch base' was to use one of the three telephone booths situated in the corridor just outside the bar.

At regular intervals throughout the evening, each bloke would take their turn. The ritual was the same every night, as was the script (and its real meaning):

1. I love you too. (Yeah, OK, maybe)

2. I miss you too. (*I miss you a little bit, but I don't miss that you can't tell me what to do, and I feel like I'm my own boss for the first time in ages.*)

3. Yes, it's hard work. (*I muck about during the day and stay up drinking at night, so I am bloody knackered because I'm only getting about three hours sleep.*)

4. Yes, learning about securities is boring. (*That doesn't matter because I'm not paying much attention anyway.*)

5. No, most of the other people here are boring bankers. (*There are loads of really liked-minded blokes here who are well up for a piss-up.*)

6. No, it's mainly blokes. (*Well, it is, but there are also a few fit women here.*)

7. Yes, I can't wait for the weekend either. (*I need to come home to get some bloody sleep.*)

8. I must go, we've got some project work to finish before 10p.m. (*I must go, there are about four pints of Guinness with my name on them sitting on the bar, and a game of poker is about to start in ten minutes.*)

Apart from the inconvenient weekend at the end of the week, the course whizzed past. I drank, played cards and laughed a lot, and also learned a little about charged and uncharged securities. I made some new friends and even discovered that underneath the bravado, Adam was a half-decent bloke. I never did tell him about being given his feedback by mistake, that would have been churlish.

Despite having to use all of my own words, I passed the exam, meaning I was allowed to start in the securities role when I returned to the branch, which Ray was pleased about because he would be getting an extra pair of hands in what was a busy department. Getting to the office suffered another challenging period with the trend of going on strike continuing into 1989, with British Rail implementing an overtime ban, while the underground came to a standstill for a few days with fears of redundancies and concerns over safety. The good news for those who couldn't be bothered to try and get into work was that after *Homes Under The Hammer*, they could now watch The House of Commons as it began to televise live debates, allowing people who should have been working to have a quiet snooze, while watching a bunch of people who were working, also having a quiet snooze.

The French were also at it as their air traffic controllers walked out, making the prospect of the new Channel Tunnel even more attractive. Unfortunately, that would be delayed due to 500 workers going on strike in protest against pay and working conditions. I find it strange that, having signed up to dig a tunnel 250 feet below the sea bed, they had an expectation that there would be effective air conditioning and a load of soup-dispensing vending machines, but there's the British and French worker for you. Maybe they had a poorly covered pool table as well.

Fortunately, all the travel disruption had cleared up when it was announced that the WWF would hold its first-ever event in the UK at the London Arena. This was exciting for me, as I had always had a soft spot for pandas, particularly since seeing Chi-Chi at London Zoo on a primary school trip. So, I wasn't amused when I arrived at the Isle of Dogs only to find that there was just a load of blokes, including Hulk Hogan, parading around in swimming trunks pretending to have a fight. If I'd wanted to see that sort of thing, I would have gone to Benidorm for my holiday. I am joking; of course, I would never go to Benidorm.

The best example I know of someone (genuinely) going to a 'gig' under false pretences was when my mother-in-law skipped off to Hampton Court Palace one Christmas to see Frankie Valli and *his* Four Seasons. Having looked forward for weeks to spending the evening doing the funky chicken to Sherry Baby and Walk Like a Man, she was understandably devastated to end up listening to The London Philharmonic Orchestra belting out *Vivaldi's* Four Seasons instead. It's an easy mistake to make, I guess. *Oh, what a night, late December back in 1763...*

Working in the securities team wasn't exactly exciting, although the guys were fun and we had a laugh. I only spent about six months taking several 'charges' over residential properties, lending loads of money against many endowment policies, and learning why freehold property was better security than a leasehold, before moving on to a role called Managers Assistant, which meant supporting the senior manager in the branch, Stan Lewis. 'Stan the Man' was in his late fifties and was a true master of *his* craft, lending money. He oozed class and was clearly a wealthy man, confirmed to me when he casually admitted that he'd lost a six-figure sum on the stock market crash on Black Monday.— I understood now why he hadn't rushed to congratulate me on getting onto the Management Development scheme the following day.

My job was to help him lend money to big corporates and wealthier personal customers; I'd swapped cutting up plastic cards for analysing balance sheets and selling stocks and shares. Although Stan held legendary status, he did have the frustrating habit of keeping me sitting in his office for about an hour late in the afternoon at the end of each day while he had long telephone conversations with various important customers and then, in the end, asking me if I could photocopy something in the morning. 'You could have told me that before the phone calls', I would mutter to myself, never actually saying it loud enough for him to hear. I did consider asking his long-serving secretary, Maureen, whether she might be able to hang around to do this, but I was neither that stupid nor that brave. Not even Stan messed with Maureen Smith, and picking a fight with her would be as futile as John Craven asking Lemmy from Motorhead outside for a scrap — it would be dangerous, messy, and there'd only be one winner. She was a curious woman of an age I couldn't work out, but definitely over 50. She never bothered coming in when there was a train strike or adverse weather because, as she explained to me once, that would mean walking from Victoria, meaning her thighs would rub together and cause her severe chaffing, creating blisters, that would potentially result in more days off. It was kind of her to share the details, but I wish she had just pretended to have a cold or something similar, as it's an image that, 35 years later, I still can't get out of my head.

I worked for Stan for about a year and considered it a privilege to spend time with someone so skilled at his art. I managed to complete my banking exams, even if most of what I learned seemed irrelevant to the roles that I'd been doing or indeed to the twentieth century, including that it's legally possible to write a cheque on the side of a cow, not a resource freely available in central London. But I'd ticked the box and proved that I hadn't just been watching *Homes under the Hammer* every Wednesday.

It was decided by the folks at Head Office I needed a different role altogether and I was offered the chance to move to the London Training team, working for a guy called 'Beamo' based at one of the bank's new regional offices in Chandos Place, just off Strand. Maybe if I did well I might, one day, get a photo of my smiling face up on a wall somewhere . . .

Self-assessment: The 'West End' years

'My time at Hanover Square has been fun, and I've really enjoyed the West End buzz. I've learned lots of new disciplines and skills whilst I've been here, including not smiling when cutting up a customer's credit card and how to make a plastic horse mural. I'm pleased that I passed my banking exams, which, even if they are likely to be of absolutely no value whatsoever, show that I still have the capacity to learn. I'm more amazed that I managed to get onto the leadership programme and I'm really grateful to Kev for believing in me, probably more than I believe in myself. I'm pleased, too, that working closely with Robert has scared me away from blaming others when things don't go well, as I really don't want to develop a victim mentality. I know too that I need to take criticism more positively and be more tolerant of people who might not be like me. Whilst I'm still not entirely sure if I'm suitable for a career in banking, the prospect of a leadership role at some stage is attractive. I am ready for a change though, so I'm looking forward to starting my new job in training, even if the thought of standing in front of groups of people and pretending to know what I'm talking about scares the crap out of me. I also need to think about getting a new car; the Escort looks seriously shite.

Part 4

The 'Branching Out' years

(1990-1997)

16

'Anything that you wanna do, anyplace that you wanna go, don't need permission for everything that you want'

Inflation was at its highest level for eight years, and the country had slipped back into recession. Neil Kinnock, who had become the longest-serving opposition leader in British political history, edged nearer to his dream of getting the top job as Labour surged ahead in the opinion polls. There was an increase in IRA activity on the British mainland, with several high-profile bombings across the country, including at the London Stock Exchange. Travelling into central London with the constant threat of terrorism was scary, but, like many things, one eventually becomes blasé about the risk. And however nervous I felt, it must have been nothing compared to Salman Rushdie, who had his fatwa renewed by the new Leader of Iran, Ayatollah Khamenei. Then again, I hadn't written a book at the time that had pissed off loads of people.

In time-honoured fashion, I was about two hours early when I came up from the tube at Charing Cross, so I found a cafe on St Martin's Lane, just off Trafalgar Square. Being early, it was still quiet, in stark contrast to only a few weeks earlier when nearly 200,000 people had turned up there to protest against the Poll Tax, a levy which meant you'd pretty much pay the same amount whether you were the Sultan of Brunei living in a Palace or a West Ham Utd fan living in a mobile home on Canvey Island. The protest got messy and turned into a massive riot, the ensuing unrest creating severe pressure on Maggie, whose leadership was now being challenged by her own party. By the end of the year, she had resigned, thus ending her reign as the longest-serving

Prime Minister in recent history and sparking off a spate of street parties everywhere, especially in the North.

At 8:45 I arrived at reception and was directed to the third floor, where I met Beamo. After the usual 'Welcome To The Team' chat, he introduced me to Pete Casey, who would be my mentor for the first few weeks. I could immediately tell that Pete was no shrinking violet. He was confident and loud and had a mischievous twinkle in his eye. In order to learn how to run a training course, I would be observing Pete deliver The Effective Supervisor programme, aimed at people who did what Janet did at Walham Green.

I watched Pete all week as he helped the participants understand how to motivate others, be assertive, and deal with difficult team members. It was the standard entry-level leadership training content, but his ability to turn dull subject matter into something engaging and entertaining was impressive. I had been given a copy of the trainer notes, the script that Pete was following, except he didn't use it once, instead preferring to freestyle, to do it his own way. He knew his stuff, and it worked.

The following week, I would have my chance. Pete would observe me, help me when necessary, and provide me with feedback on my training delivery skills. I spent the entire weekend studying the material, but even that wasn't enough to calm my nerves when Monday morning arrived. I got to the training room about an hour early to ensure everything was ready, including putting the chairs in the right places, testing that the overhead projector bulb and the TV were working, and that I had enough pens and paper. It didn't help my shaking hands when I looked down the list of participants and saw that every one of them was female.

When the first of the 12 middle-aged ladies entered the room, there was no sign of Pete, and there was still no sign of him half an hour later when the other 11 had arrived, and I was standing in front of them feeling like a teenage boy on a diving board whose swimming trunks had fallen down. *Here goes, mate, take a deep breath, and let's give this training lark a try.*

I spent most of the first session, like on most courses, explaining what were known as the 'housekeeping issues'. I attempted a joke that there was no planned fire drill, so if the alarm did go off, to run. When Pete had said the exact words the previous week, everyone laughed, when I said them, there was nothing but an embarrassed Graham Pannett-shaped tumbleweed blowing across the grey carpet tiles of London Regional Training Room Three. Not a particularly impressive or confidence-boosting start to my training career. I quickly moved on to the more serious message that 'You will only get out of the course what you put into it', a weak attempt at begging the group to listen to me or else the entire week would be a total waste of time for everyone, before then asking the participants to introduce themselves to me and the rest of the group, including the answer to the big question at the beginning of every course: 'Why are you here?' Pete had told me that the answers to this question were always an accurate indicator of how well the week would go — if there were too many 'I don't know' or 'Because my manager sent me' responses it might be a long few days. Training is only effective when someone *wants* to learn *how* to do something. It is not a substitute for motivation and won't make someone unable to do something suddenly become capable. Too often, organisations waste masses of energy, resources, and money training people when, at best, it will only make a marginal difference to how well they do their job.

I tried to explain the relevance of understanding *performance root cause* on David Mellor's *606* radio programme one Saturday evening when I was travelling back with the boys from seeing Chelsea get beaten two-nil at Nottingham Forest. The original purpose of my call was to express my frustration with the behaviour of the Forest fans, who had decided that it would be amusing to wind-up the visiting supporters by making helicopter gestures, mocking the death of the club's part owner and fans favourite, Matthew Harding, who had tragically died in a helicopter crash only a few months earlier. My expectation of football fan behaviour was already very low but I didn't need VAR to tell me this went clearly over the line. Worse was the apathetic police response in dealing with the tension that was building and with it the risk of things boiling over and becoming dangerous.

David Mellor, the Conservative MP and probably more famous for (allegedly) shagging Antonia de Sancha while (allegedly) wearing his Chelsea shirt, had been hosting the sports phone-in programme for a few years. With more hope than expectation, I dialled the 606 number on my precious new Nokia 3110, and bugger me, an operator who triaged the calls to see whether the point was 'air-worthy' answered the call, thanked me for phoning and said I would get a call back if they wanted me to go on air. Five minutes later my mobile rang. 'Hi Graham, we'd like you to make your point to David if that is still OK?'

'Of course,' I said, 'I'd love to,' trying hard to conceal that I was a bit pissed, having had a few beers before, during, and after the match.

'Hold on, and David will invite you to speak when he's ready, but as it sounds like you are in a car, can you please pull over and turn your radio off as it will cause feedback.'

'Of course' I said again, panicking that we were somewhere on the M40 near Bicester.

'Pull over!' I screamed at Dickie, which he immediately did, not bothering to look in his rear-view mirror as usual. 'And turn the radio off,' I said as we sat on the hard shoulder, although as soon as I said it, I knew what was coming.

'Fuck that' he said, 'we want to hear this. Get out of the car so we can listen, you muppet'

It was January, and it was freezing. I stumbled onto the tarmac, and the deafening roar of the cars and lorries thundering past would mean David and the listening public of the UK would struggle to hear me, and I would struggle to hear David. My only option, confirmed by the fact that Tom had already locked the car doors by this point, was to head inland. I climbed over a small wooden fence and into a pitch-black field, from where I could eventually hear, through my phone, an ongoing discussion between David and the current caller, talking about the pressure and stress of being a football manager, a topical debate at the time following the resignation of Kevin Keegan from his managerial post at Newcastle United — apparently, being paid hundreds of thousands of pounds to do a job that you love, then, when you get sacked because you got bored of it or you were hopeless, receiving an enormous payoff and ending up somewhere else three months later, having done a bit of television and radio punditry work in the meantime, is stressful.
'Now, we have Graham on the line,' announced David, 'a Chelsea supporter who wants to talk about the behaviour of the Nottingham Forest fans.'
'Hi David,' I said, 'nice to talk to you'.
'Where are you from Graham?' he asked
'Well, I'm from Twickenham, David, but I'm currently standing in a field near the M40.' I talked about helicopter crashes, untimely deaths, poor policing, and the dangers of winding up 4,000 beer-filled football fans with limited IQs. My views resonated with David, and, with my newfound radio confidence, I grabbed the opportunity to make a further comment. 'While I'm on David, I wonder whether I could talk about the Kevin Keegan thing?' I asked, half expecting that I had already been cut off.

'Go ahead, Graham,' David said, allowing me to explain that, in my opinion, being a professional football manager could only be stressful if you weren't *capable* of doing the job. I didn't make my point very clearly, so I turned to the power of analogy to make it easier for David and the listening millions to understand it.

'Imagine David, I asked you to run across the pitch at Stamford Bridge and gave you five minutes to do it. I doubt you would get stressed because you would be more than capable of doing so. If, however, I chopped off one of your legs, put a load of hurdles in the way, and then asked you to do the same, you probably *would* get stressed because you would know that you *couldn't* do it because you just wouldn't be capable.'

An analogy is effective when it is relevant and makes sense but I had failed on both counts, although David, the consummate professional, was gracious enough to say that he thought I had made an 'interesting point' before hastily moving on to the next caller to talk about how shit West Ham were.

When I got back to the car, frozen half to death and with cow shit all over my Timberland boots, the boys were still pissing themselves with laughter. 'A one-legged man!' exclaimed Dino, 'Fucking priceless'. I explained to Dino about the importance of understanding the correct root cause of performance issues, about the difference between knowledge, skill, motivation, and capability. He reflected for a few seconds, nodded, took a sip from his can of Budweiser, and told me he had absolutely no fucking idea what I was banging on about.

Back in the training room, Pete arrived just as I was about to start the next session, which made me more nervous, a bit worrying as he was supposed to be helping me. I delivered the material as it was scripted in the notes, and it landed OK, but nowhere as well as when he had done it. But, each day felt better than the previous one, and at the end of the week, Pete told me I'd done a decent job for a beginner, even if I had let the 'fat bird in the lemon tracksuit' talk too much. I also got feedback directly from the course participants via the end-of-course questionnaire, known as a *'happy sheet'* which everyone was asked to complete before buggering off home or up the pub. The comments on my inaugural performance included 'He seemed nervous' 'Nice arse' 'Quite funny' 'A bit too young for me' and 'Knows his stuff'. Despite being flattered by the more personal comments (those were the days), I was genuinely more pleased that someone thought I had the faintest clue what I was talking about, especially when I saw that it had come from the citrus-flavoured velour lady. It proved a point Pete had made to me that, regardless of how little you might think you know, the people on the course will most likely know even less. Mix in some confident bullshit, and the illusion is complete. I had a long way to go to be like Pete, but I reckoned I would enjoy trying.

17
'Lights going out and a kick in the balls'

The one frustration about delivering training was that we never really knew if we were making an *actual* difference. Regardless of how positive the *happy sheet* comments were, we rarely found out if any of the people we trained got any better at what they did when they returned to their day jobs, the acid test of our effectiveness. It made me realise the importance of knowing that you've made an actual impact, putting meaning and purpose behind the effort.

Now that Margaret Thatcher had finally lost *her* meaning and purpose, an ex-banker with three 'O' levels called John Major emerged as the front-runner to succeed her. I wasn't aware what the minimum qualifications were to become Prime Minister, but you needed at least four 'O' levels to join the bank, so on this basis, bankers must have to be more academic than leaders of the Western world. He managed to get voted in with fewer votes than Maggie had received when she got booted out, but he was only up against one bloke called Douglas Hurd, more rhyming slang than a politician, and another known as Tarzan.

Despite the earlier strike and delays, British and French Channel Tunnel workers finally met 40 metres beneath the English Channel seabed, establishing the first land connection between the UK and mainland Europe for 8,000 years.

'Hello Monseur Rosbif, ' said the pioneer French tunnel chap, in perfect, if very French-accented English, 'Congratulations on your historic achievement.' 'Hello Mister French tunnel chap', said Monsieur Rosbif. 'Le Singe est dans l'arbre'

Back above sea level, and to help with the cost of living, Poundland opened its first store, creating the opportunity for endless streams of people to ask. 'How much is this?' only to be told by increasingly fed-up Sales Assistants: 'It's a bloody pound, everything is'. Just like a phone call at Walham Green.

I too got used to repeatedly saying the same things as I delivered loads of Effective Supervisor courses, albeit eventually without needing the script. I'm not saying that I was anywhere as good as Pete, but I did my best to make them fun and engaging. Finally, I was asked to train other subjects, and, even better, Beamo told me I would be the lead for a new lending course and, in order to learn the material, I would need to attend a 'Train the Trainer' event, at which I would learn the material and then, on my return, train the rest of my teammates to do the same. The really good news was that it would be a three-week residential event at the Goodwood Park Country Club and Hotel near Chichester. And, not even a hint of sharing a room with anyone. Not that long ago, I was scraping the shit out of the banking hall at Walham Green, helping Tom Cross withdraw his last £3.52, and getting abused at the Post Office, now I was being paid to learn a little bit of training material in between playing golf, sitting in a jacuzzi with my fellow trainers and drinking the bar dry every night. If good luck is when hard work meets opportunity, I must have worked bloody hard.

Three weeks whizzed by, and I returned to London to train our team, which now included a guy called Dave Rawle, who had recently joined, like me, from a local branch. In the way that Pete had shown me the ropes, I did the same with Dave. He was Welsh, a front-row rugby player, and I realised I wouldn't want to get on his wrong side. Most of the time, I'm a good judge of who you should mess with, apart from one notable exception when Dickie, I and a couple of mates had been to Langans restaurant in Green Park for a very pleasant if expensive evening out, and as we spilled out onto the Piccadilly pavement, a rather unsavoury character was aggressively saying to a guy, much smaller than him, 'So you think I'm a twat do you?'

In a rush of public spiritedness, I stepped between the two of them and said to the aggressor, 'No mate, leave him alone, he doesn't think you're a twat, . . . but *I* do'.

It all happened so quickly. His massive, solid forehead thrust forward into mine, and all I remember is hitting the ground and rolling into a pile of helpfully positioned dustbin bags. In a Monty Python-esque attempt to save face (literally), I muttered something about 'Come back and fight like a man' as the thug strutted off with his girlfriend towards Piccadilly Circus, laughing and pointing at me writhing on the floor and gently holding my now twisted nose that I assumed made me look like a Picasso painting. Or Peter Beardsley.

Dave quickly got to grips with delivering the courses, unsurprising as he was super-bright and frankly far more professional than me. We spent a year training together, taking participants to the pub, competing for the best *happy sheet* scores, and becoming good mates. Dave has been running a highly successful global training business for many years now so I can only assume that his success is due entirely to his brilliant teacher.

Outside work, things were going well, too. Between us, the money that Lisa and I were earning had started to afford us a decent lifestyle, albeit we were helped along the way by the generosity of her family. When I first met Lisa, I quickly realised they had more money sloshing around than I was used to; that's not a complaint about my upbringing, but it was certainly different from what I'd been used to and also eye-opening. Her house, located in the delightfully named Strawberry Hill and conveniently on my cycle route to and from school, was the largest I'd been in without needing to pay an entrance fee. It had a double garage (housing a beautiful Audi Quattro) and in the back garden, a swimming pool, again, something I was only used to paying for. Although it wasn't a massive pool, it was the first time I'd been allowed to spend more than an hour in one without being made to get out because I was wearing a blue wristband. I got another clue that I was in a different world from the one I was used to when Lisa told me her Aunt was undertaking extended babysitting services because her mum had gone to Barbados for three months with her new partner. I nearly had a coronary when I was told they'd gone by Concorde.

A few years later, Lisa and I were invited to spend two weeks in Barbados. Compared to the glamour of Devon and The New Forest, Barbados seemed so far away, literally and metaphorically. I'd seen pictures of it and even dreamed about going there when I first heard the song by Typically Tropical and wanted to believe that Coconut Airways was a real airline. (I imagine the crew would undoubtedly have been more cheery than your usual grumpy BA stewardess.) The excitement of going to the Caribbean was unbelievable and it didn't disappoint. I've been fortunate enough to go back many times since, and I now think of it as my second home. I might even write a book about going there. I have friends I still see today who I met on that first trip all those years ago, as well as many others I've met since. Oh, and in December 1992, Lisa and I got married there.

18

'Lights go out and the walls come tumbling down'

Despite the continuing increase in unemployment, the Tories had managed to win their fourth consecutive term in Government when John Major and his three 'O' levels won the general election, causing Neil Kinnock to finally resign and be replaced by John Smith as leader of the opposition. It was a challenging time for the Buckingham Palace spokesperson, who had to announce that Fergie and Andy were splitting up after six years of marriage (presumably because she rumbled that he had some very dubious mates) and then later in the year, that Charles and Diana were also going to separate.

Coming back to work as a married man didn't change much, other than I now had double tax relief on my mortgage payments and that my plan to spend the rest of my career in head office had been blasted out of the water when it was decided that I needed to get some direct leadership experience and was given the role as manager of Westminster House Branch. I had really loved my time in training. It had allowed me to be creative, think on my feet, and be flexible and was the first time I had felt truly empowered to work in my own way, in my own style, to *be me*. I can't remember how many videos I played, how many times I told people that role plays were good, or how many Friday nights I was knackered after being on my feet all week, but it was all worth it.

My disappointment at being sent back to the 'real world' so soon was tempered by reflecting that I had reached branch manager, higher up the ladder than I ever imagined, certainly much quicker than I had ever expected. The sense of pride at knowing I would have my own front door, staff, customers, and business to run was immense.

Westminster House branch was tucked away in a quiet square close to The Houses of Parliament. A week before starting, I met with the outgoing Manager, Brian Pearce, so he could give me an overview of what to expect. Brian was an odd-looking bloke, only about five feet tall with a hunched back, but he knew his stuff. He had a dry, cutting sense of humour and he certainly knew how to swear. 'This is Winnie,' he said, introducing me to the cleaner who, coincidentally, was from Barbados. 'She's the only fucker in this place who has a clue what she's doing.' It seemed a little disrespectful to the other 15 team members, but I had to admit the branch was incredibly clean. Brian spent the next hour telling me why none of the staff were 'any fucking good'. I listened but chose not to take too much notice, deciding that, even though he had many years of leadership experience, I would make my own judgement on how good the team was. He might be right about them, but they deserved a fresh start, and maybe he may have even been partly to blame for their 'totally shit' performance. Brian was at the end of his leadership career, I was at the beginning of mine, and I pondered whether being so different from him might be a good thing for me, and for the folk at the branch.

Like parenthood, there's no instruction manual or class that can fully prepare you for your first leadership role. I needed to learn unfamiliar systems and rules, bond with my new team members, and tackle new, everyday tasks. Finding the right balance between these things felt intimidating. But, after Brian, I *had* to fix the culture — the habits and norms of behaviour among the team — and as I had inherited such a de-motivated team, there was lots to do. My best guess was I needed to give the people some belief, some purpose, and some pride.

My return to the front line coincided with a time of significant change for High Street banking; more competitors had started to emerge, and reducing interest rates meant that banks could no longer rely purely on fees from money transmission and the margins between lending and savings. The expensive branch network with millions of pounds of real estate and several thousands of staff, needed to find alternative sources of income to justify its existence and did so by focusing on new, insurance-based products. Traditional, stuffy institutions built on the foundations of caution and care were being forced to transition into modern, dynamic sales businesses.

Understandably, the impact on colleagues was enormous. The competencies of numeracy, attention to detail, and judgment that had been so valued for three hundred years would be replaced by product knowledge, overcoming objections, and a desire to be the best. 'I didn't join the bank to sell' was heard multiple times up and down the country, as anxious staff realised they would need to adapt to something they never thought they would have to or ever wanted to do. It wasn't easy — even before the acronym **PPI** stimulated the bile glands like it does today, persuading customers to buy insurance products that most neither wanted nor knew they needed nor could afford was tough.

Banks had to find ways of persuading their colleagues to do what was now expected of them, so they developed a range of solutions, each aimed at the different root causes of performance. To help colleagues understand *what* was now expected of them, the banks introduced annual, monthly, weekly, and even daily sales targets. To help them know *how* to do what was expected, they were given sales training, and to help colleagues *want* to do what was expected of them, they had a carrot dangled in front of them and a stick held behind their backsides — sell lots, and we will pay you more, don't sell enough, and we will need to go for a stroll in the car park for a serious chat.

Rewarding people for doing well makes complete sense, but it creates the risk of the unintended consequences of doing so. If you reward people for doing something or punish them if they don't, human nature means they will try and do more of that thing. And, because humans are not perfect, they may not always do that thing *'in the right way'*. Greedy people get greedier, desperate people become more desperate, and those in between end up going one way or the other.

In the right way — it's a strange expression to use in the context of a bank. I'll always be super-grateful that the surgeon digging inside my kidneys did his job in the right way and that the many pilots who have flown planes taking me to Barbados did so in the right way, but in banking, people needed reminding occasionally, which tells me something must be wrong with the culture. Although the consequences of doing it the wrong way in a bank might not be as serious as buggering up a vital organ or causing a major air disaster, it can create significant financial customer detriment. CS Lewis described integrity as 'doing the right thing, in the right way, even when no one else was watching' and I would suggest that the general public should expect integrity from the people working in their banks.

The likelihood of staff *not* doing something in the right way is directly correlated to the integrity (or otherwise) of the person in charge and in my case, this was a guy called Peter Dacombe. He wasn't everyone's cup of tea because he was different from his (senior) peers. He was quirky and a bit unpredictable, which is why I really liked him. Peter was the first maverick leader I worked for, and he showed me that you can 'get on' and still be true to what you believe in; you don't always have to act like one of the proverbial sheep. But, despite my respect for him, he still had a reputation for being tough. Every Friday morning, he would review performance and if a branch had not had a strong sales week, he would often make the dreaded 'How's it going?' call, code for 'What the bloody hell is happening and what are you doing about it?' Fortunately, I'd never had a call — until now. Denise, my PA, stuck her head into my office. 'Peter is on the phone; shall I put him through?'

'Well, you better had, he is the boss',' I said as I slid the metaphorical Yellow Pages down the back of my trousers to soften the blows of the beating I was about to get.

'How's it going, Pannett?' he asked, a rhetorical question if ever I'd been asked one.

'Well, Peter, it's not been our best week, and if I'm honest, I don't really understand why,' I replied, realising that I might have just shot myself in my now horribly corporate black-brogue-covered foot by appearing to not understand my business, to not being in control.

'We're selling financial products, Pannett, not bread, and you can't do the same level every week. I know you're doing all the right things, so I was phoning to say thanks for everything you *are* doing, and I hope you have a fantastic weekend.' Then he hung up. In an era when macho leadership was 'de rigeur,' I thought it was sheer class. Peter trusted me because he understood that in sales, there isn't always an underlying reason why things don't fall into place. Sometimes, that's just how it is. It's the same occasionally when it goes really well, too — no need to pretend you have done anything special, that's called bullshit.

    I *did* have a fantastic weekend, and in the following weeks, we delivered some of our best performances ever, all *in the right way*. That's what trust does for you. But, unfortunately, not all leaders in the bank had Peter's level of emotional intelligence nor his belief in doing things ethically and whilst it may not have seemed that serious to them at the time, it certainly did a few years later when the shit of PPI really hit the fan.

I was still a rookie and I needed to learn many things, but my first foray into leadership was proving reasonably successful and enjoyable too. I quickly realised that my job was to make the team *want* to do what was expected and that we could do that while also having fun. I tried to create an environment in which everyone was clear about the part they played and their contribution to the whole— treat grown-ups like grown-ups, play to their strengths, and celebrate doing your best; simple, if not always easy. But, despite my early progress, it wasn't long until the walls came tumbling down.

I spotted some 'strange' activity on the account of a member of staff. I had never forgotten the 'Clive Sanders experience,' so when I saw what Dave was up to, I needed to deal with it quickly. I confronted him, and he denied any wrongdoing. I confronted him again, and he admitted that he had 'just *borrowed* some money from a few customers' accounts for a short period'. He told me he would immediately repay it and begged me not to tell anyone. I didn't sleep well that night. I got angry he was prepared to put me in this position, that he would expect me to even think about keeping quiet, and to risk my own career to save his. I liked the guy a lot, but not that much. Dave resigned the next day, we never saw him again, and he didn't get a good reference.

There I was, thinking that this leadership lark was easy, and in the blink of an eye I'd learned not to be complacent, that as much as you want to trust people, sometimes you just never know what they're up to. It was a sudden and sobering lesson and whilst I didn't suspect any other staff had been involved, the trust had gone, and the team dynamic had changed, and it would never be the same again.

19
'The wine will be flat and the curry's gone cold'

Lisa and I had bought a new house, with full access and with our own electricity supply. This time, she kept more than a few pairs of shoes there. Having gotten used to not having to tell my mum where I was, I now had to let Lisa know when I might be late home. And I no longer had any excuse not to, as I was the proud owner of my first mobile phone. Not all technology is necessarily a step forward: losers *and* winners.

Lisa has always been OK with me going out socially, which isn't the case for a few people I've worked with — it's sad to see grown men making up ridiculous stories about taking their dog to the groomers or having to go to the dentist at 8 p.m. rather than risk incurring the wrath of their other half by going out for the occasional beer with the lads. But there was one notable exception when Lisa did (almost understandably) get the raging hump with me, meaning a few of my subsequent 'passes' were temporarily revoked and even I had to take the dog to the groomers on a couple of occasions when the boys were going out for a pint or five, and at the time, I didn't even have a dog.

The festive season was an enjoyable time to work in the branch, despite the traumatic spectre of the Christmas Party. Christmas Eve, in particular, would often get messy because branches closed at 12:30, and everyone would hit the boozer shortly afterwards. A good few hours to get on it before disappearing for a few days with families. On this occasion, we 'got on it' in a few pubs around Piccadilly Circus and Regent Street. I was due home at about 5 p.m. as we had friends coming over for dinner, but since I was finishing work at 12:32, there was plenty of time for a few and to still get back home in time. Leave the West

End at about 3:45 and get the 4:15 train from Waterloo. All planned out, all in hand.

After a few pints, my judgment on how long it takes to get from one place to another can become a little impaired, as it also did about how much it would matter if I was a little bit late home. I remember thinking, at about 4:45, that I really should get the tube and then thinking the same again at 5:45, which I did, I'm not a complete arsehole. I phoned Lisa with my Nokia 2110 and explained that it wasn't my fault that I was running a little bit late ('I was with the team darling, and as the boss, I do need to be there for them'), but the really good news was that I was now on my way. I also made the very valid point that an hour or so wasn't a big deal in the grand scheme of things and I was sure that my best mate Dickie, and also Jackie, Ian, and Tracy wouldn't mind either. I also suggested that to get home earlier, I would get the fast train to Twickenham and that, potentially, she *could* pick me up from the station.

Having received what I can best describe as 'short shrift' and a helpful suggestion that I should get my 'useless drunken arse back home fucking pronto,' I looked up at the giant, but slightly fuzzy departure board on the main concourse at Waterloo, to see that there was indeed a Twickenham train leaving in five minutes from platform 17. I zig-zagged towards it with a feeling of smug accomplishment that I'd had a boozy afternoon but now was safely on my way home and believing that I had already received the majority of the bollocking that I was unfairly going to get.

I rarely used my mobile in those days, as before the benefit of all-inclusive calls and texts, each minute cost about £4.50, however, I did the right thing and called Lisa to let her know that I was pulling out of Waterloo and, subject to there being a taxi outside Twickenham Station (for some reason she hadn't taken up my offer of picking me up), I should be home within the hour.

Thoughtfully, I also asked how Dickie and the rest of our guests were, at which point she hung up on me; she understood how expensive calls were.

Unlike Robert at Hanover Square, I've always tried to avoid being a victim of circumstance, however there are rare occasions when things do happen that are simply not your fault. How was I to know that the train I boarded wasn't the fast train to Reading (3rd stop Twickenham) but the significantly slower service known colloquially as the Twickenham Loop line? Secondly, as is often the case after a few hours of drinking, I do get a little sleepy, especially when on a train, but 97 times out of a hundred, I wake up in time — we've all heard the ridiculous stories of people allegedly ending up hundreds of miles away when they fall asleep however, I knew I would be OK because this train was only going to Twickenham before returning to Waterloo via Wimbledon. It was called the Twickenham Loop for a very good reason.

It's difficult to describe the confusion I felt when I woke up just as the train was pulling back into Waterloo Station about an hour and a half after I'd left there, until I worked out that during my little nap, the train had completed its 'loop' journey back to London. I also had nine missed calls from Lisa and notwithstanding the cost, I thought I had better phone her back.
'You really are not going to believe this', I said as I tried to explain what had happened and why it was a mistake anyone could have made. 'But, the good news is that the train is leaving Waterloo again now, so I should be home within the hour'. I didn't even get a chance to ask how Dickie and the others were.

I surprised even myself when I fell asleep *again*, missed the stop at Twickenham *again*, and woke up at Norbiton, five stops and about twenty minutes past Twickenham. £65 quid and a half-hour cab ride later, and shortly after 9:30, I stumbled through my front door and tried to style it out with 'Hi guys, sorry I'm a bit late, but you'll never guess what happened!' Dickie thought it was hilarious, but nobody else seemed to. Lisa disappeared to bed shortly afterwards, and the others left not much later. Dickie and I spent the rest of the night in the kitchen drinking Mount Gay Rum and singing loudly to our favourite Curtis Stigers CD, one of my better Britannia Music Club purchases. Unfortunately, on Christmas morning, fate conspired against me again — unusually for me, I had been less than creative with my Christmas shopping and Lisa's main present was a set of attractive and highly functional saucepans; on a cold and frosty morning . . .

Although none quite as serious as this occasion, there have been other train/drinking/getting home much later than I should have incidents, especially when I endured an unfortunate phase when my yeast intolerance (medically diagnosed rather than some made-up excuse) was at its height, impairing my ability to hold down certain fizzy drinks. Some of my mates have pointed out 'It's got bugger all to do with any intolerance, more that you've done ten pints', but I do feel that I have been dealt a bad hand on this one. Usually, I would make it to a toilet, field, or a bucket, or other suitable receptacle of some description, however on one awkward occasion, I was in a black cab on the way to Waterloo after a pleasant and long night out when I felt the acid reflux starting to kick off a bit. Before I knew it, my Cornish pasty from earlier started rising to the surface until I was sick in my mouth. Unable to hold it in for much longer, and knowing how precious black taxi drivers are about soiling their cabs, cleverly, I let it all come out inside my shirt which I had quickly ensured was well buttoned up and tucked in. Genius, not to mention considerate on my part.

I threw a tenner at the cabbie as I ran as fast as possible away from the drop-off point and to the waiting Shepperton train, congratulating myself on successfully negotiating a potentially tricky situation. I think it was before we'd got to the first stop at Vauxhall when people started moving away from where I was sitting while mumbling something about the stench and 'what a drunken twat'. It was a long and lonely journey home that night, albeit I had plenty of room to stretch out and enjoy a little snooze.

Thankfully, over the years, my yeast intolerance started to wane, however, I became burdened by a new, even more painful and inconvenient post-drinking challenge — the relentless need to pee. I know I am far from alone in suffering from this debilitating condition, but I think I have a fair excuse, given my kidney challenges, although I've yet to receive much sympathy when I've attempted, with piss running down my leg, to explain my medical rationale to fellow passengers.

If you are outside it's not too difficult to find a tree, a bush, a stairwell, or a phone box (before BT unhelpfully started to remove them) but it is definitely tougher when you're on a train. I have pissed in drinking bottles and rubbish bins; I even managed once to get off the train at New Malden when the doors opened, have a slash on the platform, and then get back on the train again before the doors closed. It was so impressive that an old guy slumped in the corner of the carriage gave me a polite round of applause; it takes one to know one. If I'd been a bit richer and lived in Ascot, I could have travelled home on one of those posh trains with toilets, but such luxury facilities are not provided on the *Shepperton Express*.

I didn't get the chance to get home late from Westminster House too many times after Christmas, as early in the new year, I was told I would be moving to another branch, Southampton Row. Here we go again. Where the bloody hell is that?

Despite the continuing economic recovery, at the beginning of 1994, the Conservative Government was lagging way behind Labour in the opinion polls.

The appointment of Tony Blair as their new leader following the sudden death of John Smith deepened this gap. Mobile phones became much more widely available, and access to the internet increased significantly, so a new concept, 'technophobia' emerged. The introduction of things being considered 'not user-friendly' highlighted the big disconnect between the ambitions of tech companies and the realities of humans learning how to use them. For the first time, people started to worry about junk mail, online privacy, and whether stores (and banks) would disappear completely, taking away the fun of squeezing a tomato (or their cashier); losers *and* winners.

I found out that Southampton Row is just north-west of Holborn Circus, neither West End nor City, and, as a result, it felt like it suffered from an identity crisis, and the colleagues at my new branch seemed similarly confused. My role was to manage sales and lending across four branches in the Holborn area. Because the branch was much larger than Westminster House, it contributed a much higher proportion of overall income, so consequently, the expectation to deliver sales was much more significant. I had a supportive new boss in Steve, but he too was under considerable pressure from his seniors, and this meant that doing things *in the right way* became less important than it should have been. Too many people, especially senior ones, failed to ask enough questions to satisfy themselves that they knew what their staff were saying when they sat with their customers.

PPI was the ultimate example, the daddy of all banking cock-ups. Frankly, I don't care less whether the Senior Executives of the time claimed (either then, or now in retrospect) that they didn't know what was happening because they did. And even if they didn't know, then, like I'd been accused of when Clive was playing his lunchtime games at Walham Green's finest casino, they bloody well should have. Complicit or negligent? Either way, it simply wasn't good enough. But in big organisations, it is possible for senior people to be so far away from the customer that they can also distance themselves from any wrongdoing and let the front-line colleagues take the rap. The hierarchy has many benefits, especially if you're a long way up it; winners *and* losers.

I still feel guilty about being part of what happened with PPI, and wish I hadn't allowed it to take place on my patch, on my watch, even with the relatively small numbers I was directly or indirectly responsible for. I have never considered myself dishonest (other than the football kit at Walham Green) so the question I ask myself now is whether I was a rotten apple or a good apple who found himself in a rotten barrel? Was it my fault that I allowed something that wasn't right (for the customer) to happen, or was I a victim of a culture that made me do it? Whatever the answer is (and it may well be a bit of both), it's a period of my working life I try and pretend didn't happen, even though I ended up spending over two years in the job.

20

'Like a perfect stranger, you came into my life, then like the perfect lone ranger, you rode away'

A lot had happened in the real world while I was at Southampton Row. Despite an earlier ceasefire, the IRA detonated a truck bomb in The Docklands, blew up a bus in London, and set off a device in Manchester. The introduction of the National Lottery had drained the country of its one-pound coins, and in one live broadcast, the ball machine broke down, delaying the draw by nearly an hour. The resident psychic, Mystic Meg, later said she had been predicting the malfunction all day; not the first or last time that the BBC didn't listen to what they were being told. It didn't 'Come Home,' despite being promised a million times by Baddiel and Skinner that it would, instead, it was '*Ir War Nach Hause*' as Germany won Euro 96 after they had turned us over on penalties in the semi-final. The Channel Tunnel officially opened, although not before it was forced to close due to several electronic failures and, on one occasion, a fire, causing havoc for thousands of French and English travellers. It wasn't the only time there was a bit of Anglo-French tension, as King Eric Cantona launched a kung-fu attack on a Crystal Palace fan on his way to the changing room after being sent off.

On the topic of changing rooms, the TV programme of the same name, presented by the appropriately named Carol Smilie and assisted by the annoying fop, Lawrence Llewellyn-Bowen, started its eight-year run on the BBC. Houses up and down the country had their living rooms ruined when their next-door neighbours were allowed to paint them aubergine and cover everything in MDF. At the same time, blokes started wearing frilly, oversized-cuff shirts and growing their hair. Including my mate Dickie, who, to be fair, had been doing that for a while.

I first met Dickie (or Richard Fernand Cesar Boulert, to give him his full title) early in 1991. I wasn't formally introduced to him, but I didn't need to be. Lisa and I were meeting some friends at our regular Chinese restaurant in Twickenham, somewhere I would go to often, usually on my way home from work on a Friday night to grab a take-away, and have a laugh with the eccentric owner, *Chinese Pete*. I remember going in there once on a Saturday, not wearing my usual weekday suit but instead, a pair of ripped jeans and an old tee shirt. As I walked in, Pete asked 'What happen you, Gwaham, you gone all fucking cwap?' Always nice to be given a warm welcome. On this occasion, we'd been told that a friend of a friend called Richard had been invited and that he was a tad flamboyant, so when we turned up and a guy was sitting at our table with long, Jesus-like hair, wearing a pair of leather trousers and a purple frock coat, I assumed it was him.

We talked, and he made me laugh. We had plenty in common; we were both Chelsea supporters, we both loved vinyl records, and we both enjoyed a drink. After an evening of prawn crackers, crispy aromatic duck, and some (aching) ribs, we agreed to catch up for a beer, possibly before a Chelsea game. A couple of weeks later, we did hook up, albeit he was half an hour late, something which, over the years, became a permanent feature of meeting with Dickie; if I had a pound for every half-hour I waited around for him, I'd have £278. We quickly established that both of us went to Chelsea, often on our own (sad but true), so it made sense to start going to games together and we cemented that arrangement when we bought season tickets for the 1992/93 season.

As well as going to Stamford Bridge, we also did some 'away' trips, mostly involving me driving and Dickie getting pissed in the passenger seat, although I didn't drive to our most memorable 'awayday,' a trip to Sweden to see Chelsea against Stuttgart in the 1998 European Cup Winners Cup Final. Stupidly, I left the travel arrangements to him and it wasn't *that* surprising when he announced he had booked everything and we were going and coming home via Amsterdam; more of an 'away-three-days'. Chelsea won one-nil due to a second-half goal by the legend that was Gianfranco Zola and I bought Lisa back a 'thank you for letting me go' present, a hand-painted, scale-model Dutch windmill. At the time, I thought it was a thoughtful gift, in retrospect, it was the second worst present I've ever bought.

I remember little of those three days, mainly due to the Olympic level of alcohol consumption and reasonably priced class B substances, most memorably the slightly odd-tasting Battenberg, which, months later, Dickie tried to re-create on a New Year's Eve trip to the New Forest. I can still taste the lumps of hash squashed into a Sara Lee Chocolate Gateaux today and I have no idea how I made it to the restaurant buffet, let alone back to my room.

Over the years, we watched Chelsea most weeks and going there was rarely dull — football fan 'fashion' has changed a lot over the decades, from the suited and flat-capped gents of the first half of the century, the mod and rocker look of the sixties, the cropped jeans, Doc Martens, and scarf-attached-to-the-wrist of the skinhead seventies, to the exotic clobber of the eighties casuals to the modern day trend of football shirts and club branded tops. But it was never acceptable to go to a match, let alone a Chelsea versus West Ham game, wearing a cream, double-breasted, crushed velvet suit. The atmosphere at these games, the tube ride there, the walk from the station to the ground, and getting home can be a little tense, *(The smell of brown leather, it blended in with the weather)* so why not make the whole experience just that little bit edgier by dressing like Oscar Wilde? But, somehow, he always got away with it. He didn't see half the looks he got or hear half the comments made about him, and those he did, he didn't give a toss about.

I learned so much from Dickie; many good things, some less so. I learned what it's like to not give a fuck what other people think about how you look or what you wear — it's their problem if they disapprove of what *being you* looks like. He wouldn't have thought twice about wearing brown shoes. I learned what it's like to laugh, often about the most ridiculous things, I learned that white linen trousers don't fair well in wet sand, and I learned what caring deeply about a mate felt like, even if he could be a total pain in the arse. I also learned what it's like to see someone give the impression of not caring less about life but, deep down, struggling with some deep-rooted insecurities. I learned that sometimes it's good to allow conflict to happen rather than try and avoid it all the time (the reason why he was almost always late was because he hated to say, 'no' to anyone and would end up arranging to be in different places at the same time) and I learned that going out for a drink can be fun, but a bottle of vodka a day isn't good for you.

And so the 'sweep it under the carpet' approach ultimately let him down. His drinking had moved along the scale from 'heavy social' to 'out of control'. His wife, Jacqui had left him, and he only saw his eight-year-old boy, Louis, occasionally. His family paid for him to spend some time at The Priory to dry out, but I knew it wasn't going well when he texted me one night to say that he had persuaded a nurse to bring him in some booze. He became difficult to be with, and I hate to say it, but I started to find reasons not to see him, especially if my kids were around, as his behaviour became inappropriate and often embarrassing. On one occasion, at Chelsea, he nipped off for a drink at halftime and he got lost. We'd sat in the same seats for the best part of 20 years, yet I had to go and find him.

In the end, the inevitable happened. Lisa called me to say that the 'brother I never had' died the previous night, alone in bed, except for the bottle of Smirnoff he'd choked on. I was devastated but not surprised. He was a total one-of-a-kind, and I'll never meet anyone like him again. He may have been a twat sometimes, but he was my twat. I miss him like fuck and think of him most days, usually with a smile. I just hope there's a bar up there, or else he's going to be so bored

Self-assessment: The 'Branching Out' years

'I really enjoyed the training role as for the first time I felt liberated to do things in my own style, even if, as feared, it was bloody scary to start with. I learned the value of confidence and how that can come from knowledge and being prepared. When I started in the bank, I had no idea that I would ever reach branch manager level so to have had 2 manager positions already has surprised me, but I'm pleased with what I've achieved and I guess that I'm starting to believe that I have a future in the bank, albeit I'm still not sure whether I'm any good at it. The incident with Dave really knocked me and made me question who you can trust; that's the second time that I feel personally let down and taken advantage of. I struggled to stay motivated at Southampton Row where it became all about counting sales, and I am incredibly disappointed that I didn't do more to prevent some of the behaviours that were going on, and that some customers may have been detrimentally impacted as a result. Maybe the branch network isn't for me? I do feel that now is the right time to get back into a head office role. I'll think twice before being a hero again as my nose still hurts from that head butt; perhaps I should have spotted the West Ham tattoo on his neck.'

Part 5

The 'All About The People' years

(1997-2001)

21

'And you find out life isn't like that, it's so hard to understand, why the world is your oyster but your future's a clam'

The country fell into mourning following the tragic death of Lady Di. A style icon, she was replaced, in part, by Charlie Dimmock, whose sizeable and uncontrolled breasts become a weekly feature on *Ground Force*, the new gardening extravaganza. No garden would ever be without a water feature ever again. The other sad breaking news was that in his efforts to stop the A30 extension in Devon, Daniel Harper, aka the Eco Warrior Swampy, had died. This was quickly followed by the relief that this wasn't the case; the rumours that he'd had a heart attack because he'd refused a bypass were unfounded. However, the rumours that after nearly 20 years, there was now a Labour government were true, as Tony Blair convincingly won the general election, consigning John Major to only making *Spitting Image* appearances. Of course, he might have lasted longer if he had tried harder at school. The new Tory leader was 12-year-old William Hague. In medicine, a new cure for insomnia is piloted. It's called a Harry Potter film, and they prove to be a complete success, as watching any of them is guaranteed to put you to sleep within 15 minutes.

Things had gone OK at Southampton Row, I even looked after Tony Blair's bank account, but for whatever reason, I didn't ever connect fully with what we were being asked to do. It had become almost entirely about sales management, and that wasn't my thing; I just didn't get a kick out of counting widgets. Although I had enjoyed the benefits of climbing further up the hierarchal ladder, I began to worry that I had leaned the ladder against the wrong wall by mistake. Peter had left, and I could feel the culture was changing, in my opinion, not for the better. So when I saw an opportunity to get back into Head Office, I jumped at it with both feet. The job I was interested in was within HR (or personnel as it was still called), primarily because I really liked the guy who would be my new boss, Chris George, whom I'd met when I was on the training team. His skinny physique and thick-lensed glasses reminded me of Syd Little, one-half of the shite comedy duo, but he exuded an air of knowing his stuff while not giving a fuck what other people thought. He was very comfortable to *be him*, which made him someone I wanted to work with. I applied, he liked me, and I got the job; *Supersonic*.

It was a time when the bank needed to make significant reductions in the 'sub-manager' population, guys like Roy and Chris Harper, so my job for the first six months was to convince as many of them as possible that they would be better off taking a redundancy payment now, rather than hanging around and being managed out. Chris explained how to do it in his broad Sheffield accent:
'Imagine I'm you, and you are one of your victims', he said, grabbing a pencil, an ashtray, and a half-full glass of water.
'We're here to talk about your future,' he said, as he pushed the pencil across the desk in front of me. 'This is you today,' he said. Then, sliding forward the ashtray, he said, 'And here's your performance, which isn't very good' before sliding the glass of water towards me, saying, 'And here's 35 Grand.'

After a brief pause, he re-gathered all of the items. 'Now let's look at what the situation is likely to be in about six months. Here's you again' he explained, pushing the pencil forward once more, ' and here's your performance,' he said, placing the ashtray in front of me. 'It's still pretty shit'. This time he just sat there, arms folded, silent, staring at me through his smudged spectacles — no glass of water, no 35 grand.

After a few seconds, I thought I had better say something. 'So basically, we're telling them they can leave now and take a redundancy cheque with them, or hang around and probably get sacked, in about six months, with no money?' 'Blimey, you're quick,' laughed Chris, 'but yes, you've got it'. Although it was only my first morning on the job, I had already started my Institute of Personnel exams, so I had obtained a basic level of knowledge about employment law. I could see how his approach would be effective, if not entirely legal. 'I do get it, Chris', I said, 'but wouldn't that be classed as constructive dismissal?'

'Of course it wouldn't', chortled Chris

'Why not?' I asked, still convinced that it definitely was.

'Because, old son, if any of them ever make an issue out of it, you deny that you ever said it. I've done it loads of times and never lost in a tribunal. Now bugger off.'

Six months later, I'd helped dozens of experienced and tired gents to find happiness elsewhere, sometimes using the technique that Chris had taught me, sometimes not. I used many props along the way, including cups, fountain pens, my wallet, a packet of crisps and the good old pencil, ashtray, and glass of water. I even asked one chap to remove his glasses, using them to symbolise his shit performance, which in retrospect was a bit harsh, but needs-must. Most people understood the reality and were happy to take the deal. I didn't need to bother with any props at all with some of them as the sales culture we were in, which was only going to get deeper, just wasn't for them, so they were more than ready to get out with a decent slug of dosh. My only regret was I didn't get to perform my influencing trick with Chris Harper. Having said that, he probably would have thrown the (half-empty) glass of water over me.

After I'd spent a big chunk of the bank's redundancy budget, I was asked to run the programme that supported the development of the guys recently taken onto the Management Development scheme. Things had gone full circle. A vital element of the scheme was the provision of a mentor, usually a senior leader who would commit to spending time to help structure the mentee's thinking in an independent, non-threatening way. I've benefited from several effective mentoring relationships over the years, and the truly memorable ones were with guys I respected, who I looked up to, and who genuinely wanted to help me. I had always considered Kevin a mentor, even though he was also my line manager. Not only had he backed me and gambled on me, but he'd also shown me what being an inspirational leader looked like. Guys like Richard Palmer, whom I met while working in the training team, would take time to give me a different perspective, sharing his wisdom built up over many years. Richard's still a mate to this day, and that's the point; the relationship, the trust you build up when you get it right, is deep, valuable, and long-lasting.

My mentoring sessions with Richard usually involved a beer or two, not least the night when, after visiting several establishments in the West End, we got turfed out of a Russian vodka bar at about 3 a.m. Richard announced he would walk home as we stumbled onto a deserted Knightsbridge High Street. 'You're having a laugh, mate, your house is miles away,' I said, and based on the fact that he was zig-zagging across the pavement and effectively doubling the distance he was going, I reckoned it would take him about ten hours to make the eight miles to Ealing. My idea was much more practical. I opted to head back to the branch in Southampton Row, which was no more than an hour's stagger away. With my judgment in tatters after a very long night of vodka drinking, I overlooked that letting yourself into a branch was, and still is, very much against the rules but I had a front door key, and the chair in my office was too comfortable to resist.

I woke with a start a couple of hours later when I heard Des marching around the office doing the early morning search. Unsurprisingly, he nearly shat himself when he saw me as I quickly apologised that I'd not followed protocol and did my best to convince him that I had just come in early to prepare for a big meeting later that day. I thought I'd gotten away with it, until, in our morning huddle, one of the team commented that I was wearing the same shirt and tie as I had the previous day and that my office had a strange smell of Smirnoff.

As well as *being* mentored, I started mentoring colleagues, and it felt significant that I'd reached a point, both in life and in my career, when other people would be mildly interested in what *I* thought, what *I* would do in their situation. Over time, especially towards the end of my career, mentoring others became one of the most rewarding things I did. Whether I made any significant difference to anybody, I don't know, but, if just one person out there thinks of me as 'their Kevin' or 'their Richard,' then I've done a good thing, and it was time well spent.

My career (in what was now called HR) was progressing well, and Lisa was doing well too. She had moved to Lehman Brothers, having fortunately left Baring Brothers shortly before it had collapsed due to a minor cock up by Nick Leeson, one of their traders, who made Chris Sanders look like a kid nicking a lollipop from the tuck shop, by managing to lose about $1.4bn. We were enjoying life as boozing in the City became a regular occurrence and I would often meet Lisa and her workmates in Corney and Barrows in Broadgate Circle — I think she eventually arranged for her salary to be paid directly to them, cutting at out the unnecessary step of going into a bank account first. And, regardless of the time we rolled in, our ability to get up at 5:30 a.m. was never tested more, but we always passed.

Although we were having fun, including going on regular holidays abroad and earning good cash, things had somehow become predictable. Something was missing. We'd talked about having children, but I didn't feel entirely convinced it was what I wanted, not because I didn't like kids, nor because I didn't want Mrs. P to stop earning decent money, but because I didn't want to turn into my mate Cheads, or at least into the life that he seemed to have adopted. Cheads was a long-time, good mate and was the first of our 'gang' to have a child. Understandably (certainly in retrospect), he and his girlfriend were besotted by baby Annie, and so were we. He was, and still is an excellent dad, but he showed me the sacrifices needed, and I just wasn't sure whether I was ready for the upheaval that having a child would clearly create. I recall the day when I had a spare ticket to watch the mighty Blues demolish some second-rate outfit in the FA Cup, and, knowing Cheads was a Chelsea supporter, I asked him if he would like to come to the match with me. No charge, it was on me, and I would buy him a few beers beforehand too. All he had to do was to meet me before the match at The White Horse (aka The Sloaney Pony) in Parsons Green.

'I can't, mate,' he said, 'we've got to go to Kingston and buy a new buggy for Annie'.

'Surely you can do that in the morning, mate? You won't need to leave for football until about 12, and we'll still have plenty of time to get a few pints in.' Apparently not; even though he had been a lifelong follower of Chelsea and hadn't been to watch them for over ten years, he couldn't get the buggy in the morning because that would 'muck up Annie's routine'. Bugger that, is this how it is when you have kids? But deep down, Lisa and I knew that Cheads was right, and I started to enjoy each home game like it might be my last for a while.

22

'Golden rain, will bring you riches, all the good things you deserve and now'

Like most people, we had just under nine months to prepare. Of course, it's impossible to be completely ready for the arrival of your first child, to anticipate the feeling of caring for something more than you've ever cared about anything else. And, you realise that until that point you hadn't fully appreciated how much *your* own parents cared about and loved you.

At 1:50p.m. on 23 October 1997, Jack Charles Freeman Pannett popped into this world. Slippery little fella, with big blue eyes and a good barnet. Saturdays for me were no longer going to be spent singing 'Blue is the Colour' but instead agreeing with Lisa that blue was the colour for Jack's new pyjamas. We would only go out and buy stuff in the afternoon because we didn't want to ruin his routine. But please don't tell Cheads.

Now consigned to staying in, I was able to enjoy watching the TV a lot more, and was delighted to see my old mate Carol Vorderman winning the first celebrity special of *Stars in Their Eyes*, when she said the famous words 'Tonight Matthew, I'm going to be . . . Cher.' It was ironic that she should choose Cher to be her alter-ego now that a few years on and a considerable amount of plastic surgery later, there's nothing left of the original version of either of them. Maybe it would have been easier and cheaper if they could have just *Turned Back Time*.

I worked with Chris for another six months before moving into the central HR team based in Bristol, a long way from Hampton, where we now lived — 118 miles each way, to be precise. I was lucky to be a able to recruit someone to work with me, and I found a guy called Paul, an ex-trainer who was up for the challenge. Although he was bright, he quickly acquired the nickname 'Trigg' (as per Only Fools and Horses) due to his occasional 'blond moments', his most famous example being when one night, he seriously asked me 'What was the name of the horse in Champion the Wonder House'? Classic.

It was a busy time as the bank had recently merged with another, based predominantly in the north of England. Having always worked in London, I'd never really met any colleagues from 'up there' so I was surprised when some of them were actually decent people, and that a few didn't even bother to disguise their northern accents. The bank also merged with a building society from the West Country, and going there reminded me of my childhood trips to the Isle of Wight — it was about 40 years behind the rest of the world, and everyone looked remarkably similar.

Much of the work that Trigg and I were doing involved liaising with the bank's unions, and although I'd worked alongside local reps like Stuart at Hanover Square, this was a new experience for both of us. I shuffled into the office for my first my negotiation meeting and was told, by a fat guy with a red complexion and a broad Glaswegian accent, 'You sit over there,' as he pointed to the opposite side of the long rectangular boardroom table.
'Oh, OK,' I said, 'silly me for thinking it was a normal table,' as we sat in silence for ten minutes until both his and my colleagues arrived. There's nothing like breaking the ice to help lay the path for a constructive discussion.

Quickly realising that we were dealing with a bunch of twats, I said very little throughout the meeting, listening, for the most part, to the union guys using their privileged position to deal with their own personal issues rather than those of their members that they were supposed to be representing. They seemed more up for a fistfight (which they definitely would have won) than a sensible, grown-up conversation, so, unsurprisingly, we didn't manage to agree on the terms of the pay deal we were negotiating, meaning we would need to go to independent arbitration and a trip to ACAS. I'd only heard about ACAS when it was occasionally referenced by John Suchet on The News at Ten, usually if the Government had failed again to agree with the Teachers or the Rail worker's unions about a pay deal or working conditions. Scott in our team who had regularly been to their offices in Southwark told me that if I was expecting to meet Kofi Anan, I would probably be disappointed, as it wasn't particularly glamorous or sophisticated and was 'just some old geezer with a clipboard shuffling between different rooms'.

A week or so after our negotiating impasse, we spent an evening at ACAS. We offered a 4.5% pay rise, the Unions demanded 11%, and we ended up 'agreeing' on 4.6%. But I did meet Harold, a lovely old fella with a clipboard who clocked up loads of steps shuffling between our room and theirs, and, as well as agreeing a decent deal for the bank, we also had some fish and chips and a few beers. I visited ACAS a few times in my HR capacity but never imagined that one day I would be going there to talk about myself.

12 million people now had access to the internet, and sales of DVDs had passed the one million mark. However, VHS tapes remained the most popular home video format. And while smug VHS owners were watching their recordings of Judith Keppel being the first winner of the big prize on *Who Wants to Be a Millionaire*, sad Betamax owners could be heard crying as they threw their already-useless machines into the nearest skip. There was more *breaking-ground* TV when BBC One aired a millennium special of Ground Force in which Alan, Charlie, and Tommy spent the BBC licence payers' money on a drug and alcohol-fuelled trip to the South African village of Qunu where they designed and built a new garden for Nelson Mandela. Fortunately for Charlie, Nelson was well known to love a water feature. However, the plan

for Carol Smilie and Lawrence 'Frilly-Shirt' to also pop out was shelved when Mr. Mandela revealed he had no desire to 'change rooms' with his near neighbour Archbishop Desmond Tutu due to his allergy to brightly coloured shirts and an extreme dislike of MDF.

Sadly, Rod Hull, one of my childhood 'ever-presents', died when he fell off his roof while trying to adjust his TV aerial. TV was his life, but ultimately the cause of his death too. I've always been curious whether Emu attended the funeral and, if so, who took him. Presumably, Russel Harty didn't volunteer. After 32 years, Ford stopped production of the Escort, another mainstay of my formative years; it's the end of an era for boy racers everywhere. Rover car sales also fell rapidly, although the rumour that the bank is responsible for this due to changing the salesforce company car scheme is unfounded. Instead, it was because everyone realised that they were crap.

One person who wasn't emotionally attached to *his* Rover 200, or evidently the bank's either, was Tim Pocock, a member of the bank's regulated salesforce who had to be 'let go' when an audit identified that many of his sales didn't have much legitimate paperwork. In fact, none of his sales had any legitimate paperwork whatsoever. Before being allowed to leave gracefully, Tim was asked to take his company car to a local centre for collection but, in a final rebellious gesture, chose not to do that, preferring instead to ask the bank to pick it up. This wasn't the first time a disgruntled salesman had left his car somewhere for collection, but it was the first time that one had been left in Moscow. I thought that Tim was a bit of a tit, but I was impressed with his final act of rebelliousness. I couldn't remember for sure, but I bet he wore brown shoes.

In addition to the building society and the 'northern bank' (or, to quote one of my more traditional senior managers, 'that load of fucking dustmen, milkmen, and postmen'), we'd also taken over a large insurance company based in Scotland, so I would go up there regularly for meetings. On the first few occasions I flew to Edinburgh, I felt very important as I skipped through the airport with my briefcase and all the other important business people, but the novelty of getting up at silly o'clock, taking a taxi to the airport, jumping on a plane, and staying in depressing, Scottish hotels, quickly wore off.

I remember being surprised one afternoon when I was up there with Trigg, and Mum's home phone number flashed up on my Nokia 6510. It was Dad.

'What's up?' I asked.

'Your Mum wasn't feeling 100%,' he replied in his usual matter-of-fact tone, 'so I took her to the hospital. Anyway, where are you?'

'I'm in Edinburgh, Dad. Is she OK?'

'Well, I think so,' he replied. 'But as you know, I'm not a massive lover of hospitals, so I've left her there and was wondering whether you might be able to go and check on her?'

I got the next flight back and took a taxi for the 40-minute journey to Kingston Hospital. After some vague instructions from the Accident and Emergency receptionist, I headed in the general direction she had pointed to and found Mum parked on a trolley in a corridor. 'What the bloody hell's going on, Mum?' She was confused but coherent enough to tell me they thought she'd had a heart attack. Bloody hell, Dad, I know that you have a phobia of hospitals, but really? When I eventually found someone who had the foggiest idea what was going on, the junior Doctor told me that they believed that she had indeed had a heart attack, albeit a mild one, and that she was reasonably stable. I wanted to rant about the suitability of a 65-year-old woman who'd nearly died being left on a trolley in a corridor, but the exhausted look on the

Doctor's face suggested it would have been both futile and unfair. Besides, Mum, being the most stoic and empathic person I've ever known, said that it was 'no big deal and not to worry' as she was fine being in a corridor as it was 'nice and warm' and she felt sorry for all the staff because they were obviously 'so very busy'.

After three hours of standing in a corridor talking to Mum about how picturesque Edinburgh is (I had to guess because apart from the airport, the office, the hotel, and four boozers, I hadn't actually seen any of it), a porter eventually came along and announced that he was taking her to a ward, prompted I think by the fact that I'd threatened to push her there myself if it helped. Mum said she'd be OK and told me to go home, but 'Could you give your Dad a ring and let him know?'

'Of course, I will, Mum,' I assured her, but hoped that she was too far down the corridor on her way to the ward to hear me mutter, 'As long as he's not too fucking busy to pick up the phone.'

I popped in to see her on Saturday morning, and she was bright. 'How's your Dad?' she asked.

'Oh, holding up, I think,' my sarcasm sailing over her head like a Harry Kane World Cup penalty over a French crossbar. Being the weekend, the likelihood of much happening on the doctor front was minimal, so after checking she was comfortable, I drove home and left her chatting with Vera in the next bed about flower arranging and the time when, in 1971, she flew, head first, through the windscreen of her Ford Escort and 'funnily enough' nearly died on the very same ward.

At around lunchtime, still knackered from a stressful, late-to-bed Friday, I was sitting on the sofa with Jack, now nearly two, wondering how it was possible for Thomas the tank Engine to have developed a Scouse accent, when I noticed that his breathing had become laboured, his little, pale chest looking like it was working extra hard on every breath. (I'm talking about Jack, not Thomas.) I called Lisa in, who at this time was the best part of nine months pregnant with our 'second,' and she agreed that he didn't look right. Within ten minutes, Jack was lying on the bed in the GP surgery, with the Doctor listening to his chest with a stethoscope, pulling facial expressions that didn't make us feel overly reassured that everything *was* OK. 'I think you had better take him to A&E,' said Dr. Vinton, 'he doesn't sound right.'

We had an anxious afternoon and evening while the doctors undertook loads of tests on Jack, at one point suggesting that he might have meningitis. Thankfully, he became more stable, albeit they wanted to admit him to a ward. For obvious reasons, Lisa took herself home while I stayed there for the night, occasionally popping over to the other side of the building to check that Mum was OK and hadn't bored Vera, literally, to death.

By Sunday morning, Jack was looking much brighter, if getting a little restless at being in a strange bed in a strange place. I didn't help much when I told him I would need to go soon as Chelsea were playing Manchester United but that his mum would be coming to sit with him soon. In case you're thinking, I wouldn't have left him alone for that long; I'm not a monster. But hey, it was Man U. Just as I was about to tell Jack to stop crying, Lisa phoned: 'I think my waters have broken,' rightly assuming I knew what that meant. It would be 20 minutes at least before I could get back home and then another 20 or so to get back to the hospital, so we agreed to ask her mother to bring her to the hospital. Jack stopped crying when I told him I wasn't going immediately and that his Grandma Lynda was coming to see him soon but started again when I explained that he would hopefully have a little brother by the end of the day. By mid-day, Lynda had arrived and relieved me of babysitting duties, allowing me to run to the maternity unit for baby birth duties. I didn't even stop en route to check in on Mum. Although I had lost £40 on my unused Chelsea ticket, I guess I was getting decent value for money from the NHS!

Everything turned out OK as we won five-nil, our biggest-ever win over United. Oh, and Mum was able to go home on the Monday after a few checks; Jack was discharged with a diagnosis of bronchiolitis and given a couple of asthma inhalers, and Charlie Frederick Freeman Pannett (A.KA. 'Charlie Five-Nil') was born just before the final whistle and came home with his Mum and I later that day. Having a second child really is very different from the first. It's not a case of loving them any less, but when we first bought Jack home from the hospital, we couldn't have been more careful with our precious, new cargo, carefully placing him in a pre-prepared space in our lounge. When we bought Charlie home, we left him on the kitchen floor with the shopping bags from Sainsbury's, where we'd popped into on the way home. My sister Sue, who has two kids, had told me this would happen, explaining to me whenever her first, Rachel, dropped her dummy, she would take extra care, immediately removing the now contaminated pacifier from the area and immediately replacing it with one of the several others that were already sterilised and ready to use. When my nephew, Adam, born a couple of years later, dropped his dummy, Sue would get the dog to pick it up and give it back to him.

I stopped going to Edinburgh shortly afterwards but spent another two years commuting to Bristol. Although I didn't have to go there every day, I wished they'd given *Avios* points for driving up and down the M4. My main job was to support the Managing Directors of what was known as the 'Regulated Sales Team' and also the 'Retail Compliance Function'. Their attitudes, behaviours, and cultures were at polar opposite ends of the spectrum; the Salesforce guys were the 'Jack the Lads', the big earners, the risk-takers, the compliance guys were far more conservative, sensible, and risk-averse. The 'business prevention' guys, as they were colloquially known.

The managing directors were equally as different as their teams. The head of the Salesforce was a guy called Geoff. He was larger than life, not physically but with more than his fair share of charisma, and he threw himself entirely into his role, epitomising the work hard, play hard mantra. He had a keen sense of mischief and fun, which I liked, and so did his people who followed him like a king. Trevor was the head of Compliance, and although he may not have been quite the party animal that Geoff was, he had his own sparkle in his eyes and a penchant for the finer things in life, including a love of all things French, especially wine.

Working for both was fun, even if the tension between them meant I had to tread carefully on occasions. I felt more naturally aligned to the Salesforce than I did to Compliance, but I also felt strongly about doing the right thing, and some of what I saw the sales guys do pushed the boundaries of 'in the right way'. Conversely, I found many of the guys in the compliance function to be very serious, too 'police-like' with their power, albeit they were clearly right-minded. I made the mistake of setting up a meeting between the senior leaders of both functions to try and create a more collaborative working relationship between them but instead of achieving harmony and an agreement to work more closely, they all spent the day arguing and throwing rocks at each other. When I eventually gave up trying to facilitate the session, I think they hated each other more than before I'd started; Kofi Anan would not have been impressed, nor I doubt would Harold at ACAS.

My lack of facilitation skills made me realise that as much as I enjoyed the job, I wasn't achieving very much, and that I was lacking meaning and purpose behind the effort. I'd become good mates with Trigg and really enjoyed working with him, but when, out of the blue, I got a call from my old mate Chris George about an opportunity to work with him again, I jumped at it

23

'Found myself in a strange town'

There was more civil unrest during 2001, with anti-capitalist demonstrations in London turning violent and race-related riots in Burnley, Bradford, and Brixton. And probably a few other places beginning with B. And Peterborough. Anne Robinson livened things up a bit when she suggested that Welsh people should all be consigned to Room 101, a comment that, while vaguely amusing, was considered too close to the boundaries of acceptability, although not racist. If only she had narrowed it down to Shakin' Stevens, she probably would have gotten away with it.

In a delightful show of self-restraint and role model behaviour, Deputy Prime Minister John Prescott reacted well to a bloke throwing an egg at him by punching him in the face. Thank goodness it wasn't Chris Harper throwing a stapler, Big John would have probably killed him. Fortunately for the Labour Party, his outburst didn't damage their image, and they secured a second landslide General Election victory. On the back of the thrashing, William Hague, who no doubt would have had a good few of those in his time, resigned as leader of the Tory Party before his 17th birthday. Music takes a turn for the worse when shows like *Popstars* and *Pop Idol* introduce us to a new level of awful, with fabricated bands like *'Hear'Say'* and *'The S. Club 7'* hitting the top of the charts. Evidently, talent is no longer required, unlike when I grew up listening to punk.

The main objective of my new job working again for Chris was to design and deliver a remuneration package for the financial advisers who helped the top-end customers. I was to be based in Haywards Heath, the other side of Gatwick from London and compared to travelling to Edinburgh or Bristol, the idea of a short jaunt through the West Sussex countryside sounded straightforward. As I passed the Burrell Arms Pub at the bottom of Perrymount Road on my first morning, I could tell that Haywards Heath was an old-fashioned place and I thought I may have done a Marty McFly, activated time travel, and gone back 50 years. Or I was in the Isle of Wight by mistake.

My project wasn't due to start for another month, so Chris told me to 'keep busy', which I did, mainly by frequenting the Burrell Arms, in between not doing much else. It was a grubby boozer with sticky floral carpets stained by years of spilled drinks and dirty shoes, round tables with peeling varnish and chipped edges, a couple of quiz and fruit machines, but a decent beer garden. Well, it was a garden, and I could drink beer in it and although I didn't drink too much because I was driving, it was a pleasant way to spend an hour or five.

The following week, a grim-faced Chris said he needed an urgent chat. 'It's all gone tits-up,' he said. 'The sales team is being made redundant, so they won't need a new remuneration package, but they're not announcing this until November, and because the change is potentially sensitive enough to impact the bank's share price, we're not allowed to tell anyone.' I looked at Chris, and he gave me a knowing look back as he saw that I had realised we were going to have to spend the next six months going through the motions of running a project that had nothing to achieve, to negotiate with the unions the details of a pay package that was never going to be implemented, and to get paid to do a job that was a total waste of time. Part of me was gutted; another part smiled that the silver lining in this particular cloud would probably be made from Guinness. To soften the blow, Chris introduced an old London HR rule that, during the winter months, if you were in the pub after 1 p.m., it was not acceptable to go back to the office until it was dark, and when you did get back, it should be to delete emails only. I admired the sentiment, and it just didn't feel appropriate to mention that it was 9 June, so it wouldn't get dark until about 9 p.m. But he was the boss, and rules are rules. On the way back to the office, I had a sneaky peek at the summer train timetables.

I've always enjoyed getting a tan, and it was better in the summer of 2001 than most years. The beer garden might have been crap, but it wasn't in the shade. Rather inconveniently, Chris and I had to occasionally meet with the Unions and pretend — there are few meetings more bizarre than when we sat in Lombard Street, on the *opposite* side of a glossy oak desk, arguing about the nuances of something that only we knew was never going to happen. Although it was a charade, it was a good sport, especially as my old red-faced mate was there. That'll teach him to be a grumpy twat.

One Tuesday morning, while preparing one of many pointless presentations for one of many equally pointless meetings, I heard a commotion in the office next door as everyone, with shocked expressions on their faces, gathered around the small TV screen mounted on the wall. I'm sure we all remember where we were when the first plane hit one of the Twin Towers on 9/11. It was chilling beyond belief, and as things worsened and the true horror of what was happening started to sink in, my thoughts turned towards the Missus and the kids at home. All I could think was that I needed to be with them for no logical reason other than if the world was going to end, it should be with us together. I've since reflected that it was selfish to think about me, about them, rather than the immediate victims of the atrocities, but that's what I did.

Shortly after the second plane had ploughed into the second tower, I couldn't hang around anymore, so I jumped in the car and drove toward home, my head spinning with the shocking brutality of what I had just witnessed. Having spent most of my working life in London, I'd been used to terrorism, most notably when working in Regional Training and Dave and I were told that there was the risk of an IRA mortar attack nearby and that we should stick tape in an X shape across the windows so that if there was a blast, the glass would be more likely to blow outwards than inwards. It felt as pointless as hiding under the stairs four minutes before a nuclear strike. The attack happened, but our windows were spared, so maybe it worked. We left the tape on the windows for a couple of weeks just in case. But this, even though it was 3500 miles away, felt completely different, far more scary. Like so many people that day, I felt sick and, later, while watching the dreadful events repeatedly on the TV, cried my eyes out.

The world had changed forever, and my world was about to change even more. As the *war on terror* continued, two days before the US invaded Afghanistan, our first daughter, Rosie Grace Freeman Pannett, was born. I really did have to question what kind of a world we had brought her into.

Not long afterwards, the truth about the changes and the redundancies became public knowledge, and everyone worked out why Chris and I had been doing bugger-all for most of the summer, over and above any other summer. And although I'd always known that the job wouldn't last forever, I now needed to find a new one fairly sharpish. Fortunately, I'd kept in touch with Trevor throughout the Haywards Heath debacle. He'd become a mentor to me, and I enjoyed his company, his wine, and his knowledge and love for France, which had piqued my interest in visiting our cousins across 'Le Manche,'. Now, with a family, Lisa and I had put on hold our annual trips to Barbados, primarily because we couldn't afford it, but also because I know the face I would pull whenever I got on a plane before an eight-hour flight to find that there was a noisy kid in the seats in front; the thought of taking three of them under the age of five was too much to contemplate.

I found a place on the internet (no more hours spent in a travel agency going through a load of bloody brochures), and we set off for what turned out to be the longest drive of my life, eventually arriving at *The Comptoir*, in the tiny village of Paulmy, bang in the middle of absolutely nowhere. As we pulled into the small driveway at the front of the gite, a guy with long scraggy ginger hair, holding a tumbler half filled with red wine and smoking a cigarillo was leaning against one of the gite's eau-de-nil painted window shutters. He approached the car as the kids fell out of the back seats and introduced himself as Jean-Pierre, the owner. Having previously struggled to explain to the attendant what petrol pump I'd used when we'd stopped for fuel on the journey down, I was delighted and relieved that he spoke decent English, even if it was in a ludicrously French accent.

Jean-Pierre led us inside and into the main room, which looked spookily like an old bar-cum-restaurant, which is precisely what it had been until about three weeks previously when Jean-Pierre had decided that running an old bar-cum-restaurant was too much like hard work and that he'd make much more money renting it out to 'rosbifs' looking for a bit of culture. We were his first guests. Running along the back wall was an aluminium-topped bar, longer than the one at Lombard Street and at the All Bar One in Richmond that I'd been drinking in the previous evening with Dickie (note to self: don't drink too much the night before a 12-hour journey in a country you've never driven in before) and more chairs, glasses, plates, and cutlery too. The tiled floors and the thick stone walls, randomly daubed with different ages of plaster, made the place intriguingly quirky, if not particularly warm or luxurious. The kids, in their excited holiday impatience and disinterest in admiring the masonry, ran out to inspect the small heated swimming pool, which, although not massive, was big enough to accommodate the five of us.

Before Lisa and I had finished taking in the beauty of the late summer afternoon sun reflecting off the stucco courtyard walls, we were dragged by Charlie over to the enormous old barn in the far corner, the reason for his eagerness becoming quickly evident as he excitedly showed us the games room with table tennis table, dartboard, table skittles, and a pool table. The only thing missing was a *Foosball* table to complete the full suite of *Indoor league* 'sports'. If you are not familiar with *Indoor League*, you should be — aired during the post *Watch with Mother* lunchtime slot between 1973 and 1978, it was hosted by 'Fiery' Fred Trueman — any TV programme that is fronted by an ex-England and Yorkshire cricketer wearing a beige and brown cardigan, smoking a pipe and drinking a pint of light and bitter throughout and involves a load of out-of-work fifty-something blokes from Leeds playing darts and arm wrestling (not at the same time as far as I'm aware) has to be worth a look-up on YouTube. 'I'll see thee.'

It was lucky that the kids would be able to create their own barn entertainment as, in truth, there was bugger all else in the small village other than a trip to the tyre repair place, a boulangerie, and a small bar. While the boys were on their seventeenth game of pool and Rosie was becoming increasingly confused by the term 'winner stays on,' I decided to set off on the 20-second stroll to check out the local hostelry, which, according to the rusting metal plaque at the bottom of the concrete steps leading up to the entrance was called *Jackie's*. Eager for a pint of something, I skipped up the steps and through the door that was almost entirely hidden by the overgrown ivy that covered the entire front of the small building. Reminiscent of the scene at the *Slaughtered Lamb* in the film *An American Werewolf in London*, the three massive French blokes sitting at the bar and the slightly smaller fella behind the bar, presumably

Jackie, stopped their game of dominoes, turned and glared at me, albeit more with looks of curiosity than with any menace.

'Bonjour, I'm Graham, Je suis staying chez Jean-Pierre's avec my wife and trois enfants. It's tres bon to be here, it's lovely to meet you all, and I wonder whether je peut have a pint of *Kronenbourg*, silver plate?' I shouldn't have been too surprised that they were all 'very French,' only spoke French and just looked at me *'comme le poisson hors de l'eau'* that I was. Jackie at least understood the word *Kronenbourg* as a small glass of beer was thrust onto the bar top. I downed it, pretended to understand the nuances of dominoes, said bonjour again, left 5 Euros, and hurried the 50 steps back to The Comptoir.

Over the next 'quinze jours' we spent many hours at Jackie's. The kids learned how to play dominoes and that the rest of the world doesn't necessarily speak English (and nor should it); I learned that drinking pints is uncouth and 'seize-cent-soixante-quatre' tastes much better from a 275 ml glass, even if it still tastes like piss. We saw very few tourists while we were there, which was a good thing; there's nothing better at ruining a cultural holiday in a French Gite than a group of Liverpool football shirt-clad yobs. Actually, there's not much that they wouldn't ruin. We did get a lovely old couple from Edinburgh wander through the front door of the gite, sit down at the bar, and wait patiently for a drink. Nobody had told them Le Comptoir was no longer a restaurant, so why wouldn't they? Apparently, they'd been there for ten minutes before I wandered in from the swimming pool, but after I'd got over the shock of two strangers casually sitting in my holiday home, I was able to explain the situation and we agreed what an easy mistake to make it was.

'Well, now you're here, what would you like to drink?' I asked them. We drank red wine for the best part of two hours, talked about how pointless Scottish football was, and eventually, after a couple of games of dominoes (I'd learned the proper rules by this time), our new best friends, Greg and Mary, left. I stood at the door and waved them off into the distance, half pissed and as close as I'd been to my dream of owning my own boozer.

We returned to *Le Comptoir* seven years in a row, and Jean-Pierre became a friend, even inviting Lisa and I to stay there for a long weekend to celebrate his 50th birthday. As a present, I took a vintage *Foosball* table I had bought a few years earlier to allow him to complete the I*ndoor League* set. He appreciated it, and we played a couple of games. He absolutely spanked me with an air of satisfaction as if the French rugby team had just turned over England at Twickenham. I'd let my country down but reacted in true English style by proceeding to get completely smashed and talking very loudly to a load of French farmers in the genuine belief that they understood me.

On a couple of occasions, my dear mate Jimmy 'Snooksie' Snooks and his lovely wife Lou and kids Olivia and Elliott came and stayed with us. Between dominoes and buying cheap antiques at local *Brocantes* (a French car boot sale which the kids really enjoyed, a bit like a trip to a Devon pottery on a rainy day), we visited a Zoo in Beauval. As usual, on the way out, I hurried the kids through the gift shop in the hope that if we were quick enough, I wouldn't have to waste any hard-earned Euros on some over-priced tat, but failed miserably, in particular with Charlie, who fell in love with a long-armed, fluffy toy monkey. He carried it everywhere, so maybe it wasn't a bad purchase, including when we went out for dinner one evening. As was the norm when we were in France, the grown-ups ate nicely whilst the kids played noisily in the nearby square, chasing each other around the fountain as the late-night summer sun slowly faded behind the jumble of charming old houses. Just as I was tucking into my plate of *escargots*, an inconsolable Charlie came running towards us, accompanied by his concerned brother and sister; something dreadful had happened — Charlie had 'accidentally' thrown his new toy into one of the many olive trees that decorated the now near-dark square.

A disaster on this scale needed swift and decisive action, so Snookisie and I rushed to see what could be done, only to find that it was so high up that we would need some steps to retrieve it.

'I'll ask the non-English speaking restaurant owner for some ladders,' I told Jimmy, 'you explain why we need them'. He looked at me, confused, before a massive beaming smile broke out across his face,' Le singe est dans l'arbre!', he exclaimed. 'I knew it would come in handy one day!'

I think Trevor was pleased that I had fallen in love with France. I told him how the job in Haywards Heath had been a total waste of time, that I had spent more time in the boozer with Chris than I had in the office, and that I now needed to find a new role. He told me there was a vacancy in his Compliance team and that I should apply. It was a promotion, and although I had supported his function with HR stuff, I knew very little about actual Compliance, but for some reason he thought I could do it. I'll never know whether it was because he thought of me as the son he never had or because he genuinely believed that I had the competencies to do the job, but, remarkably, after going through a straightforward application process, he phoned me late one afternoon in 2002, while I was in the pub to tell me that I had got the job. When I eventually returned to the office to delete some emails, I told Chris the news. 'We'd better celebrate then', he ordered, and we returned to the boozer. I left later than usual that day and remember little of the train journey home. Two weeks later, I was looking up how to get to Chatham in preparation for my new job as Head of Compliance Oversight, whatever that meant.

Self-assessment: The 'All About The People' years.

'It's been a real eye-opener moving into HR as it has allowed me to see more about how organisations work and how in reality it can be quite brutal. I'm grateful to Chris for giving me the opportunity and I'm pleased that I've learned a new discipline, even if, according to Lisa's boss, 'It's a job for fucking Sheilas'.

Working with Geoff and the sales force has been great fun, if occasionally close to the 'edge', and I've learned from him the power of getting people to buy into your vision and to want to follow you. Supporting Trev has been different, but also enjoyable, and he's taught me loads about France. I've definitely realised that you need to adapt your influencing style in order to navigate through the politics of a large organisation. Although I met some special people, working in Haywards Heath turned out to be a total waste of time and as much fun as spending the day in the pub was, it made me realise the importance of having meaning and purpose at work and being able to see that I'm having a tangible impact, something which may become increasingly more difficult as I continue to work in head office roles and further away from customers and front line colleagues. Trev has offered me an opportunity to move into compliance, it's not a move that I ever had in mind, I know very little about risk and compliance but I'm happy to give it a go, especially as it's a promotion and I don't actually have another job at the moment'

Part 6

The 'Wilderness' years

(2001-2004)

24

'I don't know what I'm doing here, 'cos it's not my scene at all'

There are four places in the world I would not advise going to — Cabot Cove, Midsomer, the Caribbean Island of St Marie, and Chatham. Statistically, you are highly likely to get murdered in all four, although only three look lovely, and only one has a problem with abandoned Lidl shopping trolleys and mobility scooters being driven aggressively by fag-smoking women in their thirties.

I try to convince myself that I'm not a snob, and if ever I find myself lapsing into being one, I do my best to reign myself back in. So, despite being told that Chatham made Liverpool look like Belgravia, when I set off for my first day there I did so with an open mind. I negotiated my way to London Bridge and jumped on the Ramsgate-bound train, empty carriages as usual due to travelling in the opposite direction to the rest of the working population. As the train got nearer to Chatham, I was already dismissing its bad write-up, as I enjoyed field after field of green and yellow rural beauty; by the time I had reached Rochester, with its pretty cathedral nestled on the banks of the River Medway, I started to believe that I might even enjoy the Garden Of England; Charles Dickens liked it here, so why shouldn't I?

The train pulled into Chatham Station, and, with a new-job spring in my step, I rushed up the exit stairs at the end of the platform and out into the delightful, bright Medway Town sun. Sadly, that was as good as it got and any 'Great Expectations' rapidly started to fade away. When I walked down the hill and through the syringe-strewn car park of Wickes, where I was enthusiastically welcomed to Chatham by three gents enjoying an early morning breakfast of fag-butts and Special Brew, I realised why those who had told me it was a shithole were right. I hurried towards the cobbled street of the town centre, where I found the mandatory Primark, Superdrug, H. Samuel, and a Poundland, but nowhere to grab a coffee, so I ventured into the horribly seventies-style shopping mall, amusingly called the Pentagon Centre, presumably named after its shape rather than any link with the US Defence Department. After a nano-second of being in there, I wondered whether Al Qaeda, just a few months earlier, had got their plans mixed up.

Eventually, I found a small, independent cafe, ordered a coffee, sipped the cup of lukewarm brown water, and gazed across the soulless courtyard of shit shops, starting to ask myself what the fuck I'd done. There is one school of thought that the word 'Chav' derived from Chatham although the Oxford English Dictionary has suggested that may not be true. I think that if the bloke who made that decision spent some time in the Pentagon Centre once the indigenous population had come out for the day, he might change his mind — I'm not quite sure what could be more *chavtastic* than two teenage mothers having a full on fist fight following a particularly nasty triple buggy road rage incident. Then again, being pushed out of the way at the bottom of the escalator when on your way to McDonald's for three Happy Meals and a Big Mac for breakfast *is* a big deal in Chatham and a punch-up is an obvious way to sort things out.

After half an hour, I set off for my new office and entered the drab concrete building called 'Mountbatten House'. I took the lift to the 12th floor, where Trev was waiting. After a cup of actual coffee and a quick chat about what he wanted me to do on my first day, he showed me to my office, a large bright room with a massive glass window on one side, affording me a pleasant aerial view of the bus garage and The Pentagon Centre whenever I wanted it. Trev left me alone to 'sort myself out,' and I realised I had no clue what I was supposed to be sorting out, as I had no idea what I was doing. It was evident from the attitude of some of my new colleagues that they knew that as well. I was experiencing a massive feeling of imposter syndrome, especially having come from previous roles that I was not only qualified for but could do in my sleep, or indeed pissed, which is what I was most of the time.

In time, I started to understand the job but found it dreadfully dull. I took some comfort that I was learning a new discipline, but I hated Chatham and I didn't particularly like the people I was working with either. I'd been allocated a parking space, so at least I could now drive rather than risk the walk from the station to the office again. The best part of every day quickly became seeing the *'Welcome to Chatham'* sign disappearing in my rearview mirror as I headed towards the safety of the M20 and the joys of the M25 beyond; I knew the job couldn't be right when going for a pee and paying nearly a fiver for an Americano at Clackett Lane services became something I genuinely looked forward to — the coffee was ludicrously overpriced, but the toilets were very pleasant. I even considered buying a pair of boots two sizes too small so at least I could have some pleasure every day when I took them off.

It was my fault. I had completely ignored the advice that Kevin had given me many years before and I had chased a grade, a promotion, rather than find a job that I was interested in. I knew I had made a mistake, but Trev had put his faith in me, even gone out on a limb to give me the opportunity, so I couldn't just bail out. I was stuck. Salvation eventually arrived after a long and less-than-enjoyable 18 months when, out of the blue, Trevor announced he was leaving the bank. I never did find out why — there were rumours that it was under a cloud, but regardless, his departure meant I had nothing holding me back from finding an escape, apart, of course, not having another job to go to. Fortunately, not long after Trev had left, the bank announced a restructuring of the compliance and risk functions, allowing me to negotiate my way out of Chatham and join a team back in London based in Chiswell Street. I was still working in Compliance, but it was based in Barbican, just around the corner from the Brewery Bar and Restaurant, one of my favourite places to drink. 'That'll do', as Dickie used to say.

Technology had continued to move on at pace, and an estimated 40 million people now had access to the internet. Sales of DVDs took the largest share of the home movie market, signalling the beginning of the end for the VHS format and meaning that I'd have to get rid of my vast collection of recordings of Vic Reeves's Big Night Out, The Sky at Night, and Saturday Superstore. As an 80th birthday present, the Queen got the pleasure of being painted by Rolf Harris. Fortunately it wasn't her annus horribilis.

Despite the change in location and the absolute joy of hopefully never having to go to Chatham again, I still wasn't loving the job — same nonsense, different building, if a better one in a much better location. I didn't label it then, but I realise now that I was going through a mid-career crisis, unsurprising as I was about to turn 40. I realised the illusion of immortality was precisely that, an illusion. I knew that my opportunities weren't endless and that time was finite, so I started to question again whether I was doing what I really wanted to. I couldn't ignore the feeling because I knew, like the mole on my arm, it would get bigger and worse and probably become a problem. But, I didn't want to give myself the excuse to be a victim, the employee who's been wronged, who's not to blame, for whom everything just wasn't fair, like Robert.

The key to sorting it out was to understand the root cause of why I felt like I did. Was it the job? Was it the boss? Was it the culture? Was it something else? And, most importantly, what *did* I want to do to achieve career fulfilment? It's not easy to re-think your course at a time when you have more non-negotiable commitments to consider than at any other time of your life — kids, big mortgage, social expectations — although ironically it was these constraints that made my thinking more precise and realistic; despite my very brief experience of being a bar owner in France, running a beach shack in Barbados sounded like a magnificent idea, but it wasn't going to happen.

Moving to another company would be a wrench as I was generally happy at the bank, even if I was miserable in my job. At a practical level, I could have tried to make small changes to make a difference, such as getting involved in a side project that stretched me, but that didn't seem as though it would be enough. Another cause of my mid-career de-motivation was simply boredom with a job that I found dull, so there was the option of changing roles, not necessarily a promotion; a sideways move into an exciting role would have been fine, but there weren't many opportunities out there that I was either interested in or, just as importantly, would be interested in me. As these strategies weren't working, maybe it *was* time to make a more dramatic change. I guess, even if subconsciously, I knew this when I next met Trev for lunch.

25

'Climbing, forever trying, to find your way out of the wild, wild wood'

We were in one of Trev's favourite places, Swithin's Fish and Oyster Restaurant in the City, and as we sat on the luxurious red leather stools that were screwed to the floor around the brightly illuminated glass bar, he was educating me on which white wine best accompanied a mixed seafood platter. I'd met him for lunch a couple of times since his departure from Chatham 12 months or so earlier, during which time he'd done very little and had clearly enjoyed his break. He had then got a call from a competitor bank who needed someone of his experience and a person of his reputation to do a six-month contract, sorting out the mess left by the previous incumbent. He jumped at the opportunity to get 'back in the game,' especially following a somewhat hasty exit from the old place.

A big part of his positivity had come from discovering a newfound freedom in his work. Now that he was a contractor, without a pension at stake or the risk of losing a large redundancy payment, he was more liberated, more liberated to be himself. Without the jeopardy that had previously constrained him, he could now tell senior leadership how things really were and not worry whether it was what they wanted to hear. The stakes had changed, the grip of the hierarchy had loosened, and Trev was the best he'd been for a long time. 'So, Graham,' he asked, as I was enjoying the first sip of a perfectly chilled, crisp Sancerre, 'Exactly how firmly seated in the corporate saddle are you?' 'Well, not that firmly, to be honest, Trev, but you know how it is, I'm earning good dosh, and I need to look after the family and all that stuff'; a pathetically non-committal answer that took us nowhere, other than confirming to him that I was not enjoying my current situation.

He explained that as they had been so impressed with him, the bank he'd been contracting at had asked him to take on a permanent role and that he was now recruiting a new team, turning to some of his old direct reports as potential safe bets to help him. He told me more about the job, including that it would be in Canary Wharf, which, as he explained, had an authentic French wine bar and a swish rooftop restaurant that served a very authentic Confit de Canard. A fresh start, an exciting job, fine wine, and a duck. It was very tempting.

'So, how much would it take to loosen you completely from the saddle?' he asked, the glint in his eyes reflecting off the brightness of the bar. I had no idea what the correct answer was, panicked, and plucked a number out of the air. 'Ok,' he said, 'that should be fine, let's make it happen'.

I squirted lemon juice into my eye rather than onto my prawns. 'Fucking hell, Trev, really?'

On the train journey home that evening, numbed from a bottle and half of fine wine, a couple of sneaky pints of Meantime Pale Ale I'd grabbed at the Fire Station Bar just outside Waterloo station, and the surreal conversation I'd had with Trev, I knew that I'd have to think long and hard about what to do, both about the job offer and also whether I'd make it back to Hampton without needing a piss. Moving banks felt like such a massive risk, especially as nagging away at the back of my mind was the possibility that soon, someone might be having a conversation with me armed with a pencil, an ashtray, and a half-empty glass of water; there had been several redundancies in other teams, and I'd seen a few mates walk off with big smiles on their faces, and big cheques in their pockets. Conversely, at my age, time was no longer forever, so the postponement of doing something worthwhile also felt costly. If not now, when? And, if I was being honest, I struggled to think much past the salary that Trev was offering me. I spoke to Lisa and explained that I needed to make a decision one way or the other; she gave me direct, honest, and ultimately common-sense advice. 'Do what your heart tells you, but whatever it is, don't be boring'.

The next day, I spoke with my boss. 'Off the record, Richard, what are the chances that I might get a pay-off shortly?' I asked him.
'Minimal,' he responded, which, although disappointing on the one hand, did at least make me feel good that they still wanted and valued me, that they thought too much of me to let me go.
'There's no budget,' he continued, 'otherwise, maybe we could have sorted something'. Bugger. Not only was I in a job that I didn't like, the bank wasn't even that bothered about keeping me.

I disappeared to lunch, glugged a pint or four at The Jugged Hare in Chiswell Street, and contemplated my predicament. I'd been at the bank 24 years, all my working life, so any decision to leave felt enormous. I even briefly told myself that going across to a competitor was disloyal until I realised that was, of course, nonsense. I've seen too many colleagues claiming loyalty to an organisation by staying with them for several years, but, I don't buy that — when you work for a large organisation, it's a very straightforward arrangement — you work for them, and they pay you. That isn't loyalty; that is just a deal, a contract. Staying put in one organisation is arguably more about laziness and being cozy than it is about a (misguided) love for each other. And, it makes no difference who you are, how good you are, or how good you think you are, the organisation will spit you out if it wants to.

I took my own advice for a change and chose to sleep on it, but a restless night did nothing to change my mind; from the moment Trev agreed to my salary 'demands', deep down, I knew what I would do. I saw Richard in his office and told him I'd decided to leave. His screwed-up face suggested a level of mild disappointment if not exactly devastation. I walked back out into the main office feeling positive I had been assertive enough to make a decision, but shitting myself about the reality of stumbling, not for the first time, into an unknown future.

Later that day, Richard's boss, Catherine, phoned and asked me what it would take to change my mind. Maybe they did want me after all? We talked, and I explained the deal I was being offered and about the job I'd be doing, and she told me that she thought I was doing the right thing. It made me a little more comfortable with my decision and I was grateful to her for trying. Richard had the mild hump with me over the following days. I realised that this was less about me deciding to leave and more because, only a couple of weeks earlier, I had somehow managed to persuade him to pay for me to attend a 'Leaders in London' conference, literally over the road at the Barbican Centre. Despite my hatred for conferences, this was different. Costing nearly two grand a ticket, it included several high profile speakers — my favourite business mogul, Tom Peters, the explorer Sir Ranulph Fiennes, and the ex-leader of the Soviet Union Mikael Gorbachov. That is what I call an eclectic and impressive lineup.

I loved listening to the speakers, each fascinating in their own way. Peters continued his passionate quest to show the value of personalised in-touch leadership in providing excellence in customer experience, Fiennes talked about being committed to a cause, even when you have to lose a couple of toes along the way, and Gorby, through a translator, spoke emotionally about his work with Ronald Reagan in effectively ending the Cold War, and thus, with it, the need to shelter under any stairs Each of the them made managing risk in a

High Street bank feel pathetically insignificant, which, of course in comparison, it was.

But the best was saved to last, albeit *only* via satellite link — the 42nd President of the US, Bill Clinton. He talked about some of the challenges of being the most powerful man in the world for eight years, and all but one of the audience listened intently to every compelling word he said. While he was halfway through talking about the opposition he had encountered when championing gay rights, a lady in the audience kept shouting a question about the *Monica Lewinsky* scandal. Everyone else in the auditorium was annoyed by the heckling and its inappropriateness, and she got shouted down and almost removed from the conference room by security. Unfazed by the commotion, President Clinton continued to talk until it was announced that he was on a busy schedule and would have to leave. Clinton stopped the guy facilitating and said, 'I think there was a lady in the audience who had a point to make that the rest of us failed to appreciate. Can you give her the mic, please?' The lady asked her question, and he spent ten minutes talking to her and the rest of us about the most challenging time in his life; you could have heard a pin drop even though there were a couple of thousand people in the room while he was a couple of thousand miles away. I felt privileged to have witnessed a masterclass in empathy, in listening, in humility, in giving people an opportunity to express their views, even if they might be different from your own or difficult to talk about. Sheer quality. I bet you need more than three 'O' levels to be President of the USA. Oh, wait a minute . . .

I arranged my leaving do for the Friday before Christmas so that if nobody turned up, I could blame it on people having previous commitments. Fortunately for my ego, a decent number did come along to Browns in Eastcheap for a few beers and some fancy food, a far cry from the first leaving do that I had been to many years earlier at The White Hart in Fulham Broadway. If *vol au vents* had still been a thing, I would have ordered some.

I enjoyed catching up with a few guys I had not seen for a while, and it was fun to reminisce about some of the stuff that had happened over the years. But the reality was, as much of an impact as I may have thought I had, I would be quickly forgotten when I walked out of the door. What was a landmark in my life was not much more than another leaving-do for everyone else. As I staggered towards Bank station and down the steep slope leading to 'The Drain' to get to Waterloo, I had an overriding feeling of anti-climax; I hadn't expected a firework display over the Bank Of England, but I thought I'd feel more of a sense of occasion or a level of sadness at leaving an organisation that I had spent all of my adult life in, but I just felt nothing. I was going home late on a Friday night, a little bit pissed, and it didn't feel much different to many other Friday nights, as much as I wanted it to. At least I had a couple of weeks off before venturing a couple of miles further east to Canary Wharf and into my next new beginning.

Self-assessment: 'The Wilderness' years

'What the fuck did I do? In my desperation to get a job and to satisfy my ego's need for progression, I ignored Kev's advice from many years ago and chased a promotion, but to a job that I wasn't interested in and in a location I hated. It was all my fault albeit that ironically it has opened up the opportunity to move into a new organisation; I hope I'm making the right decision with that too. Having said that, I do need a change, and now that I know that my current bank is hardly desperate to keep me, it has got to be worth a punt. Maybe one day I'll look back over this period as one that may not have been my most enjoyable but one that did prompt me to seek a fresh start. Only time will tell'

Part 7

The 'New Beginning' years

(2004-2013)

26

'They let you think you're king but you're really a pawn'

It was a strange Christmas and New Year. Not much happened other than Jack and Charlie decided, in their curiosity about whether or not to still 'believe' to utilise the latest technology and set up video surveillance of the lounge fireplace, resulting in Lisa making me dress up as Father Christmas and get 'caught' on camera as proof that the *big fella* was still a thing. I would have thought that watching Polar Express 12 times would have been sufficient for them to *believe*, but evidently not.

Being in between banks, for the first time in a long time I was off work but not worrying it, as I had nothing to actually worry about. I no longer had to worry about the Queen either, as the TV documentary *The Queen by Rolf* showed Mr. Harris doing her portrait, and she seemed relaxed enough for me to take enough comfort that no funny business had gone on. Like many at the time, I'm not sure Liz realised what a narrow escape she'd had. Unlike some of Rolf's previous work (admittedly done with a full-size Wickes fence brush), the portrait was so shite, I'm not convinced that when he asked, '*Can you tell what it is yet?*', she would have had a clue.

'One has no fucking idea who that is supposed to be, Mr. Harris.'

Navigating my way to my first day at my new bank wasn't too challenging — I knew where Canary Wharf was, albeit I had not been there since a school geography field trip about 25 years previously. At the time, what was known as the *London Docklands Development Corporation* was not much more than a massive patch of wasteland. When the 'guide' professed, 'One day this will be the financial capital of Europe,' most of the class thought the bloke had lost the plot. Funny how things turn out.

The journey to Canary Wharf was straightforward. An eight-minute stroll to Hampton Station, 53 minutes to Waterloo, straight down the escalators opposite Platform Five, and onto the Jubilee line. The 'silver' line was the only stretch on the London Underground, with sliding doors between the platform and the train - very posh, very new, and very shiny. As I turned left at the bottom of the escalator onto the front of the platform, I saw from the anxiety-relieving indicator board that a Stratford train was due in one minute, so no need to worry about waiting and staring down the track in expectation. 15 minutes later, the packed tube emptied onto the platform at Canary Wharf Station, and I started the ascent up what seemed like miles of (Japanese tourist-free) escalators along with thousands of other suited commuters carrying their Costa and Starbucks coffee cups. Even though it was only 7 a.m., everyone still looked purposeful and keen. I emerged into the glum January daylight of Canada Square, searched for somewhere to get my own coffee, and, in the absence of anything more independent, settled on a Neros. Canary Wharf, it seemed, only did the big chains.

Compared to the out-dated offices of Chiswell Street, the Wharf was impressive with its intimidating cluster of skyscraper banks surrounded by shops, bars, restaurants, and the ubiquitous, ever-winding River Thames. The building I was to be based at was impressive — only opened about seven years earlier, it reached high up into the docklands clouds, almost like it was in the tallest building competition with the others. At 31 levels, it wouldn't win the 1st prize, but the panoramic views from the top were no less stunning. I stepped into the enormous marble-floored reception area, the steel and glass decor as contemporary as the smartly uniformed security guards strategically placed at various security barriers and exit points. It was as posh and shiny as the new as the Jubilee Line, just without the tramps. I doubted that any customers had ever had a dump in here.

I waited in the queue for the reception desk behind a long line of impressively dressed ladies and gents: high heels, snappy suits, and even an occasional brown shoe. Although nobody was in the slightest bit interested in my arrival this time, there *was* at least a security pass waiting for me that would give me access to the lifts and for my onward journey to the sixth floor to meet Trev for my second 'first day' working for him; fortunately unlike in Chatham, there was no smell of wee this time or the sound of little Britneys and Chardonnays getting told to 'Fucking behave yourselves' as they headed off for their daily trip to Wilkinsons.

Sue, Trev's PA, was waiting for me and took me over to the far southeast side of the building — the office was so big that knowing your compass points was helpful for navigation. Trev was at his desk drinking a black coffee and, by the look of his already semi-filled ashtray, smoking about his tenth fag of the morning; he might not have been in Sir John's league, but he did like a puff nonetheless. He introduced me to some of the guys I would be working with directly and a few others who worked in different teams within the department. I would be running the team whose job was to check that the folks in the branches were doing things '*in the right way*'. Classic poacher turned gamekeeper, but, as they say, *you can't kid a kidder.*

My new bank seemed bigger in every way, unsurprising as it was a global business compared to my previous employer who had been ostensibly focused on domestic banking. But that's where the difference ended. In essence, all the banks had the same issues, concerns, and risks as each other, almost as though they had gathered in a darkened room one day and agreed on all of the things that they could potentially fuck up. Same shit, different (much larger) building.

The main issue of the day was still PPI, and the magnitude of the problem had become worryingly evident, following several years of colleagues effectively being forced to sell a potentially toxic product which had left the banks and their reputations in tatters. Ironically, it was a decent product for the right customer in the right circumstances — unexpected events do happen, so to have insurance that can clear someone's debt if that did happen is a sensible option for many. But for those who didn't benefit from it, couldn't afford it, or didn't know they had it (or, in some instances, all three), it wasn't.

It's easy to question why so many customers were *that* stupid to end up with an expensive product that they didn't want or get value from, but herein lies the crux of the scandal as it was the use of clever and not always ethical sales tactics that allowed it to happen. Whether it was making the insurance a condition of taking out the loan (no insurance, no loan, no dream car), not disclosing the price upfront and allowing the customer to believe it was the cost of just borrowing money, or simply the blatant request to *'just sign here please'* without any mention of PPI at all, the truth is it was not always sold *in the right way*. Layer that on top of many customers' vulnerability, either financial or cognitive, and it wasn't hard to do. And with the industry ending up paying out nearly £50 billion in remediation, it happened an awful lot, whatever a Senior Executive might tell you.

A challenging part of my new role was to help Trev convince the industry regulator, the FSA (as it was called at the time), that, 'Honestly, we haven't done anything that bad at all'. It was like fighting off an oncoming tank with a stick. But, despite taking a regular beating from a group of very solemn-faced middle-aged ex-bankers turned big gamekeepers, I was excited by the challenge of my new adventure, nearly as much as Mum when I gave her my new business card proudly displaying my job title *Compliance Monitoring Director*.

Personally, I couldn't have given a toss what I was called but I had already learned that in head office, job titles were a primary way of showing other people exactly how important you were. Which, apparently, was a very important thing to do.

The first criteria for an impressive job title is that it must clearly demonstrate the size of the empire over which you reign. Being in charge of a branch is commendable, of an *Area* is impressive but it's significantly better if you can boast *Regional* responsibility as that shows everyone that you've risen above the menial, day-to-day life of the front line and are likely in a strategic role. If you can claim to have *National* responsibility, you are incredibly important, but the ultimate is to be able to boast *Global* accountability; not only does that make you one-down from royalty, but it also adds a level of glamour and intrigue that being responsible for 'Harrow and Edgware' could never quite conjure up. I remember asking a Senior guy where his 'patch' was, and he replied 'The Northern Hemisphere'; what an absolute dick.

It would be more fun if people's job titles described what they *actually* did. *Chief Fannying Around Officer, Global Head of Making Crap Up or Managing Director of Turning a Blind Eye* would all be more descriptive and also sound impressive on LinkedIn. At least we did manage to keep things simple at The Jolly Coopers Book Club, at which, in accordance with article 5 of the club's formal Constitution (agreed at our inaugural Thursday night meeting held at the boardroom table underneath the dartboard) it was explicitly stated that:
(5) You will only be referred to by your book club name, until that gets boring (usually after about ten minutes) when reverting to real names is allowed.
Steve, who ran the fabulous Cheese and Wine shop in the village was called *Cheese*, Martin, a 'diamond geezer' and a really good mate of mine was a postman and therefore known as *Post* and Nick, another great guy who was a

very successful corporate lawyer was known as *Law*. Amongst other things, I was called *Bank*. In the early weeks of the club, we also had a member called John, who was a gynaecologist. We decided just to call him *John*.

As well as having an impressive job title in the bank, there were other ways to demonstrate importance, techniques that were a crucial part of the survival kit needed to navigate effectively through the political minefield of a large organisation:

- Always use 'I' whenever talking about a successful piece of work. If describing something that has gone tits-up, the correct pronoun is 'they'.
- Tell others you either 'lead' or 'head up' somewhere or something. Anything less means you're a subordinate, or worse in an operational role.
- If possible, only lead or head up projects that are so sensitive they require a non-disclosure, confidentiality agreement. Be sure to let junior people know you can't tell them anything about what you're working on or else 'You'll have to shoot them'. Then, shortly afterwards, tell them all about it. All the worst-kept secrets in big organisations are confidential.
- Avoid doing any work that the 'higher-ups' won't notice or give you credit for. There's no point in doing low-profile activity or something simply because 'it's the right thing to do' as this is a total waste of effort.
- Do not get involved in any projects that have a high risk of failing.
- Never be afraid to steal others' ideas and claim them as your own or take credit for achieving something you had absolutely nothing to do with. Pin the blame back onto the original owner at the first sign of somebody important not liking the work.

- If you are in a lift and asked 'How are you?', always reply with 'Busy'. It doesn't answer the question but will justify your existence and make you feel better.

If you could master using these tools, you stood a good chance of creating the most important corporate survival condition there is — being Teflon. Famous for being the basis of non-stick items such as saucepans and frying pans, as well as linked to the poisoning of loads of farmers in Ohio and West Virginia, Teflon is a coating that provides high resistance to chemicals, solvents and being made redundant. It does this by ensuring that nothing negative ever sticks to you, protecting mediocre performing colleagues against the risks of the relentless cycle of organisational change. It's particularly helpful for those people who do very little actual work other than just falling in love with whatever is next, especially if whatever is next is very shiny and new. A quicker way to become Teflon is to get hold of some photographs of the boss in a compromising sexual position; works a treat (apparently)

Not that long after starting at my new bank, in the early morning of October 29, our fourth child, Evie Rose Freeman Pannett, arrived and, in doing so, broke the World Birth Speed Record, being born in minus 20 minutes — apparently, it's not uncommon for number 4 to 'slip out' relatively easily (not my words!) and Lisa was only in labour for 40 minutes, 15 minutes into which the midwife climbed onto the bed and put the clocks back by an hour, signalling the end of daylight saving and the start of winter, proving that, unlike Cher or Carol Vorderman, it is actually possible to turn back time.

And, although I'd only been working in Canary Wharf for a short while, I had realised that in my new, shiny, 31-floor building of 5000 colleagues, a surprisingly large number of them should have just been called *John*.

27

'Stop apologising for the things you've never done'

I spent two years trying to keep the grown-ups and the Regulator happy by checking that our branch colleagues were doing things *'in the right way.'* I *felt* we were making a difference, reducing the risks for our customers, but I was too far removed from them to *know* that we *definitely* were, regardless of what the countless graphs, charts, and dashboards told me. Too many leaders in large head offices will rely purely on data and so often get stuck in a cycle of perpetual analysis — although validating performance with data makes total sense, it can also be a good idea to go and see for yourself what's going on, which can't happen if you are permanently sitting in the literal and metaphorical comfort of your Ivory Tower.

Unfortunately, even when the head office folks did manage to get out, the power of the hierarchy would often mean they wouldn't see the reality of working on the front line. On too many occasions, senior people in particular would only experience the sanitised version of the truth because the local leader was too shit-scared not to make everything look pristine, and would have spent the previous week spring cleaning everywhere. It's the same reason that the Queen thought the world smelled of paint. I get that people don't want to let others down, but papering over the cracks will never allow problems to get fixed, and it is disingenuous for branch staff to create a false image of how things really are.

Senior people losing touch (or, in some case, never being in touch in the first place) with what is really happening is not uncommon, yet if your job is to help front-line staff to help their customers, you should, at the very least, have a basic understanding of what life at the coalface is like; it provides context and an appreciation of the challenges and helps close that gap between the spreadsheet and the truth. To try and mitigate this risk and in an attempt to show customer-facing colleagues that Head Office people really *did* care, the bank developed a 'back to the floor' initiative, which, if nothing else, would allow people wearing proper suits to spend a day making tea for colleagues wearing spontaneously combustible uniforms, whilst trying their best to hide their smug relief they didn't have to put up with any of the crap that they did.

I was lucky enough to be allowed to be part of this programme, so I was keen to give it a try, especially as one of the options was to visit the branch in Babbacombe, just outside Torquay in South Devon. It may sound excessive to make a round journey of 400 miles to hand out custard creams to depressed branch staff, but I had an ulterior motive — to re-visit Babbacombe Model Village, a truly magical place I had visited every time I'd been on holiday to Devon as a kid.

Compared to the long, sick-inducing journeys of my childhood, the drive down was relatively uneventful and I didn't even have any marmalade sandwiches before I set off at 5:30. My favourite road, the never-ending A303, was so empty I had to slow down to fully enjoy the arc-shaped beauty of my favourite oak tree that sits majestically in the central reservation just before Andover and I even drove past Stonehenge without waiting two hours for the pleasure.

Shortly after 9:30, I arrived at the branch, introduced myself, and could immediately tell that the colleagues there had no expectation that I would be of any help whatsoever, which was absolutely right on their part. I was obviously not considered particularly important either, as, thankfully, judging by the messy state of the office, they hadn't bothered to have a spring clean before my visit. I spent about four hours making awful tea and feeding the staff with doughnuts from the bakery next-door before announcing, much to their relief and mine, that I was off to visit the model village. The nostalgic draw of this place meant I'd thought about little else all morning, particularly the exquisite scale version of Wembley Stadium that, back in the day, had the diminutive model figures painted in the team colours from that year's FA Cup Final. In the summer of 1970, a few months after my team's first-ever FA Cup win, I remember staring proudly at the Blue of Chelsea (and the white of Dirty Leeds); 37 years later, we'd won it again, this time beating Man U in the final. I was giddy with anticipation as I said goodbye to the branch staff, reflected on how grateful I was that I no longer worked in a branch, thanked them for putting up with me and dashed through the traditional olde English seaside cobbled streets, desperate to re-visit the site of many amazing childhood memories.

I paid my £12 entrance fee (prices must have really rocketed as there was no way Dad would have paid that for each of us) and started to wend my way down the main path, edged by exquisitely manicured midget topiary, leading me to the magic of this miniature heaven. The wave of disappointment hit me quickly, and I realised at once that I should have re-calibrated my expectations of how impressive a place would be that I hadn't visited for 30-odd years. It was still magnificently designed, built, and maintained, but it was, well, small! I know it was supposed to be, but I'm not talking about the models (that would be incredibly churlish), it was the size of the overall Village itself that was disappointing — what used to take a whole glorious summer evening to wander through was going to take me about ten minutes.

But even that ten minutes got cut short. It hadn't occurred to me that there was anything remotely dubious-looking about a suited middle-aged bloke wandering around a model village on his own during a Tuesday afternoon in

September when the only other people there were coach loads of young kids on early term school trips. When a teacher ran up to the two girls I was pointing out the model train to and dragged them away, I panicked and as a defensive gesture, started to show the teacher a photo of Rosie and Evie on my new iPhone 3G saying, 'I've got daughters of my own you know.' I think it possibly made matters worse and in my increasing embarrassment, hurried out of the Village before I'd even made it to the Wembley Stadium model. So as well as being accused of being a paedophile, I didn't get the pleasure of seeing a two-inch high plastic figure of a sobbing Cristiano Ronaldo.

The issues that have emerged from *Operation Yew Tree* are disturbing, disgusting, and highly sensitive, and I would never want to appear flippant about them in any way. However, I can't believe I'm the only person of a certain age who thinks too that they've been a victim of a few of the most prominent public figures who were a massive part of our growing-up years because they just weren't what and who we thought they were. In truth, they were a million miles away — I spent many evenings cheating at cards against the old ladies at Fernham, laughing *with* Stuart Hall on *It's a Knockout*; I was in awe of Rolf's clever paintings (well before the disastrous Liz portrait) and his weird musical instruments, and what a decent bloke Jimmy Savile was, that ever-present likeable, caring do-gooder. And although, unlike the many that have, I didn't suffer in any way, I am still miffed that a small but constant part of my early life was a scam, that I had been cheated, that I fell for the entertainment world's equivalent of **PPI**. And not unlike PPI, senior people must have known what was going on, and if they didn't, then they bloody well should have. Complicit or negligent?

Then again, we all knew that Gary Glitter was a nonce.

It was a long drive home from Babbacombe, and the traffic was heavier, but at least this time, I could stare at Stonehenge for about an hour and spend a bit more time appreciating my favourite tree again. Despite my hasty and embarrassed exit from the model village, my visit had certainly stirred many memories of summers past and how lucky I'd been to have spent so many sunny and contented weeks in that beautiful part of our country. But I couldn't get out of mind the look on that teacher's face, when she ushered her pupils away from me. Maybe I should have anticipated it, but nonetheless, it was a sad indictment of the world we were living in.

As 2007 stumbled to an end, not even the torrential rain and gale-force winds that caused havoc to public transport and electricity supplies would be enough to stop hardened smokers huddling in doorways of pubs and offices following the ban on smoking in all public places, which also introduced the new workplace habit of 'just popping out' for 15 minutes about ten times every day. Clown Boris Johnson became Mayor of London as most (sensible) people reflected on the ridiculousness of how such a buffoon could secure such an important position. My old mate Tony Blair resigned as Prime Minister, having never recovered from his obsession with Iraqi smoking guns. Little did we know, there was an *actual* smoking gun in the financial world that was about to fire . . .

It started in the States and, as most things do, came over the pond and buggered us up too. The first time we took any notice of what became known as *the financial crisis* was when *The Northern Rock Building Society* needed bailing out by the Bank of England. Unsurprisingly, in a country where a lockdown threat causes a run on toilet rolls, this caused a run on the bank. We were bombarded with constant TV images of anxious customers queuing in the street, desperately waiting to withdraw their cash. Customers of other banks became similarly spooked, resulting in widespread financial panic. Throughout the early part of 2008, world stock markets fell sharply, albeit they temporarily recovered when an old couple from the US, *Fannie Mae and Freddie Mac*, helped everyone out by investing about $200 billion in buying dodgy mortgages from banks. It later emerged that Fannie and Freddie weren't a sweet pair of hick farmers from the deep South but a US government-backed enterprise. However, as long as shares were going back up, nobody gave a fuck.

It was a difficult time for many, especially those working in financial services. The spectre of bank collapse and redundancy loomed large, and unsurprisingly, few people outside the industry felt sorry for those within it. Being a banker was never the most popular occupation — one up on the 'twat index' from an estate agent and one down from an MP — but now 'normal' people (non-bankers) were directly impacted by the apparent greed of the city boys, the animosity deepened, forcing a whole sector of people to pretend they were accountants for fear of being lynched. Politicians were quick to put the boot in as well, not least my local MP and Deputy Leader of the Liberal Democrats, Vince Cable, whose comments suggested that he thought all bank employees were to blame; I thought it was harsh to lay the world economy turning to shit at the door of Vijay, a cashier at East Ham. It also seemed ironic to have a dig at *us* at a time when MPs had just been found out for claiming travel expenses when they shouldn't have. Mum had voted for Vince for years, and he'd also opened Jack's school Christmas fete a few weeks earlier, so I felt it only right that I should tell him of my concerns. I penned a vitriolic letter about transparency, fairness, and hypocrisy and accidentally pressed the send button late one night after a few beers.

I didn't expect him to reply, but to my surprise and to his credit, he did. Handwritten and on top quality House of Commons headed notepaper, his letter explained that he hadn't meant to blame the 'workers' and apologised if he'd come across that way. He also sent me a signed copy of his book *Storm* and told me that his true thoughts and opinions were explained within its 987 pages. I started to read it, but it was too heavy for me (both literally and literarily) and I got confused after the third page. But respect due to the fella for responding. A few years later, when he was making his own comeback, after being unceremoniously dumped by the electorate in 2015, I bumped into him (literally) at our local Classic Car show, at which he was making a royal visit, albeit nobody had tried to repaint the grass on our village green. I'm not proud that, fuelled by quite a few cans of Neck Oil, I repeated, less eloquently than in my letter, the same points. With an impressive level of politician's expertise, he politely thanked me for my thoughts and was almost excited to tell me that interestingly, I wasn't the first person to raise this very issue with him, having received a letter a few years earlier from someone making very similar points. He said he'd sent that person a signed copy of his book to explain his perspective and asked whether I would like a copy too; I was going to tell him, but even in my inebriated state, I didn't want to hurt his feelings, so a couple of days later, I became the proud owner of my second signed copy of his book, which I've also not been able to read yet.

The financial challenges continued into 2009, impacting several banks and financial institutions and also hitting the High Street. After the best part of 130 years, *Woolworths* closed the doors of its last store, consigning cheap Christmas TV adverts with Jimmy Young and the original 'Pick and Mix' to a fading memory for millions. Not as high-profile was the (ironic) collapse of the low-quality furniture chain *MFI*. On their last day of trading, there was no denial from the liquidators that the company name really was an acronym for 'Made For Idiots'.

Whilst all hell was breaking loose in the world around me, I'd left the Compliance Monitoring team when it got disbanded and moved by Trev into a new role. Still within his department, the new job was even more office-based and involved reviewing and re-writing compliance policies and procedures. It was actually even more boring than it sounds which forced me to search outside the office for excitement to relieve the acute tedium. I found it at the unlikely venue of Waitrose in Canary Wharf —being one of the John Lewis Partnership's flagship stores, there were two things here that were only found in some of their shops — a wine bar and a steak bar. The Wine Bar, tucked away in a corner between the toilet rolls and the bin liners, served all the available wines in the shop — take it off the shelf, hand it to either Lynn or Lynda, and tell them how many glasses you needed. If instead you wanted a cold white, you could choose from the chilled selection available directly from the fridge. They also served a small selection of tapas dishes prepared and plated for you if you ever felt a little peckish. Perfect. And Naz, Sally, and the rest of the team were happy to join in

The bar area was small, with four round tables and a few high stools. Admittedly, on the first couple of visits, it did feel odd sitting on them having a drink while other people were wandering around picking up their shopping albeit we quickly got used to that. The only downside was that the toilets (wine plus reduced kidneys = essential) were on the other side of the store, so you had to hurry through the frozen meat aisle and part of the dairy section to go for a pee. It was a small price to pay and also helpful if you were stuck for something for dinner that evening. The steak bar was situated more conveniently near the toilets. It was a simple run of 12 swivel stools along a metal top, behind which Nick, the chirpy chef, would cook to order your cut of choice.

As the work became duller, the wine bar became an increasingly regular haunt, both at lunchtimes and in the evenings and my personal consumption of Villa Maria Sauvignon Blanc and The Ned was putting a severe dent in the grape supply of New Zealand. Visits to the steak bar were less frequent, usually saved for an end-of-the-month Friday lunchtime as a treat for having worked so 'hard.' One memorable lunchtime, five of us trooped down there at 11.30, leaving the office early to get five stools together, only to find that most were already taken. Seeing our disappointment, Nick suggested that we go to the wine bar, and that when five in-a-row stools were available, he'd give Lynn a call, and she'd let us know. Aware that Trev was visiting the FSA that afternoon and wouldn't be back for a while, it seemed a sensible plan. We headed past the yoghurts and to the wine bar, where we proceeded to tuck into a couple of bottles of reasonably priced Pinot Noir.

I hardly noticed that it was over an hour and a half before the phone rang, and Lynn told us that we could head over to the steak bar when we were ready. Carrying my glass and a half-empty bottle of red (wine bottles are always half empty), I and the others headed towards our much-needed beef fillet and triple-cooked chips. I think it was at the minced lamb freezer when I saw Trev out of the corner of my eye, shopping basket in hand and heading straight towards me. How was I to know that his meeting with the FSA had been cancelled and that he would be picking up his weekend provisions at that moment? All I could think to do was to raise my glass and say cheers as I sped up and disappeared across the supermarket to get away from his gaze. He said nothing, but his look of disgust and shaking head meant that I didn't enjoy my steak very much.

28

'Some people might say that I should strive for more'

Despite Trev's love of wine, catching me drinking it in the middle of Waitrose when I probably should have been writing a fascinating compliance policy brought to the fore a conversation that I had suspected for some time that we were going to have. He suggested I consider moving to a different role as, clearly, I wasn't enjoying the one that I was doing for him. I agreed because he was right. It had been nearly four years since I'd met him at St. Swithin's Fish bar, and he'd flattered me and offered more money to go and work for him than I could ever imagine. It was the right decision at the time, but again, I'd found myself in a job that paid well but wasn't suitable for me. My adventure had started with a few bottles of crisp white and looked like it would end with a half-empty bottle of Red.

I don't think I had ever really recovered from the conversation I'd had with Trev a few months earlier when he said, to me ' I've lined you up for a meeting with Phil; he's got a vacancy, and I think you'd be good at it.' Phil's job was a small promotion, which may have meant a little more money and was certainly a fresh start but it was dull, and I no longer wanted to do a tedious job, that's what my current role had become. "Thanks, Trev, ' I said, 'but I don't think I'm interested. Not sure it's quite for me.'

Trev looked at me disapprovingly and said, 'Oh, I'm surprised; I thought you were more ambitious than that.'

Ambitious? At that moment, it struck me that Trev and I had very different views on what that meant and what was important. To him, ambition clearly meant promotion, progression, advancement, climbing the hierarchal ladder, and doing what he and the business (and the culture) expected me to do. It had taken me nearly 30 years to realise it, but my interpretation of ambition was achieving what *I* wanted to do, not everyone else. From that point on, I vowed to *be me*, not what I was expected to be.

In truth, it was a convenient decision to make as I'd probably reached my ceiling in terms of grade, mainly because I wouldn't be good enough to get promoted to Managing Director but also because I wasn't prepared to sell my soul to the devil which seemed to be what was necessary at that level. But regardless, it's unhealthy to keep on measuring personal achievement by metrics that are not ours — success is a highly individual construct, and what gives me pride and joy won't necessarily spark happiness for others (or for Trev); if we chase criteria that are borrowed then we can end up pursuing someone else's dream, raising the risk that, in the end, we'll reach an arbitrary finish line, very unsatisfied. Additionally, if *our* 'targets' are not within *our* scope of control, our outcomes more dependent on luck than skill, we'd be placing the fate of our happiness in someone else's hands, which is a dangerous thing to do.

Kev had told me all those years ago that there is another scorecard, weighted more in favour of internal factors than external circumstances, so focused more on the process than the outcome — who we are as we pursue our goals matters and we should always be mindful of the cost of what we were willing to do to get to the finish line and recognise the collateral damage it took to get there. Did I hurt anyone along the way? Winning isn't just about what we get or what we do, it's about who we are on the path to where we're going.

Making a decision to focus less on status and more on being my best, being a better steward, felt liberating. The beauty of reaching this stage is the permission or freedom it gives you to *be you*. Be yourself. Do the right thing, not necessarily what your boss wants you to do, or worse, what you think your boss wants you to do or be; it was time to find something I wanted to do, not something I'd fallen into.

The financial misery continued into 2010, with European regulators introducing something called *Basel II* for banks. An interesting directive which *'increased capital ratios, limits on leverage, narrowed the definition of capital to exclude subordinated debt, limited counter-party risk, and added liquidity requirements.'* Don't worry, none of us understood or cared less what it meant either, so Trev had to recruit a specialist into the team, a bloke called Steve, who was already an expert. Steve was super-intelligent, liked by the ladies, and undoubtedly knew his stuff. However, from day one, he told me that his real passion was for politics, not for banking and that one day he would be a senior member of the Conservative Party. While it was only a pipe dream, and I thought he was an arrogant twat, I admired his focus and the clear path that he'd laid down for himself — he had an ambition, which was very much his own, what he wanted to do, nobody else; not even Trev.

I'd seen a job advertised within the telephony function, and it interested me, even if, at the time, these guys were considered the enemy by the folk in the branch network. The threat of branch closures was made more significant by the emergence of the telephone as a viable alternative for customers, and the number of calls the bank received each day was increasing rapidly. Despite the apparent customer convenience, call centres were not held in particularly high regard then or even now. I agree that call centres can be a pain, especially those that undertake cold calling to sell you something or, even worse, scam you somehow. If you want to get rid of them, ask them to provide you with *their* date of birth and mother's maiden name before agreeing to talk anymore; they quickly hang up. It's similar when I get cold callers turning up on my doorstep, often *Jehovah's Witnesses*, when I tell them 'I'm really sorry, but my Mummy and Daddy aren't in now, so you'll have to come back later'. They never do.

The big boss in the bank's call centres was Raymond, an assertive and scary Scottish guy with whom I'd done some work previously. Despite his direct approach, he talked common sense and I got on well with him. Although the interview process was rigorous and challenging like him, I was delighted when he offered me the position, which involved working with the colleagues in the bank's telephony centres based in Coventry, Liverpool, Sunderland, and Glasgow, and so I spent a couple of weeks just travelling to these sites, meeting lots of lovely people, learning about the challenges that my job would bring, and feeling that I'd made an excellent decision to move across to the 'dark side.'

16 days after starting the role, I got an email sending me (literally) to Coventry the following Monday morning, a message I instinctively knew wasn't great news, not to mention ironic. My intuition was proved correct when, after 19 days of being the Head of Telephony Operations, I was told there would be a restructuring and that my role no longer existed. Liz bloody Truss lasted longer than I had, and I didn't even meet the Queen. My Mum hadn't even got round to putting my new business card on her fridge door.

The meeting was short and sweet, and I managed to grab Raymond before I left. 'You must have known when you took me on, right?' I asked. He said that he honestly didn't, and I believed him. As tough as he was, he appeared genuinely sorry for me. Being four days before Christmas, it felt brutal, but then again, there's never really a best time to be told that you've lost your job, and from the bank's perspective, the fact that Santa is on his way isn't a good enough reason to delay a cost-saving change.

As I drove back down the M40, not even my favourite festive song, Chris Rea's *Driving Home For Christmas*, could cheer me up, in fact the words almost rubbed in the reality of what had happened. Yes, Chris, I am driving home for Christmas, and yes, Chris, I am top to toe in tailbacks so yes, Chris, there are red lights all around. But, no, Chris, I can wait to see their faces, especially when I tell them that I'm about to be made redundant just after starting a new job and just as the roof had been removed from the house in preparation for our loft conversion. When I did eventually get home, I did tell them, and the dog and none of their faces showed that they were bothered, seemingly more interested in what presents they would be getting in a couple of days. But then again, they weren't bothered by the melting snow dripping through the kitchen roof onto the washing machine either.

I could have blamed myself for having made the change as if I'd stayed with Trev, then at least I'd still be in a job, and the boys might have got the latest release of FIFA that they'd been after for Christmas. But I reminded myself that sometimes shit happens, and it's not necessarily personal nor your fault— don't waste energy regretting decisions you make unless they were made pissed or without any rationale, and in this instance, I'd made the best decision based on what I could reasonably have known at the time.

I bumped into 'Basel Steve' at Waterloo Station after he'd been to the Compliance Christmas Lunch, and he seemed a bit worse for a few shandies. I asked him how his quest for political stardom was going, and he told me he was working on it. That's a lie, he was far too pissed to talk, and I just left him slumped at the bottom of a pillar opposite platform 15. As I write this, Steve (Barclay) is the current UK Health Secretary. I'm curious how his knowledge of 'all things liquidity' helped him understand the many challenges of the NHS, but fair dues to him for achieving his goal. Having said that, the nurses and junior doctors are currently on strike, so maybe he should have stuck with capital ratios.

Self-assessment: The 'New Beginning' years

'The new place was so big, and everything felt posher, shinier and more American but the issues were the same, just on a larger scale. I had to learn quickly that the higher you move up the organisational hierarchy, the more political things become and the more skilled you need to be at navigating your way through the corporate bullshit; sometimes it seems that it's more important to be seen to be doing good things, rather than actually doing them and that there are some senior people who really do know how to play that game.

I enjoyed running the monitoring team and it felt as though we were making a difference, so it was disappointing that I had to move into the policy role, which frankly was the most boring job I've ever had, so making the decision to leave compliance was the right one, even I lasted last less than 3 weeks— I've been on holiday for longer than that. It really has struck me that I've spent too long in jobs that I don't enjoy and that's not sensible — if you don't love what you're doing, how can you be your best? Maybe I'm getting old, but meaning and purpose are definitely becoming more important to me than status and pay, and more and more I'm becoming less inclined to do what other people think I should — maybe it's time to go out and buy a new pair of brown shoes.

I've also learned that it's not a great idea to walk across a supermarket with a glass of wine without first checking who you might bump into'

Part 8

The 'Back In The Game' years

(2013-2019)

29
'Daylight turns to moonlight, and I'm at my best'

Ding-Dong The Witch is Dead. Regardless of your political views, it seemed harsh that the death of Margaret Thatcher, the longest-serving Prime Minister in recent UK history, should prompt loads of street parties and a record in the charts to celebrate. But then again, any excuse for a piss-up and a sing-song . . . There weren't the same level of celebrations when Nelson Mandela also passed away, and I hoped that they found someone to look after his water feature. Prince Philip was admitted to hospital for what was described as an 'exploratory operation', and although there was no formal announcement of the results, it's believed that he was indeed found to be a decent, yet undeniably racist Greek bloke.

After 13 series and 70 episodes, Agatha Christie's TV series *Poirot* ended, allowing David Suchet to finally stop wearing that ridiculous false moustache. I met his brother John, the ITN Newsreader, late one night while queuing for a coffee at Waterloo Station. I had a decent conversation with him about a few things, and it was going well until I asked him how he felt about his brother being more famous and more successful than he was. A potentially insensitive question but one which everyone else who was a bit worse for wear and standing in that coffee queue wanted an answer to. He looked at me dismissively and said he wasn't bothered at all, especially as he was Alistair Stewart. Newsreaders all looked the same in those days, except, of course, Kirsty Young.

Following several years as a successful children's entertainer under the alias of Jimmy Krankee, Nicola Sturgeon succeeded Alex Salmond as leader of the Scottish National Party. *Fandabidozi*. And in the world of complete irony and proof that anything is possible, Andy Murray won BBC Sports Personality of the Year.

Alan Turing, the 'Enigma' codebreaker from World War Two, who wasn't Scottish, receives a posthumous pardon for being chemically castrated and convicted for homosexuality. I can only hope that if ever I get wrongfully chemically castrated, I get a bit more than a 'really sorry about that' 60 years after I've popped my clogs. It was bad enough having a vasectomy, one of my least pleasant and more bizarre experiences, which I assume was less painful, if not less humiliating. I will never forget lying in the freezing room with my bits out as some bloke attacked them with a soldering iron, while a charming Chinese lady, whose job it seemed was just to look at my genitals and have a chat with me, sat at the best seat in the house and did nothing other than just look at my genitals and have a chat with me. It's hard to talk about anything too worthwhile when you're under that kind of scrutiny, although I did agree with her when she said, 'It *is very* cold in here.'

In the banking world, after allegations of drug taking, inappropriate expense payments, and the use of rent boys, the former Cooperative Bank chairman, Paul Flowers, sets a perfect example for the 'ethical' bank when he is subsequently convicted of possessing cocaine, methamphetamine, and ketamine. I'd loved to have read his 'leaving' note to colleagues; I can only imagine 'I want to spend more time with my family' wasn't part of it.

I didn't have to worry too long about not having a job. The bank's process of looking for a 'suitable alternative role' offered me a position based in Hatton Garden, running a team that checked branch colleagues were following the internal rules and policies. It was less about sales more about process, and in truth, it wasn't a job that I would have chosen or even arguably be suitable for and it certainly wasn't in line with my new objective of only doing what I wanted to, what I would enjoy, but with four kids, a big mortgage, and still no roof on the house, needs-must. It was that or a redundancy cheque, and I certainly wasn't ready for one of those. The best thing about the new job was that I found an old disused table tennis in an even older disused office. My new team, Andrew Brown, Adrian 'Uncle' Hester, Daz Lovelock, and I took every opportunity to sneak in a few games of doubles during the quieter moments of the day. As the prevalence of teleconferences increased, I even occasionally managed to get a few rallies going while on mute during the really dull ones. By the time, 2 years later, that one of the grown-ups realised that Andrew would be much better at running the team than me and I got moved on, Daz and I were 'up' by 928 games to 925. And clearly now, Brown definitely was, very much for town.

I was asked to work on a short-term project looking at ways to help more customers embrace digital banking, an increasingly popular method of undertaking basic transactions now that access to the internet and ownership of mobile phones had become significantly more widespread. Many customers had embraced the faster, more convenient way of managing their finances as the use and demand for cash declined sharply.

And it wasn't just banking that was becoming digitised as the way we bought music shifted from the joy of finding, picking up and playing a vinyl record (or, to a much lesser extent a CD) to the undeniable convenience but the less satisfying experience of downloading music from the internet. That same need for the familiarity of the physical ownership of things had made digital banking a step too far for certain parts of the community. Of course, we'd had 'virtual money' for many years as, contrary to what some people, including Tom Cross, believed, the balance of their bank accounts wasn't kept in individually named shoeboxes stored in the downstairs safe of the branch.

Nonetheless, just because the banks were keen to move customers away from the comparatively expensive branch network, it didn't mean everyone wanted to join in. So it was our job to come up with ways to encourage customers to try alternative methods of banking rather than going into a branch, which, in 2013, was still happening 175 million times a year across the country in our bank alone.

I knew little about why customers still used branches, so I had to learn. I had to research and talk to experts from within and outside the bank who could help shape our thinking. I was given the budget to create a team and called upon some old buddies to help, including my table tennis partner Daz and Deano from Liverpool. Great guys and a strong team. And to give us focus, because we loved a target, I was given one — cut the number of counter transactions in half within two years. Easy! It was daunting but exciting, too, and I was looking forward to being allowed to be proactive and creative. It was out of my comfort zone, but bang into my agenda of 'doing something worthwhile.'

The options for customers were to use online or mobile phone banking, or if that was a step too far, self-service automation in-branch, whether a simple ATM or one of the new-fangled multi-functional devices recently developed and installed in most of the bigger branches. The customer reasons for resisting automation and mobile banking were often illogical, emotional, and deep-rooted, and so convincing about seven million of them to change how they'd been doing their banking for many years, in some cases, all their lives, wasn't going to be easy.

For many, using technology was just too scary. If you trust the person at the bank more than you trust yourself, why wouldn't you want them to carry on doing it for you? And, from a customer's perspective, if you, the bank, make a mistake, I can blame you; if I make a mistake, you might blame me. For others, it was more a case of 'why should I change? It's my money, and as long as I have a choice, I'll carry on using the branch'. For others, continuing to use the branch was because they genuinely believed that if they started using alternatives, the branch would close, and the staff would ultimately be out of a job. It is not a ridiculous thing to believe even though ironically the opposite was true as, if banks continued doing millions of manual, colleague-assisted transactions every year, they'd have no choice other than to reduce their costs, and usually that *did* mean closing branches with the resulting staff losses.

There was also a big raft of branch users, often elderly, for whom talking to someone they may have spoken with for many years was an important, often enjoyable part of their daily routine. So, a little wait to chat with their 'friend' wasn't a problem, especially as they potentially had little else to do anyway. Doing things quickly isn't a benefit to everyone in society; winners *and* losers. Jumbo Supermarkets in the US recently introduced 'slow checkouts' designed for precisely that reason.

Finally, and unsurprisingly bearing in mind there are people in the world who are still bewildered by velcro, there were those customers who just *couldn't* use the technology either because a machine couldn't achieve what they wanted to do or because they just didn't have the mental capacity to use it. This included those customers who, for example, needed to withdraw their last £8.90 but a machine doesn't give you less than £10 or people like my old mate Tom Cross who would have kept his Number 14 bus outside the branch for hours while he struggled to navigate the touch screens of a branch machine. He could barely work his own ticket machine, let alone a multi-functional ATM. The reality is that retail technology just wasn't designed for the vulnerable people in society. We underestimated this in our project, and it's still a barrier today.

Understandably, many colleagues were resisting the changes, too. I remember being in the branch in Darlington when I asked a customer why they'd queued up for 15 minutes at the counter to deposit some money when they could have done it in less than five minutes at the machine. The lovely lady told me she had known Jenny for 25 years and didn't want her to lose her job. 'Oh,' I said, 'what makes you think that would happen?'
'Jenny told me', she replied, making me realise that as well as convincing customers, we would have to work hard to influence colleagues too.

Even though, at times, it felt like senior management believed that it was as simple as just telling them to change, we settled on a much more collaborative approach based on encouraging customers, not forcing them, and focusing on making things as easy as possible. And while you could argue that the switch to the new ways of banking wasn't that complicated, we needed to try various strategies and tactics, as a one-size-fits-all approach wouldn't work. We tested various 'nudges', including using more creative signage and getting colleagues to use different language. We even tried giving names to the machines to make them feel more personal, which worked well for a while until the Daily Mail got hold of it and decided to use it as proof that we were replacing people with machines. Which, of course, is precisely what we *were* doing.

Over the two years that we ran the project, some stuff worked, some didn't, and even though it was occasionally frustrating as we didn't always see the impact, the change continued to happen, albeit slower than some senior people wanted. Today, the number of counter transactions is about 75% less than it was then, albeit the 'encourage not force' approach has now been turned on its head with branch closures, meaning for those customers still trying to hang in there, fewer options remain.

I had done as much as I could and the responsibility for expediting the change in the customers' behaviour was transferred to the branch leaders, meaning that I needed to find myself something new to get excited about.

30
"Cos time is short and life is cruel'

'If we don't get the customer experience right, we'll lose out to our competitors', bellowed Raymond as he paraded up and down the stage like a caged tiger. Even though I was struggling to concentrate through tiredness after getting up at 4:15 am to start the three-and-a-half-hour drive to our annual conference, this time at our technical development campus near Manchester, his words piqued my interest. Raymond had become the senior guy in the UK branch network, so even if I hadn't forgiven him for terminating my career in telephony after only 19 days, I'd have to pretend that I had anyway.

I loved listening to Raymond. He spoke with passion and clarity, his strong Glaswegian accent emphasising the key points. Our dismally poor ranking in the industry customer experience league tables had created our new *burning platform* and now the message was that delivering a memorable customer experience would create a competitive advantage rather than just being a nice thing to do while selling products. I couldn't have agreed more and wanted to be part of the action.

All around the room were the nodding heads of agreement of the 200 or so members of the UK leadership team, showing Raymond how they were all buying into his vision. In truth, they'd be nodding if Raymond had said that we should all dress up as chickens and serve cornflakes in the branches because we always agreed with the boss and the strategy. Fortunately, this strategy was one that I really did agree with. A week later, my direct boss at the time Ivan, a super-intelligent Czech-American guy whose brain was nearly as big as the bridal department in Chatham's branch of Sports Direct, asked whether I'd be interested in running a project to support the focus on improving the customer experience. I nearly bit his arm off.

The bank's previous attempts at driving a better customer experience hadn't, in my opinion, been that great, largely because it had focused on the measure, not the actual experience itself. Like many organisations, customer satisfaction was, and still is, measured by a metric called the Net Promoter Score (NPS), which uses direct customer feedback, via a phone call in the early days or more latterly by an email survey, to find out how they felt about their interaction. Customers would be asked to score between nought-ten against a number of questions, the ultimate one being *'how likely are you to recommend the organisation to a family member or friend?'* A score of nine or ten was classed as a *promoter*, seven or eight was classified as a *passive* customer, and anything less was called a *'detractor'*. Remove the passives from the data, subtract the total scores of the detractors from the total scores of your promoters, and you end up with your overall NPS score. In theory, the higher the score, the better the customer experience was.

This score would be used as a comparator with other organisations at a national level, so it was an important measure. And because it was important, colleagues and local leaders had been incentivised to score well, which is where the problem started, as, now, the score had become more important than the actual experience that the customer received. It was possible, in fact probable at one stage that you could go into a branch and the cashier would be wearing a big badge like one from a small child's birthday card, urging customers to 'Score me 10,'. If you have to use mind games to brainwash customers into believing they had a brilliant experience, you know that something is fundamentally wrong.

I was determined to focus on the right thing, to persuade colleagues to *want* to deliver a brilliant experience to customers. I was allowed to keep my old team and was also given permission to recruit a couple of additional colleagues from the branch network to help. After a couple of interviews, we were lucky to find two brilliant young guys, Sonam and Gopi. Impressive, intelligent people with a fantastic work ethic, too. I interviewed a third guy who I didn't take on as he was, to literally use one of my daughter Rosie's adjectives, a total melt. He wasn't right anyway, clearly chasing a promotion rather than being interested in the job, but he'd put some fake tan on, and as the interview progressed and the room got hotter, his face started to drip. I can ask a tricky question, but I'd never made a candidate literally melt away before.

We got to define both the 'what' and the 'how', and we were fully empowered to be creative, which we needed to be if we were going to develop and implement something which would make a genuine difference to colleagues and customers. Having a blank piece of paper is both exciting and scary and while I don't fully subscribe to the management term 'no idea is a stupid idea' (because clearly, some ideas are stupid, like eating ten Cadbury Cream Eggs in one go or getting the new boy stuck in a lift) if you want to come up with something fresh, something different, it's helpful not to be constrained by how odd the ideas might initially sound. Sometimes, if it ain't broke, break it.

We created a set of 'standards', beneath which a range of behaviours and actions for colleagues was designed to create a memorable experience for our customers and wrapped all this under the 'five star' banner as it was already a recognised measurement of quality and excellence. It wasn't scientific — get the basics right, connect with your customers on a personal level, and find a way of adding some value to them. We'd designed something simple, understandable, that would make sense to our colleagues. Along the way, we'd had some fun, too, and it was one of those occasions when the team just clicked, and great things happened. On a personal level, I'd found a creativity in me that I didn't know existed, or at the very least, hadn't ever felt sufficiently confident to show. My lack of bravery for so many years had potentially quashed any of it and kept me boring. Worse, it had kept me in compliance and risk where, despite the occasional opportunity to try and do things differently, I always knew that any attempt would ultimately be written off as *very nice* but not really what we want.

But then, just as it felt that all was going well and just before breaking up for Christmas in 2015 and as we were getting ready to get the programme out to the branch colleagues, I got an email from Ivan inviting me to a meeting with him and a representative from HR on the first day back in January. Well, here we go again, I thought. I might not have been sent to Coventry this time, but I feared the same outcome.

I was right to have been anxious. I arrived at the designated room on the 30th floor in Canary Wharf and was asked to come in by a grim-faced Jen from HR and sat across the desk from an even more grim-faced Ivan, who proceeded to tell me about the re-structure, the strategic (cost driven) need for it and the regrettable news that as a result my job had disappeared and that again I was officially at risk of being displaced. The good news however, Ivan told me with an almost David Brent-like lack of emotional intelligence, was that while the standard notice period was three months, I was lucky as I was being given five months, enough time for me to complete the Five-star programme.

'Am I supposed to be fucking grateful?' I thought, and to my regret afterward, thought out loud. Ivan shuffled uncomfortably before agreeing with me that I probably didn't need to be grateful and that he understood why I might not be overly delighted about what, in effect, was merely a two-month extension on death row.

On the way home, I stopped off at the bar in Natural Kitchen on the balcony at Waterloo Station, nursed a bottle of Primitivo, and did the maths, which made it clear that at the age of 50 and without access to any pension, the redundancy payment I'd get wouldn't last very long at all. I carried on drinking and woke up the following morning with a red-wine-induced hangover, feeling sorry for myself in more ways than one.

Just because you've been told you're about to lose your job doesn't mean you don't carry on with stuff. That morning, I had a meeting at our Branch in Tottenham Court Road to talk about Five Star with a group of branch colleagues. As usual, I was way earlier than I needed to be and searched for some much-needed caffeine and fat. I emerged from the dark of Leicester Square tube station and into the freezing West End air, head down and focused on finding somewhere suitably warm. As I took a left turn at the top of the steps, I was faced with a guy with an enormous smile, bigger even than Ivan's brain, inviting me to buy a copy of The Big Issue. 'Sorry, mate', I murmured as I headed up Cranbourne Street.

'That's OK, man, have a really great day', he said, genuinely meaning it.

I walked a couple more steps and then stopped in my tracks. 'You son of a bitch' I thought, 'you've done me there', and I turned around and headed back down towards him.

'Hey, here's a couple of quid; I should have bought a copy when I came out. Sorry mate. But let me ask you, how do you stay so positive?'

Wrapped in his scraggy scarf and a woolly hat that barely covered his matted dreadlocks, he smiled at me again and said, 'It's easy, man, life's too short not to be.'

Life's too short. Wow. This guy's life had seemingly, not materially at least, gone that well for whatever reason, yet, he was still able to appreciate what he did have. Now, there's a sense of perspective, especially compared to me sulking about maybe losing my well-paid job. His name was Felix and he gave me a good kick up the arse.

After I'd found somewhere to tuck into some scrambled eggs and coffee, I walked up to the lovely, warm, comfortable branch. The colleague who let me in and who got paid a lovely, warming, comfortable salary at the end of every month didn't smile. In fact, she hardly even acknowledged me. 'Cheer up', I said, 'life's too short.' I wish I'd offered Felix a job; I should have but never did, maybe because I was assuming that I wouldn't have one myself. I only had five months, and the clock was already ticking.

In the meantime, we still needed to get Five Star out to leaders and colleagues. The standard approach would have been to send the material out in a snazzy pack of shiny folders, hand-outs, and 'goodies', instead, we decided that the only way we could get staff to *buy into* this was to create a series of face-to-face events to deliver the message and so we embarked on a national programme of providing three-hour sessions to all branch colleagues, about 150 workshops in total. We toured the country, and between five of us delivered the material to over 2000 staff. It was received well, and despite my impending departure from the organisation, I loved doing it — it was like returning to my training days as I got to muck about, be creative, and occasionally make sense to colleagues.

The head of the London region was a guy called Richard, and the content resonated with him and the subsequent change in colleague behaviour had started to positively impact the customer experience in some of his branches. I ran a few sessions for one of his Area Directors, a guy called Mike who, over a beer after I had completed the last one for his patch, told me that he'd put in a good word for me with Richard and that there was a possibility, with a re-shuffle on the horizon, that there might be a vacancy and that I might be considered. 'I've been out of the branch network for a very long time, Mike,' I said, 'do you really think that I could do it?'

'Of course, you can do it', he said, 'it's a people leadership role, and you get people. All I would say is that if you're offered a job, take anywhere except East London, that's a real shithole.' I thanked him for his support, and for his advice.

A few days later, I received a call from Richard. 'Do you want a job with me?' he asked, confident I'd say yes.

'Where?' I asked.

'East London', he said.

'Shit, really?'

Richard told me that East London was changing, that it was vibrant and cool, and that I would love it. I was delighted that I'd been offered a job on the one hand, on the other, Steve's words about East London were ringing in my ears. 'OK, Richard, thanks so much. May I just think about it and get back to you?' 'What is there to think about, Pannett?' he asked

I didn't know what there was to think about, but, regardless, I managed to buy myself 24 hours.

'Guess what?' I said to Mike when I called him straight afterwards. He laughed but then started to furiously backtrack. 'Well, I know I said it's a shithole, but maybe it's not *that* bad,' he said, unconvincingly.

As I'd promised Richard, that evening I thought about it. East London was a two-hour commute each way from West London. As far as I knew, it *was* a shithole, but the job sounded like an excellent opportunity, regardless of the location. And, I needed a job, not just a brilliant one, or I'd be looking elsewhere for another one reasonably soon. 'Hey boss, I'm up for it,' I told him first thing the following day.

'Cool,' he said, 'I knew you would be. You start Monday week.'

UPDATE: I went into a branch yesterday and the badge is back! There it was, sitting in the cashier's window. 'What's that for?' I asked. '

'Oh, that's in case you get an email asking about the service I gave you today — the answer is 10!'.

Fuck me, really?

31

***'See me walking around I'm the boy about town that you heard of,
see me walking the streets I'm on top of the world that you heard of'***

The Clown Mayor of London announced that he was to campaign for the UK to leave the European Union, and bizarrely, 51.9% of the population ended up agreeing with him. Older people and racists got their own way, forcing David Cameron to resign and Theresa May to succeed him as Prime Minister. London's stock market plunged more than 8% after the EU referendum result, with the pound falling to its lowest level against the dollar since 1985. The Bank of England responded by dropping the base rate to 0.25%, the lowest ever. What a total shit show.

My 'Monday week' came around quickly, and my alarm abruptly woke me at 5 a.m. The first challenge of my new job as Area Director for the shithole that is East London was to get dressed in my new Corporate Uniform. I hadn't worn a suit much over the past few years, Canary Wharf having migrated largely towards smart casual and not just on dress-down Fridays. Richard was a stickler for leaders wearing uniforms, but I absolutely hated it. Considering it had to cater to several thousand people of all shapes and sizes, it wasn't actually that bad, except the material for the suit jacket and trousers was made of a seemingly inflammable material, likely to instantly combust if my fat thighs created too much Maureen-like friction and caused a spark. I wrote it off as a small price to pay for having a job. Fortunately, Richard was a big fan of the brown shoe and so I was able to wear my lovely new, Jeffrey West tan boots without any fear of recrimination; it seemed like it was going to be OK for *me to be me* . . .

I caught the 5:33am train from Hampton that got me to Richmond for 5:45 so that I could then jump on a District line tube for the 24-stop journey to Whitechapel, a place I only really knew of for people being brutally murdered by Jack the Ripper during the nineteenth century and more recently by the Krays. I hoped that it was a bit safer now. Even though it was early, the train got progressively busier for the first 15 stops or so as commuters piled into the carriage but then started slowly emptying out once it hit Westminster, and by the time it had left Aldgate East and Whitechapel was the next stop, it was almost empty. I'd commuted into town and then started going back out, all before 8 a.m.

Two hours after leaving home, I skipped up the stairs at the rear end of the platform and headed for the temporary exit because the Crossrail project was in full flow. I emerged into the bright East London sunshine, and my first thing to negotiate was a one-legged man huddled under an umbrella, begging for cash, food, or anything that he would be able to make use of. I ignored him, instantly felt guilty, and carried on. Life *is* too short, Felix, but for some, it's horribly tough too.

I turned left onto Whitechapel High Street to the clanging sound of scaffold poles being chucked around by the market stall holders as they erected their tarpaulin gazebos ready for a day's trading of vegetables, fish, clothes, and sweets, all very much catering to the predominantly Bangladeshi local community. Like a salmon swimming upstream, I dodged the shoals of commuters coming towards me. I was surprised that so many were 'millennials' and also that so many of them were white. It was the first sign of what I assumed Richard had meant by how East London was changing.

I had an hour to kill and spotted a few tables outside a really cool coffee shop called The Mousetail. I sat on the bench alongside one of them nursing my Cortado, having long since graduated onto 'posh' coffee, and I marvelled at the eclectic mix of characters flowing along the pavement — as well as the 'head down' commuters and the guys still assembling their office for the day, there were schoolchildren of all shapes, sizes, and colours, other homeless men *and* women, some begging, some shouting, others silently shuffling around looking for something of use. Richard was definitely right about it being vibrant. However, I couldn't have felt more conspicuous sitting amongst all of this in my shiny, flammable suit and lovely tan boots as I completed the first hour or so of my East London career.

Eventually, it was time to go to the branch. I ventured further along the Whitechapel Road and stopped at the confusing crossing area outside the famous Blind Beggar pub — famous for The Krays having a pint or two and then (allegedly) shooting someone. I ran across the road, narrowly avoiding being knocked over by a bearded chap in a check shirt on a bike coming at me from what seemed to be the wrong bloody way. Before I'd had the chance to tell him what I thought, he politely pointed out that I was 'jaywalking' on a two-way cycle lane and kindly suggested something about popping into Specsavers.

Knowing that the staff had already completed the early morning entry routine, I rang the front doorbell, and was let in before saying hello to a whole load of people I didn't know yet, and then shown upstairs to my new office, my new home. I had nearly 250 staff in total, spread across 20 branches, so although I was based in Whitechapel, I spent most of my first few weeks visiting the other branches across my 'patch' from Hackney to Walthamstow, from Stratford to East Ham and everything in between, some of the most deprived and challenging parts of the country, not just London.

It became apparent that my new colleagues in East London had a level of resilience and a perspective like I'd never witnessed before. On my second day, I got a call from the branch manager in Dalston to tell me that one of their customers had threatened to 'stab one of the female cashiers in the eye' if she didn't give him his money, which he didn't actually have in his account.

'Fucking hell', I said, 'Is she OK, and what do we do now?'

'Oh, she's fine', said Sal, 'nothing that you need to do; it's pretty normal, and she'll get over it. I just wanted to let you know, that was all.' Whilst I was impressed by his relaxed, almost flippant reaction to what had happened, I was also shocked by how accepting of it he was. There's being resilient, and there's being over-resilient. So, my first 'symbolic' gesture was to clarify that we'd have zero tolerance for any abuse and close the account, of any customer, regardless of how much they were worth to the bank, who didn't behave properly. I would get advised at least three times each week about colleague abuse of some description, and although I know that money is an emotive topic, what kind of world do we live in when this kind of thing happens so frequently? But even when faced with people threatening them, the staff still wanted to give them another chance because some had severe challenges, and we were so important to them in continuing their lives. These really were people who cared about their communities.

I didn't ever reach a point where I thought that the extreme behaviour of some of our so-called customers was acceptable, but, over time, I got used to the patch's edginess, even learning to love it. And, as well as getting to grips with the new role, I was constantly reminded of what a privilege it is to lead people —getting out of bed every morning knowing that you can make a difference, hopefully, a positive one, to many people's lives is a wonderful thing.

I learned so much, too. I learned what people working incredibly hard looked like — being based in still predominantly cash-based communities, all the branches were relentlessly busy from opening time to way past the time they should have closed if there hadn't been a queue of customers out onto the pavement. Brian wouldn't have been able to shut the door bang on time like he used to at Walham Green.

I learned what it is like for colleagues to have respect for others and to be grateful for what they *did* have, not worrying about what they *didn't*, even if they had to work in highly challenging environments. Most branches were run down, cramped, and unloved, yet nobody complained. The gleaming financial head office in Canary Wharf towered paradoxically in the skyline over many of the branches, as a constant reminder of what I'd left behind and the stark difference between that world and the one I was now in. At Canary Wharf, no prostitutes were plying their trade in the car park like they did at Forest Gate branch, there were no junkies leaving their dirty syringes over the floor of the entrance as they did at Newham Branch, and there were no bullet holes in the glass doors like the one at the old Stratford Branch, but at Canary Wharf I *had* seen people get upset because they'd stopped doing Chicken Caesar Wraps in the third-floor restaurant or that the dry cleaners in the basement was closed on a Wednesday. In East London, the guys weren't that entitled or needy and they just got on and did a brilliant job.

I learned that the change Richard had told me about is better known as gentrification, '*the process whereby the character of a poor urban area is changed by wealthier people moving in, improving housing, and attracting new businesses, often displacing current inhabitants.* It's also sometimes described as *the process of making someone or something more refined, polite, or respectable*' and it's been happening in East London for some time and will no doubt continue to do so. The risks are obvious, and I'm not sure I agree with the assumption that it will make anything or anyone more polite or respectable. And so I learned that although East London has its challenges and faults, it isn't a shithole.

I will always be grateful that East London forced me to think differently, to seek to understand diversity in all its various forms and to challenge my embedded behaviours and views. Something as sensitive, and to be honest, outside the comfort zone of many leaders, mainly middle-aged, male, white ones, is a struggle to get right; it's awkward territory to be in, not always because of a lack of best intentions but sometimes for fear of doing or saying the wrong thing.

I saw part of a pathetic, yet typical example of this when working with Trev. Jen from HR was meeting with us to see how we were doing with our plan to drive more diversity and inclusivity in the team. About three minutes before she arrived, Trevor asked me, 'So what exactly are we doing about being more diverse?' I started to worry that this might not go too well. Jen arrived, and Trev and I were waiting for her in his office. I talked about a couple of semi-believable plans around both race and gender equality, and Trev, thankfully, said nothing. I remember a meeting with him early in my Compliance career with a bunch of very Senior people, and I said absolutely nothing for the entire two-hours, and afterwards Trev asked,' So how do you think that went?' I responded with an apology that I hadn't said anything. 'Graham,' he said, 'it's much better to say nothing if you've got nothing to say than talk for the sake of talking and make a total arse of yourself'. Wise words, and thank goodness Trev was now following his own advice.

Jen seemed pleased with our plans and convinced that we were taking the challenge seriously. In an attempt to reinforce our commitment, Trev ushered Jen out of his office and into the main open-plan area. 'Just look around,' he said, genuinely pleased with himself. 'You can see that we have a real mix. For example, there's Manisha' he said, at which point Manisha gave a little wave, 'there's Ali over there', at which point Ali also gave a little embarrassed wave, 'and there's John. He's one, isn't he?' he asked, looking at me. As appalling as this was at the time, the reality is that I essentially laughed it off as a crude but nonetheless harmless incident. Of course, it was far from harmless and was a classic case of missing the point: two white blokes playing at being inclusive, thinking and believing that they were doing the right thing.

But we weren't the only ones. As an organisation, our attempts at being inclusive were barely more than paying lip service and, at times, even worse, a pure tick-box exercise. Unsurprisingly, many corporate diversity programs fail because they become more about looking good and protecting the organisation from reputational risk rather than embracing the benefits of different people of different backgrounds with different thinking. I'm not sure what's worse — pretending to be inclusive to manage that risk or having absolutely no idea what being inclusive means. But regardless, diversity and inclusion isn't an objective and shouldn't be reduced to one. I know that I risk appearing self-righteous, but I learned that you don't need a degree in this stuff to understand that people experience the world differently. Difference is beautiful, and it should be celebrated and used, and those business leaders, who really don't get this whole 'D&I thing' need to check their privilege and bias.

Sadly, even now, after awful events such as the George Floyd tragedy, I still have to question how many leaders really care. It's not about quotas, it's not about applying a lens after a decision, it's about thinking more broadly and not being lazy and it's that lack of seeking to understand that means some of our subconscious or conscious biases will never change — I'm just talking about making a little effort to understand what it means and feels like to be different from you, for better or for worse, which, at the very least, allows you to have a level of empathy, show some kindness, and broaden your perspective. Of course, the first prize would be if we removed all unconscious bias and who knows, we might actually get the right people in the right jobs regardless of anything else. I'm nervous about straying into territory here that I'm not qualified enough to talk about, but for the record, I at least tried, even if I'm embarrassed that it was very late in my career and only because somebody else threw me into an environment that forced me to think more broadly.

32

'We were so close and nothing came between us or the world'

By the time I'd started my second year in East London, the political world was in complete turmoil, primarily driven by the ongoing debacle of Brexit ending with Theresa May resigning and Clown Boris becoming Prime Minister, proving that, indeed, the world had gone completely mad. Predictably, Jimmy Krankee won pretty much every seat in Scotland, but poor old Jeremy Corbyn lost pretty much every one of his. The news broke that the Grand Old Duke of York had been getting himself mixed up in a sex trafficking scandal, not something which I imagine the Queen would have been overjoyed by: 'Andrew, one really is a fucking embarrassing bell-end.'

We achieved some great things. With a bit of focus added to the team's unbelievable energy and stamina, we shifted our NPS significantly to higher than it had ever been, one of the highest in the country, even with the challenges we faced. And we did it 'in the right way' not by gaming it, not by wearing stupid bloody badges, but by genuinely doing the best for our customers. In fact, I think we got close to being five-star. We also managed to get colleagues to take more pride in the brilliant things that they did, mainly by ensuring that everyone was clear about their purpose, how they contributed to the whole, and also, most importantly, by giving them meaning in what they were doing; when team members know they're making a valuable contribution to the world and producing work that positively impacts others they're much more likely to set their own goals and desires aside and focus on the needs and objectives of the wider team.

To help me explain this to colleagues, I used a concept known as 'Jobs To Be Done' and, in our context, specifically what jobs our customers needed to be done, or in other words, what the product we provided them with *did* for them, how it allowed them to do something meaningful in their lives. The most memorable example was in Whitechapel when the branch manager Wajid proudly told me one afternoon that Jaston had 'done a loan' for £25,000. 'That's excellent,' I responded, 'good for him'. I was genuinely pleased for Jaston but also for my own selfish reasons, as a loan of that size would be very helpful in going towards achieving our weekly lending target. 'What was the loan for?'

'Err, not sure,' Wajid said, knowing he should have known. And he should have known because not knowing meant he'd missed the fundamental point of what we were about, our purpose, our meaning.

In this instance, it turned out that the loan was to allow the customer to build an extension to his house to create an extra room for his daughter, currently living in India, to enable her to come and live with him following the death of his ex-wife, her mother. It was a significant, life-changing event, a significant job to be done for this customer, yet we'd reduced it to a loan for £25K, to a sale.

I didn't blame Waj or Jaston for focusing on the outcome for us rather than the customer because they were both ambitious and incentivised to lend money. But in my view, you *can* do well *and* be focused on the customer outcome — that's what being customer-obsessed really is, not what the bank pretended it to be. I've been to too many seminars and conferences where colleagues have been celebrated for smashing their targets, without mentioning how we'd helped our customers along the way. It may sound overly altruistic, but be honest, if your other half or your kids or your mates asked you what you've done today, would you prefer to say a loan for 25K or that you'd helped a father who'd lost his ex-wife to create a new life with his daughter?

It's a simple approach. I'm a massive believer in giving colleagues context, but if employers continue to insist that once their people understand the facts and the logic for change, then they will simply buy into it and act, then they're missing a trick. It's about creating an emotional connection or winning hearts as well as minds that unlocks the discretionary effort that people put into their work, connects their day-to-day efforts with the broader goals of the business, and shows how their action or behaviour has in some small way contributed to the enhancement of someone's life. When we work hard for something we believe in, it's called passion, but when we work hard for something we don't believe in, it's called stress.

Despite the occasional bout of drama with a few of our colleagues, most people were buying into what we were trying to do, and we started to see some excellent results. We had our identity, a purpose, and a focus, and it felt brilliant. I had no desire to go back to the warmth, shininess, and safety of Canary Wharf, with its marble floors, multiple lifts, coffee shops, and whingeing staff. I preferred the buzz of the 'real' world, the edginess, the soul of the shithole, even if I wasn't brave enough to wear my noise-cancelling headphones in case I didn't hear someone coming up behind me in the back streets of Hackney.

My job was made a shed-load easier by having a brilliant group of colleagues, most of whom intuitively cared about others and just wanted to be given the chance to be themselves. And some colleagues were simply incredible. I had a 'deputy' called Mo. She'd been promoted to the role a few months before I arrived and was finding her feet with the demands of her new job and the patch. She was a whirlwind, with infectious boundless energy and enthusiasm, and she knew everything there was to know about how branches worked, which was helpful for me as I knew bloody nothing. We made a good team.

I first met Karen, or 'Knowlesey,' at the East Ham branch on my first visit there. It was as full-on busy as anywhere I'd been before, with demanding, vulnerable customers scattered everywhere. In the middle of this chaos was a blond lady with a massive smile, gliding around and helping what seemed like ten customers at once, all of them following every word she said. It was extraordinary to watch and showed me that even if customers have to wait for a while or might not get the answer to the question that they want, if the person helping them clearly cares so much and is doing everything possible to make their life easier, then most will be happy. And Knowlesey was the best there was at making people happy.

Then there was Jack. To use a football analogy, he was pretty much offered to me 'on a free' as, apparently, things hadn't entirely worked out for him in his previous role. Jack was a good Essex boy in his late twenties and a 'top geezer' and when I first met him, I could immediately tell he was an intelligent lad and had views on how to do a job that I liked. Over the next couple of years, Jack not only directly helped significantly shift the customer experience but also grew as an individual. I loved his unwavering confidence in his ability, which he used to help others, not just himself and I was delighted when he got a promotion, which made a mockery of his previous boss's suggestion that he wasn't good enough.

Working with Jack helped me realise that while others' opinions are helpful, it's more important to make up your own mind about whether somebody is any good guy or not. It also showed me that sometimes you just have to find a way to tune in to your people and if you do, it gives them a real opportunity to flourish.

And then there was Michael; wonderful Michael. Michael was recruited to the bank on a fantastic scheme that gave opportunities to people who suffered from mental health challenges and who otherwise might struggle to get a job, certainly in financial services. He was based at Whitechapel and again, like Knowlesy, in a banking hall as busy as anything you'd ever seen before. His job was to welcome, direct, help, and say goodbye to customers, which he did effortlessly with a smile like no other smile I'd seen before or since —even bigger than Felix's. Unsurprisingly, the customers absolutely loved him, as did all of his colleagues and as did I. Every day, as part of his coping mechanism, he would go into the office next to mine, take some time out, and relax, in peace, on his own. When he'd finished, he'd smile at me and give me the thumbs up to let me know he was OK. But despite his own challenges, on his way to and from work and during his lunch hour, he would stop outside the tube station and sit on the floor next to one of the many homeless guys, give them some food, or just chat with them and make them feel human again, if only for a brief while. Wajid had recruited an extraordinary young man.

I suppose I shouldn't have been that surprised when, just as we were really getting into our natural stride, it was announced that from May 2019, we would be moving to a new organisation structure and that I'd be moving over to the new West London area. On my last day in East London, the sun was shining brightly as it was when I first walked from Whitechapel station to the branch. I smiled as I thought about the irony of Steve's comment from nearly three years ago when he'd said, 'Take anywhere except East London', yet here I was thinking that conversely, I'd rather keep East London than go anywhere else. I passed the queue at the Post Office spilling onto Whitechapel High Street, past the Urban Bar pub outside the Royal London Hospital, full of hipsters drinking their craft beer and ran across Whitechapel High St to avoid the speeding

BMWs, Mercs, and the Number 8 bus, as well as the hi-vis, helmet-clad cyclists still seemingly all going the wrong way. As I dodged my way through the throbbing market for one last time, heading for the tube station, still with its temporary entrance and exit due to the over-running Crossrail project, I realised that I had tears in my eyes because, against all the odds, I was going to miss this place, and these beautiful people, so fucking much. I trudged over the bridge where I first saw the one-legged tramp, where Michael gave so much comfort to so many unfortunate people and I disappeared deep into the underground.

As I waited on the platform and readied myself for my last marathon tube journey back to Richmond, I tried to forget about what I was leaving behind and to look forward to next week. 'It will be cool too,' I tried to convince myself. 'After all, I'll be in West London, my home turf.' Little did I know that not only would it not be cool, but it would also be the last job of my banking career.

Self-assessment: The 'Back In The Game' years

'Leading two national projects allowed me, probably for the first time, to deliver work that potentially has impacted a significant number of colleagues and hopefully customers too. I've been able to think creatively and freely and to work collaboratively with both new internal and external stakeholders which has felt liberating and something that I've found really enjoyable.

Although I understand the rationale, I'm gutted to have to leave East London - I absolutely loved it there and it was a true privilege to work with such a fabulous group of skilled, humble and hard working colleagues. After the best part of 20 years, I didn't ever think that I'd end up back in the branch network but I am so grateful to Richard for giving me that opportunity, which as well as being fun and massively increasing my confidence, has also forced into seeking to understand different cultures and viewpoints; I'm a better person for the experience. I've also learned that sometimes, you need to find out for yourself about things rather than take other people's word and also that you shouldn't cross Whitechapel High Street without looking both ways. I know that it will feel different in my new patch, but it's a real opportunity to take some of the successes from East London and implement them in a new context'

Part 9

The 'Beginning Of The End' years

(2019-2022)

33

'You better listen now you've said your bit'

To make my departure to pastures new even less palatable. Richard announced that he would be leaving to set up a new team, looking after what was known as flexible banking, providing pop-up banking sites in areas with no branches or where we would soon be closing branches, of which there were many. He asked me if I'd go with him on what was ostensibly a three-year project but the defined end date bothered me, so I declined the offer and decided to stay put in West London, but felt good that he'd asked me. I'd actually asked for the South West London Area, but apparently, my new boss misread what I had written on my preference form because my poor handwriting had let me down again. It was a lie though, as I had sent the form by email. Unfortunately, this was just a taste of what was to come.

My sponsor had left, and a new sheriff was in town. Ironically, given the (false) allegation about my inability to write, Robin was a big believer in trust and loyalty, as I found out at one of our first monthly team meetings when, as part of a 'get-to-know-each-other' session, we were each given a flip chart and a range of materials including pens, pipe cleaners, buttons, glue, straws and asked to create something that was an 'accurate representation of you' As it didn't feel appropriate simply to draw an ageing hippy with a BMI beyond advisable limits, I launched into true 'Vision On' mode and made what I thought was an insightful collage of colour and texture, representing both my fun and sensitive side, my search for fairness and also for maintaining perspective; charming and self-righteous, and I was sure that if I *had* sent it to Tony Hart, he would definitely have put it in *The Gallery*. And yes, I know I would never see it again as they *'were unable to return any of your pictures'*, but the sacrifice would have been worth it, and I would have won a prize.

After 20 minutes of arts and crafts, it was time to share our creations with the rest of the team. After I'd explained mine, like everyone else, I got a ripple of polite applause from the group and a less-than-discreet 'tosser' hand gesture from Paul, very much in keeping with our laddish but brilliant relationship. I thought he'd peaked early with the abuse as he'd not yet had his go, but, to be fair to him, his effort reflected his balanced personality — showing his care for people on the one hand and his good old-fashioned corporate 'steel' on the other. It didn't stop me sending him a WhatsApp message calling him a wanker.

The rest of the team shared their efforts, a few of which I thought were pretty sad attempts to try and show the new boss what they thought he wanted to see and hear. Eventually, it was Robin's turn. There was no room for the fluffiness of pipe cleaners in his world, his masterpiece was pure pen and paper, a simple drawing of a circle with a few stick men in it and, alongside the circle, a rectangle with an upside person sticking out of it, legs dangling out the top. 'The circle here is the circle of trust', he explained, 'and I cannot emphasise enough to you all exactly how important trust is to me. I've based my career on trust and loyalty, and it's this that I expect of you, and in return, I'll give it back. The bin', he said, pointing at the rectangle, 'is where people end up if they abuse that trust or don't stay loyal.' The stick man in the bin wasn't wearing tan-coloured Jeffrey West boots, but he might as well have been.

Robin was right in one respect — trust *is* a two-way thing, but not something that happens by demanding it. If leaders want trust from their teams, they need to lead by example; when you openly acknowledge your failures, uncertainties, or weaknesses, then you're signalling trust in your team. This might seem counterintuitive, given that many corporate cultures reward the most self-assured, seemingly flawless individuals with senior roles, however, maintaining an illusion of perfection doesn't encourage your team to trust you. Instead, it encourages your team to feign perfection themselves, eroding trust over time.

As I prepared for my first morning working in West London, I felt less of a fire hazard, having long since confined my flammable Corporate Wear to the local Oxfam shop. I hope it ended up in a good home and I still wonder whether there's a farmer somewhere in Africa dressed as an overweight English banker. At least I didn't need to get dressed in the dark now that my new journey to work was no longer a two-hour hike across London and back out the other side but a ten-minute drive to Walton-on-Thames, a mere four miles in the comfort of my own camper van, my vehicle of choice at the time and incredibly handy to stop and make a cup of coffee if the traffic got too bad. It never did, apart from when some Eco-warriors glued themselves to the M25 when I was en route to Cobham one morning. At least I could have a nap, make some breakfast, and even watch a bit of *Homes under the Hammer* while we all waited for the police to peel them off the tarmac. And Dion really is becoming very knowledgeable about property renovation.

It felt odd that I didn't have to get on a train every day after so long of doing so — commuting is the price many of us must pay to work in London, but it can have a detrimental effect on those who do it over a sustained period. To be classed as a true commuter, specific criteria must be satisfied. The most essential of these is departing before 9:15 a.m. otherwise, you're classed as a shopper, or even worse, if you're on the 9:20 and trying to beat the peak time fare, you're known as a 'Twerly', which is punishable by a feeling of guilt at trying to beat the system, and an excess fare. There's also a minimum qualification period of one year to be allowed to call yourself a commuter, as anything less suggests that you're just on a short-term contract, and that doesn't count.

There are different levels of commuter 'accreditation' (one-three), defined mainly by the frequency and depth of the grumpiness exhibited. The primary behaviour at the basic entry-level (Level One) is tutting in mild frustration at another late train. These commuters are often younger than the average and haven't yet been worn down by relentless train company incompetence over a sustained period of travelling. They will have a higher propensity to carry a folding bicycle and, therefore, also carry a self-righteous smile because they're healthier than most and know they won't have to endure the Jubilee line when they reach Waterloo.

Level Two commuters are more cynical and may even have considered driving to work. They have a generally low level of expectation but still manage to get really frustrated on a regular basis, often heard muttering expletives at the sight of the 'train delayed' narrative on the electronic indicator board. Common behaviours also include agreeing with other Level Two commuters on how crap the service is and occasionally going onto Twitter for a sarcastic rant at the poor hipsters at @SWRHelp.

The ultimate achievement is reaching Level Three status or, as it's also known, 'super-commuter'. Many aspire to achieve this dizzy height but (luckily) fall by the wayside, recognising the signs early enough to seek help and get a local job or even pretend to work from home a few days per week. Regular behaviours of Level Three include:

- Avoiding being seen by friends they would have a beer with at the weekend for fear of having to talk to them during the journey.

- Pretending to be getting off at a station different from the one they actually are, and therefore legitimately having a reason for going to the back of the train, for the same reason as above.
- Jostling for position to stand by their secret 'mark' on the platform so that the doors of the train open right in front of them when it arrives.
- Getting the hump with level One commuters with folding bicycles ('They really should pay extra')
- Shouting 'move down please' in a loud and condescending voice and, in extreme cases, whilst banging on the window
- Pretending to be asleep to avoid giving up their seat to a more deserving passenger.
- Sarcastically offering a set of headphones to some idiot who insists on playing their phone on loudspeaker.
- Asking an 'outsider' to move. An 'outsider' is someone who deliberately sits in an aisle seat, hoping nobody will ask them to move, thus keeping one seat for themselves and one for their bag.

The regular display of these behaviours by people who, at the weekend, are normal and decent shows the true seriousness of the condition, so at least, now, I had been relieved from that burden.

It didn't take me long to realise that the journey time wasn't the only difference between my new world and my old one. Having become used to such a melting pot of demographic backgrounds, the mainly white, mainly female, and primarily 'fifty-something' colleagues were in stark contrast to what I'd been used to. They also seemed to lack energy and harbour a high sense of entitlement, which didn't exist in the *shithole*. Unsurprisingly, the customers were very different too, mainly white, largely middle class, less tolerant, less polite, and simply less pleasant. I was already yearning for the chaos of changing tubes at East Ham station to get to Upton Park rather than the comfort of my van. I was also annoyed that TFL had waited until I had stopped commuting to abolish charges to use public toilets at mainline stations; fantastic news for the current bunch of weak-bladdered commuter drunks, but too late to save me the fortune I'd spent over the years. It did, however, finally end the validity of grandparents confusing small grandchildren by saying. ' I just need to go and spend a penny' as their Nan toddled off for a pee.

Despite quickly becoming nostalgic for what I'd left and trying to take a leaf out of the East London playbook by being grateful for what I had, not what I didn't, the challenges of my new patch reminded me of why leadership is such a privilege because it was within my gift to change things, or at least within my gift to try. I might not be able to change the colleague demographic, but I could try and make people more aware of other people's challenges, and I could try and help people to seek to understand. I might not have been able to change the team's profile, but I could try and get them to be proud of what they did and feel good about doing it. And while it's not for me to judge why people feel like they do, that's their prerogative, I could also try and help them smile more.

To support me, I'd been gifted a deputy who was in a different league from anyone I'd worked alongside before. A mother of two, Michelle had been appointed as part of the re-structure, and although she'd worked in branches before, it was a while ago, and she'd not led people at this scale. But any lack of experience was completely wiped out by her energy, focus, and ability to get things done. She had a machine-like quality that, to some, was intimidating but, to me, was remarkable. Her tough exterior was mere camouflage for the real her, who was as caring as anyone I'd worked with. We quickly 'got' each other, agreed on our respective roles, and planned what to do, playing to our individual strengths wherever possible. We wanted to make our market a force to be reckoned with, a place that people wanted to work in and one where they could be the best they could be and where customers received a brilliant customer experience. Nothing complicated, the same old strategy, but not easy.

We made some progress in the early months, especially with the leadership team, who, for the first time in a while, were given the autonomy to run their own branch as if it were their own franchise. 'You decide the right thing to do, but we're here if you need support or direction'. I think we reached a point where we'd created enough trust for most of the guys to feel safe making their own decisions and mistakes. We also invested a lot of time in trying to engender a culture of collaboration in which every leader looked out, not just for their own people, but for their leadership mates too. We weren't interested in creating internal competition despite it being the norm. We weren't trying to outpace our mates but to outrun the bear, even if that bear had turned into other areas in the region rather than the *actual* competition — when you're being managed in a 'divide and conquer' way, survival becomes the primary driver.

Any feeling of positivity was given a massive jolt when I received a call from Wajid at Whitechapel. He told me that Michael had taken his own life by throwing himself from a building. This beautiful man who had so much to offer the world in so many ways couldn't battle his own demons despite the support he was getting medically, at home, and at work. I sat in a crappy little interview room in Shepherds Bush branch and cried over Michael, not for the last time.

A few weeks later, a memorial service was held in his honour. All of the staff from Whitechapel attended, as did I. Wajid, who had become an excellent mentor to Michael, spoke eloquently, passionately, and stoically about him and about how significant an impact he'd had on all the colleagues and customers that had met him. He spoke of all the good that he did for others, he told of that smile that I have tears in my eyes now thinking about. If anyone needed a sense of perspective, we all got it that day, big time. Mo, Knowlesy, and I spent the afternoon in a pub in Petticoat Lane afterward, drank a lot of rosé, and cried some more.

Months later, a quiz was held in his honour to raise money for his family and mental health charities. It was a difficult evening, and, ironically, I was on a winning quiz team for the first time; I'd rather there hadn't been a quiz at all, so it didn't seem appropriate to run around the pub calling everyone else losers as I collected the £15 beer voucher.

Quizzes and other social events are an important part of work life. It's good to let your hair down occasionally and get to know your colleagues more personally. The big social event of the branch network calendar was the end-of-year awards evening. Despite the title, these were usually held in January as room hire was significantly cheaper, and it made sense to give colleagues something to look forward to in the depression that hits us following Christmas. I was lucky enough to host two awards nights in East London, on each occasion with about 200 staff. They were brilliant fun and being at them made me feel proud to be part of their team. So I was keen that in West London we would use the opportunity to get all the colleagues together to create a sense of fun and a sense of identity.

'Come on guys, let's do something creative and different from the norm,' I said to my direct reports, and Michelle, as was her way when given a challenge, came up trumps. She discovered a place in Wandsworth called Chelsea Beach, which, in the winter, is decked out in a 'Nordic theme' with rug-filled cabins, quirky tables and chairs, different activity areas such as table tennis, a bowling alley, and air hockey, Perfect.

Well, it would have been if more than 70 people had bothered to turn up, and whilst that meant that there was an enormous whip behind the bar, which I took full advantage of, it told me a lot about the team I had inherited. The reasons for non-attendance included 'it was too far to travel', 'it would be too cold', 'I don't like table tennis' and the simple rudeness of just not bothering to turn up. But at least Michelle and I now knew exactly how much work we had to do to galvanise a disparate group of colleagues who either didn't like me, didn't like parties, or, more worryingly, didn't have the passion for being part of something bigger.

A week later, still wondering what I wasn't doing well enough, Rosie and I popped over to New York for a few days. By the time I returned to work the following Monday morning, all hell was breaking loose.

34

'Some people might say my life's in a rut'

All of the senior leaders were invited to a formal 'conference call' at which it was announced that there was going to be a significant organisational restructure and that, as a result, there would be an equally significant reduction in staff at all levels; whilst it wasn't a surprise to any of us, hearing it put so bluntly made it feel very real. But, within a few days, even this news became of secondary importance. When Rosie and I had been in the US, the story had broken about the cruise ship Anthem of the Seas, which had been quarantined in New Jersey due to a potential outbreak of this new thing called the Coronavirus. Now, this had become a UK problem too and by the end of February, we'd seen the first death from what was now being more frequently referred to as COVID-19.

People started to panic and so did the financial markets. The FTSE 100 plunged in its biggest daily drop since the Great Storm, forcing the Bank of England to cut interest rates to 0.1%, the lowest in its 325-year history. Other markets worldwide were similarly affected by ongoing economic turmoil, and everyone started stockpiling toilet rolls and booze as Prime Clown Boris advised against 'non-essential' travel and contact with others. Before long, in a memorable live evening broadcast, he announced a UK-wide lockdown with immediate effect, and I sprinted down to the Hampton Off Licence to stock up on rosé wine. Although we were expecting it, being told we were not allowed out was surreal; it was the first time I'd been told that since Dad stopped me from going to the park in 1972 when he'd caught me riding my Chopper bike with no hands.

As the seriousness of what was now being described as a 'pandemic' dawned on everyone, the reality set in that our safety was almost entirely in the hands of The Clown and the Government, which for as long as we could remember had been in utter chaos. The only person who gave us any hope or comfort that anyone had a clue what the hell was going on was Chris Whitty, the Chief Medical Officer who clearly knew what he was talking about and managed to explain things honestly and in a way which we could understand. Quite rightly, he quickly became a national hero, although that didn't stop two twats from attacking him in St James's Park — there really are some arseholes in the world.

Although I was anxious about the safety of my family, it seemed as though I might be wasting my energy as they appeared far from worried, the thought of *having* to stay at home and sit in the garden in the glorious sunshine not being the worst challenge that they'd ever faced. But Michelle and I had 300 staff that were also sitting at home watching and going through similar emotions, but, unlike my kids, were classified as 'key workers' and therefore still expected to go to work, expected to put themselves out there, in front of the general public, without knowing whether they would catch this mystery disease, which could quite possibly kill them. That was scary for them and, if I'm honest, for us, too, as we would be responsible for leading these guys through this. Our priorities changed literally overnight. Those things that we'd been focusing on yesterday became utterly irrelevant today; forget getting excited about spreadsheets and PowerPoint slides, let's worry about keeping people safe and alive.

There were times throughout the pandemic when the risk to colleagues just felt too high. It was extraordinary that customers still came in to branches to do ridiculously unimportant things. Of course, it's a judgement call about what's essential to any individual, but risking death, yours and other people's, to change a £20 note for two tenners shows some seriously flawed decision-making. I saw too many colleagues with fear in their eyes above their face masks not to know that this was gambling with people's lives. On many occasions, I just wanted to shut up shop and send everyone home to the relative safety of their own homes to be with their families. Conversely, I understood the symbolic importance of keeping as many banks open as possible. Unlike another clown, Mayor Sadiq Khan, who declared that in London the virus was 'out of control', *we* needed to give the public confidence that the world wasn't actually about to end, that while we were severely restricted in what we could do, we would make sure that the wheels of finance didn't stop turning altogether. It was the same as supermarkets, although, to be fair, if they hadn't stayed open, the world may possibly have ended.

As is often the case, a crisis can bring out the best in people, and I will always have the utmost respect for the staff who turned up to their branches day after day, putting their own lives at risk. In most cases, their resilience was extraordinary, and whatever previous view I may have had about their energy or motivation became irrelevant. A few staff didn't join in entirely in the same way — I'm not talking about those colleagues who rightly needed to shield for their own health reasons or for those that they were living with, I'm talking about a handful of colleagues who, before the pandemic, had all the bravado, all the chat, yet as soon as things got a little awkward, they disappeared as quickly as a senior executive from a project going tits-up. Some of the reasons these guys couldn't come to work were impressive if obviously bullshit. But because of the uncertainty of what was happening, it felt right to pretend to believe them, even if, in essence, it was letting them 'get away with it' as some of my peers described it. To a large extent, they were just scared, that was all. And it was OK to be scared; we all were. But those who *did* come in will understandably never completely forget their *mates* who disappeared from the trenches when the actual fighting started.

As well as fear, COVID also created lots of ambiguity. Before, most things in the bank ran in predictable cycles, but now, change was happening almost daily, sometimes intra-day. It was hard work to keep up and often frustrating but strangely exciting too. However, this constant change was stressful for many leaders who'd become so used to and comfortable with routine, with predictability. Now, we all needed to think on our feet, to be agile and adaptable. Now, there wasn't always a right or wrong, a black and white. Now there was grey, which meant we had to use that old-fashioned skill of judgement, which also meant that we might make mistakes. In a healthy culture, making a mistake wouldn't be the end of anyone's world, but we had created something that wasn't entirely healthy — even if senior people would deny that a blame culture existed, it did, meaning that too many people did too many things just because it was the safest option. That's not healthy, whatever the grown-ups might believe.

The fear of making mistakes, or of not doing or saying *the right thing* had also been magnified by the fear of the impending re-structure, even if it had been announced that, rightly, it had been 'put on the back burner for the time-being'. Some of my peers, mindful of losing their jobs once the dust of COVID had settled, didn't let a pandemic get in the way of trying to outrun their mates, rather than the bear, so much so that in a couple of cases I'm sure that they were shaving their legs in order to become more aero-dynamic.

The first full lockdown lasted nearly four months, including over one of the hottest May's on record. Sunshine, 80% pay, takeaways, and rosé wine. We quickly adjusted to our new way of living and we also learned a new vocabulary — *Shielding, social distancing, furloughs, lockdowns, PCRS, lateral flows. Self-*

isolation, 2-meter rule, r-number, contact tracing. Dominic Cummins is a dick, all entered common parlance. I still feel guilty that I preferred parts of living and working in a pandemic to the 'old world', but mostly people were kinder to each other, looked out for each other more and I felt that I was doing more meaningful work with a clear purpose, pace, and creativity. There was no traffic on the roads, and as technology stepped up and created new remote capabilities, I didn't have to go to any monthly Regional meetings and listen to a load of bollocks, I could do that in the comfort of my own bedroom. Even MPs embraced emerging technology and took part in a virtual Prime Minister's Question time via *Zoom* which I can only imagine must have been an absolute mess; a load of old duffers struggling to understand how the camera on their laptop worked, Sir Keir Starmer's dogs barking in the background whilst he's trying to slag off Matt Hancock, who in turn was probably watching something about tractors rather than concentrating on what was being discussed, and Boris pretending that he was losing his signal to avoid answering a question that he clearly didn't know the answer to, conjures up an image of utter carnage.

As working from home and hybrid work patterns became the norm, some of our more traditional leadership beliefs were challenged. For some leaders, their deep-rooted lack of trust in their people came quickly to the fore as they worried that instead of working, all of their teams were admiring Dion Dublin's much improved performances on *Homes Under The Hammer* or the various shades of walnut of David Dickinson in his *Real Deal*. Of course, if we fully trusted our people, we shouldn't have worried; we should have just trusted them to get the job done. But we weren't used to thinking that way because that's not how *we'd* been treated.

As the lockdown rules relaxed, we all relaxed too, unfortunately, too much as September saw a 'second wave' of infections. Before we knew it, we entered into another lockdown, but it was not so sunny in October; people were bored of it all, and the frustration levels started rising. To make matters worse, despite a short-term relaxation of the rules in December, London and then the rest of the country were forced back into staying home again; not a Merry Christmas and not a Happy New Year. There was, however, light at the end of the tunnel — not, as feared by many, Boris Johnson with a torch bringing us more bullshit, but a genuine light in the form of the vaccination roll-out. By February, ten million people, prioritised by 'risk profile' had received 'just a small scratch'. Being over 50 was never so good.

Again, some restrictions eased in time, and we were allowed back into pubs, albeit only in the garden, which would have been fine if it wasn't about three degrees outside; I enjoy a pint as much as the next bloke, but not enough to huddle under a blanket at 9:30 a.m. at my local Wetherspoons. I could be locked indoors for years and still wouldn't want to go to a Wetherspoons — if I wanted to spend time with the homeless and the mentally ill I'd go and work for Shelter.

Restrictions also eased for gyms and hairdressers, two other places I had absolutely no intention of going to.

As we moved into the spring, most things became easier and more relaxed, especially for Matt Hancock, who was forced to publicly apologise for breaking social distancing rules when he's caught by The Sun kissing one of his aides. *Gotcha.* He resigns shortly afterwards and starts instead to dream of being stuck in a jungle for three weeks with even lesser-known celebrities from Emmerdale. Later, it emerged that Mr Johnson himself had not acted entirely in accordance with his own rules amidst allegations of quizzes, parties, even orgies at number ten. Whilst I find the latter slightly amusing, the scandal would ultimately lose him his job, which definitely is amusing; what a tit.

June brought us brighter news when, on the first day of the month, there were 'zero' reported daily deaths from the virus in the UK, the first time since the start of the pandemic. Our national football team also tried to do their bit in the delayed-by-a-year Euro Championships, progressing to the final before losing on penalties to Italy. 31 million people tuned in on TV, the biggest single audience since the funeral of Princess Diana. According to the two blokes sitting nearly two metres in front of me in the pub, losing at football was even more tragic than a kind-hearted national icon being murdered in Paris. You just can't beat football fans for keeping a sense of perspective.

By autumn, the need for stockpiling toilet rolls was a distant memory; instead, we started to panic-buy fuel due to a supply shortage. Petrol stations started running dry, resulting in the good old British tradition of having a punch-up on a forecourt with a complete stranger because you thought they'd pushed in before you. The fuel crisis did cause me some anxiety as shortly before the first lockdown, I'd made the impulsive and, in retrospect, foolish decision to buy a Jeep Wrangler. It was a quirky car, and I liked it a lot, but it only managed to eke out a massive 16 miles per gallon on a good run. I forgot to ask about fuel economy when I was in the showroom, and they forgot to mention it to me, as well as that the car also came with a 'free' new friend — in my case called Shaun, the geezer at my local BP Garage who I became very friendly with when I saw him every couple of days when filling up.

Lateral flow tests also became in short supply, allowing those who didn't want to come to work not to bother and those who had COVID-19 to go to work and spread it to everyone else. 'It's only a cold,' they'd say, as they stood in a 5 x 5 metre office coughing their guts up.

But thankfully, as the year drew to a close, things started returning to what became lovingly known as the 'new normal'. In truth, COVID had stopped all of the progress Michelle and I had made in driving a more collaborative culture — arguably, we'd gone backwards as the branch leaders became far more worried about their own branch and their own people and therefore became more parochial again. It was a small price to pay in the grand scheme of things, but a setback nonetheless. More of a frustration was that the bank's strategy for the new normal became increasingly unclear, other than the increased pace of closing branches, and that wasn't something that I found particularly exciting. In truth I wasn't performing at my best but we didn't really know what performance was. I was becoming increasingly worn drown by the constant feeling of inadequacy and the belief that being creative was futile, even damaging. It felt more and more that I was working in a dysfunctional environment, which, slowly but surely, was breaking my spirit.

35

'Oh and it won't let you go, 'til you finally come to rest and someone picks you up, upstreet downstreet and puts you in the bin'

Getting old is tough. Things that shouldn't get bigger, get bigger, and things that shouldn't get smaller, get smaller. I think I've missed my opportunity to audition, let alone appear on Naked Attraction. (I really do struggle to try and understand what it must feel like if you had a less than impressive performance on that show and someone in the office casually mentions 'I think I saw you on TV last night . . .) Even my computer knows that I'm getting on a bit — I used to get pop-up messages and SPAM emails advising me that a lovely young Russian lady living nearby was very keen to meet me, but now I only get offers on diabetic slippers and stair lifts. The only solace I do get is that it's not just me, although having said that, I struggle to describe the devastation I feel every time I now see my old hero, Ian Botham, appearing in those dreadful TV adverts for a foot massager. He certainly looks 'Beefy', but less like Superman and more like my Uncle Derek after a long day in the office at his accountancy firm. *'Oh, Sir Ian, what happen you, you gone all fucking cwap.'*

Getting old can be tough mentally, too, especially at work, where there's the constant reminder that you've had your best days and that the young bucks are coming to get you. Understandably, the organisation switches its investment from the tired old buggers to those they hope will be around for much longer; it's a sensible philosophy, even if it doesn't always feel very inclusive if you're one of those being ignored. But, like many, as I was reaching the twilight of my career, I wasn't after investment, I was merely looking for some recognition of my situation and, with that, the opportunity to use my strengths built up over many years. I accepted the reality and simply wanted to be led in the same spirit. *Please don't treat me like you treat the high-flying 30-year-old because we bring different things. I'm not going to sell my soul for the business or work an 80-hour week anymore to please you, boss, but I can help you understand how I dealt with the same problem in another context, and I'd be delighted to show you how to make it work this time. That is, of course, if you ever bother to ask me.*

I remember during one of my rare and frankly pointless performance reviews, Robin told me that my age was irrelevant to him; I think he meant well by that, but in truth he'd missed the point — it should have mattered to him, because it mattered to me. Understanding diversity means what it says, and age is a diversifying factor, whether senior leaders, especially younger ones, believe it or not.

But it's not all bad. Although you can't stop getting older, you don't have to get old and so I decided that I wanted to age disgracefully, even if I didn't, and still don't know what that really means. But it does definitely mean being *me*, not what someone else wants me to be. It can be fun, it can be liberating and I saw it as an excuse to get another tattoo. And in addition to being top of most holiday lists, there are benefits to being an old git, including the heightened sense of perspective that comes from age and experience. I caution against an over-reliance on experience as, in a world that is changing so rapidly, simply doing things the way we've always done them, isn't always effective. We may well have 'been there, done that, watched the video, got the T-shirt', but unfortunately, the T-shirt is most likely too small now and even if we have got the video, there's nothing left to play it on. Nonetheless, that 'wisdom' does allow you to react to events in a more measured way, including recognising that sometimes shit just happens — there doesn't have to be a deep-rooted reason why. Although I didn't always react proportionately to certain things, I did learn, eventually, to file things in the right drawer in my brain.

One advantage of being older is the opportunity to be legitimately grumpy, because that's what older people do. Importantly, that doesn't have to be negative, even if it does have a negative connotation, in essence, it's practicing what is more formally called stewardship or seeking to leave the business in a better place than when you took it on. It's also called caring about things and comes back to doing things *in the right way*. It's significant for us crinklies because it provides a valuable level of self-esteem now that we've moved away from the constant need for achievement and advancement. It's *purpose for old gits*.

A large, indeed important part of being an effective steward is *speaking up*. Teams with a *speak-up* culture have greater trust and can adapt better to change and also come up with more innovative solutions to problems. When colleagues speak up, the organisation benefits from their ideas, their concerns, and their disagreements; tension is accepted, and a healthy, inclusive, and respectful culture is created. Unfortunately, in many large organisations, speaking up doesn't happen anywhere near often enough, and whilst I know that challenging the status quo can create conflict and be uncomfortable, we can't find the best ideas or reach the best solutions if we simply agree with each other all the time. And in my world, a post-pandemic world, that was what it felt was happening and it was causing me to get increasingly frustrated.

As a leader, it's our job to help team members learn how to disagree productively, to make them feel psychologically safe, so that the risk of speaking up feels surmountable and worth it. It might not always be easy, but it's not complicated either — be intellectually humble, leave your ego at the door, respect others' viewpoints, and be open to changing your mind when necessary. As Jack Welch said, *'When you were made a leader, you weren't given a crown, you were given the responsibility to get the best out of others.'* And even if you, as the boss, do know everything about everything (which you don't), it might not be a bad idea every now and then to let your people feel as though they have contributed. Even just a little bit.

We were coming out of probably the most significant amount of change any of us had been through in our lives, and the post-COVID *new normal* had given us a fantastic, almost unique opportunity to break old habits, to think differently, to be creative, but instead the spectre of the long-promised re-structure, and with it the possibility of job-losses, meant that culturally we regressed into 1980s dog fighting; survival of the fittest. Rather than people speaking up, letting senior management know what was really going on, too many leaders tried to be know-it-alls, to be the smartest person in the virtual room, continuously looking to outshine everyone else. There were colleagues of mine who not only brought their trainers into the office for a quick getaway from the bear and to leave their mates stranded, there were some who I reckon were shaving their legs too in order to be that extra bit aerodynamic.

A large part of winning that race seemed to become more and more about agreeing with Robin, as, after all, he was the person most likely to be making the decisions about any redundancies. There's nothing wrong with that, other than any challenge disappears, and with it the truth. Worse than removing healthy disagreement, it venerates the need for subordinates to relentlessly agree with everything the boss says, regardless of how nonsensical it might be; actual grown-ups with their own minds, actively agreeing with shit because they're too scared not to. Once it gets out of control, the problem, like all ineffective behaviours, becomes the norm, happens subconsciously, and ends up being the culture.

In the world of 24/7 accessibility, a primary example of how people can easily be turned into sycophants is the compulsion to reply to the boss's emails at ridiculous hours of the day or night and with a response that adds absolutely no value whatsoever other than to allow the team member to virtually jump up in the air and say 'look at me, look at me, I'm over here and aren't I a good boy or girl for being on my emails at this anti-social time'. I used to have a bet with one of my colleagues on who would be first to reply to an email from the boss and at what time. Tom was a fully grown adult with a beard and all sorts of grown-up things, but an email at 8:40 p.m. from the boss would immediately send him into a spin, so I usually had him as evens favourite to reply first. Jane was usually next at 2-1, and Wayne was a solid outside bet at 7-2. If Tom didn't make it first (maybe because he was having his dinner or he had gone to the toilet all on his own), he would rarely reply second, (nobody remembers who came second in anything) preferring instead to wait until 5:30am the following morning to impress us with his early start — sending an email before the sun has come up, just saying 'Thanks' doesn't add much to anyone; if you want to blow smoke up the boss's arse, save the effort and buy a smoke machine — you can get very reasonably priced ones on Amazon for under 15 quid, and they're compact enough to go in a small briefcase or a decent-sized handbag so you can take it to the monthly meeting as well.

But worse than just creating a load of nodding dogs, worse than suppressing finding out the truth of what's going on, in essence it's saying to people 'Your opinion doesn't matter'. When you convince people of that, you effectively stifle the opportunity for people to *be themselves*. It's that bloody hierarchy again and the fear of it biting you on the arse. Ultimately, it comes down to a risk and reward equation, which is why, as I got older, my mortgage got smaller, and my kids a little less reliant on me, I was able to be braver than many of my colleagues. If the stakes are too high for people, and they are genuinely afraid of repercussions in some way, they'll be less likely to take the risk. And I do understand that.

The constraining power of the hierarchy struck me very recently when I was lucky to be invited to a reunion lunch with many of the guys from my first bank. I felt relatively young for the first time in a long time, as most of the people there had started working well before me. But as a stark reminder of my own mortality, it was a sobering start to the proceedings when Geoff, the host, mentioned those colleagues who wouldn't be (or more accurately couldn't be) coming this year. I was devastated to learn that Kevin, my very first mentor, was one of those who wouldn't be tucking into the roasted rack of lamb with a garlic and herb crust. Rest in peace, boss, and thank you for everything.

I was eating, drinking, and talking with people who, back in the day, I had been shit-scared of, even subservient to. Now, when all of the jeopardy had disappeared, their previous importance became irrelevant. There's no hierarchy at a reunion lunch, it's a level playing field and I could now talk to them as just other human beings. It did make me wonder whether I'd allowed the hierarchy, the culture, to be an excuse to behave as I had over the years, or whether it was a real thing that did exist and did control my behaviour. I was chatting with one of my favourite old managers about this at the lunch, and I asked him whether he thought it was real or imagined; he suggested that I was making more of an issue out of it than it actually was. By the time we were tucking into the chocolate pudding, he'd talked about three of his favourite roles, and he described each one in terms of its grade and seniority and how many people he'd been responsible for rather than what he'd achieved or what he'd enjoyed. Maybe it's not just me.

There was another 'guy' at the lunch who, back in the day, had given me a tough time every now and then. Now in his eighties and clearly weak of bladder, I got my revenge by beating him to the toilet every time I saw him starting to head in that direction; I do believe in karma — what goes around does come around old son. He still has a lovely Rolex watch, although I doubt very much that he'll be at 300 metres below the surface very often and need to tell the time

In terms of my stuttering career, I was in good company — my old mate Postman Pat had also suffered from the impact of sudden changes in his structure, mainly when he ended up in the spin-off series *Postman Pat: Special Delivery Service*, in which he is promoted to Head of the SDS and had to embrace emerging technology and to adapt to changing customer demands. Rather than just delivering letters, he now had to deliver almost anything, so he ended up with a new fleet of vehicles, including a bigger van, a gyrocopter, a fuel-guzzling 4x4 Jeep, and a motorbike, all of which must have made his self-assessment tax return very complicated. But, despite the privileges of seniority, he also got a new boss, Ben, who didn't understand him, ignoring that Pat is a highly experienced colleague who has spent many years using his own initiative and making his own decisions, Ben uses a very heavy-handed, direct leadership style, which understandably frustrates Pat and causes his performance to drop. And, after two and a half, largely COVID-filled years in West London, I had reached the point with my 'Ben' where I genuinely believed that the only thing I knew more about than him was my own opinion and my own feelings, although sometimes I wondered whether he was also an expert on those.

In retrospect, I should have made more of an effort to adapt to his style, to tell him that I loved him really and that I wasn't out to get him (which I definitely wasn't). He didn't need to ask for loyalty from me because, to people of my generation, it's implicit. 'If I work for you, I'll be loyal because that's what I'm paid for, and just because we may not agree on everything doesn't mean I'm Brutus and I'm going to stab you in the back'. But before I had the opportunity to dwell too much on what to do about how I felt, my last trip to Oxford Circus had made my decision for me.

So here I was, sitting in a boozer in the West End, alone, angry, and about to be unemployed. After 14881 days, it looked as though my career in banking was finally coming to an end. It was a premature end, in my opinion, but in reality, this time around, my opinion was irrelevant. Eventually, I left the Red Lion and headed off to meet Charlie outside Stamford Bridge for the football. I felt numb, in part because I was about five pints down, but more due to the shock of what had happened only a few hours earlier. Chelsea won four-nil, one of their best performances for many years, but I don't think that I really appreciated or enjoyed it that much. Winning *and* losing

Being displaced this time was a genuine shock and it hurt. I don't think that my ego had taken quite such a battering since an ex-girlfriend had called me a few months after we'd split up and asked whether I could give her the telephone number of my mate who's she'd always fancied. When I had been made 'surplus to requirements' when working for Raymond, it was just unfortunate that I was in a role that was genuinely disappearing and when I had been 'put at risk of displacement' by Ivan, I knew that it was to genuinely reduce costs and that the person who remained in role was an excellent, more experienced and better performing colleague than me but this time, it felt personal — I may well have been the 'most shit Director' that Robin had, but I doubted it then, and I doubt it now. Additionally, Robin told me things 'off the record' (which I won't repeat here), that confirmed to me that the process had not been entirely objective. But I had severely underestimated the impact of my poor relationship with him. My fault, I guess, I could have tried harder to pretend not to have my own opinion.

I could have appealed the decision but I didn't bother because I knew I would be fighting a losing battle, and even if I thought I could win, if I wasn't wanted, what would be the point? At the time, I didn't bother asking for a copy of the assessment exercise done on me as I knew it would have been written through a glass-half-empty lens, intended to make me score below everyone else, to fit the process. When I did ask to see it a few months later (when I was considering taking the bank to an industrial tribunal), I wasn't exactly shocked to find that it was pretty much how I had assumed it would be — it twisted the truth, provided inaccurate evidence, and used examples that I'd been told wouldn't be used because they hadn't been validated. The assessment that I read really did describe the most shit Director *I'd* ever met, but in my opinion, *words and figures differed.* I asked the bank to check the accuracy of what had been said about me, but the HR Director said that he wasn't prepared to, as he 'had to trust the Managing Directors to do the assessment fairly'. Oh well, that'll be the end of that then.

So my departure from the organisation, and indeed 14881 days of banking, could and should have been more amicable and it certainly didn't happen quite how I had anticipated it was going to. I felt as though the bank had tossed me onto the scrap heap and despite me giving them the chance to check their own homework and re-consider, they weren't prepared to. To them, it was merely a neat and convenient way to reduce their headcount; to me, it was the end of my career, almost the end of this story.

On my last day, I was invited to a 'leaving brunch' at Oxford Circus (yeah, 42 years in the industry and they couldn't even stretch to lunch). On my way, I decided to stop off at the Fulham Broadway branch. It seemed appropriate to return (near to, if not the exact site) where it had all began, so many years before. The branch had been closed for a number of weeks for refurbishment and had just re-opened in all it's wonderful new, shiny glory. But there was no reference to Walham Green, now a place consigned further back in history, there was no Tom Cross now that the Number 14 bus had long since become driver-only, there was no peeling wallpaper, just beautifully slick new plaster, and there was no counter for Nora to pull her blind down on or for Brian and me to muck about on, nor was there an enquiries window to stand behind with Daz. There was no back office, no Colin, Alan or Frank and nobody was sorting up any cheques. Nobody was smoking and nobody was eating bacon rolls, besides The Bridge Cafe had been closed down for health and safety reasons about 30 years ago. But, the most noticeable thing, apart from the fact that it was a Friday and that there were hardly any customers, was that nobody was smiling, nobody was laughing, just a couple of seemingly disinterested colleagues standing around, occasionally apologising to customers that they couldn't provide any cash, instead directing them to a new machine that could do everything they needed to. There was no banter, no nothing.

Technology has undoubtedly made modern day banking far easier, faster, safer, more cost-effective, but I couldn't help thinking that it had also lost its soul. I know that it's the price of progress, progress that has to happen, but I do feel sorry that any new entrants to the banking industry won't be given the chance to enjoy what I was super-lucky to enjoy, won't be allowed to laugh like I laughed, won't be able to go out for a pie and a pint like I did; winners *and* losers.

Feeling nostalgic, reflective, and if I'm honest more sad than a man of my age should have been, I headed off to my leaving 'bash'. I'd pondered how to approach this momentous event - should I be passive, accept the gift, and gracefully disappear, or go out with a bang and dress up in a black plastic bag to give the full 'I've been thrown in the bin' effect. In the end, I chose passive, ate my eggs Benedict, spent the afternoon in the pub with a few of my *real* friends, got pissed, got cross, sent Robin an angry parting text, and wandered off into the early spring night, into three months of gardening leave.

On the following Monday morning, there was a LinkedIn post showing the Fulham Broadway branch on its formal opening launch, with proud senior leaders standing next to the new UK Branch CEO who had popped down to cut the proverbial ribbon. Interestingly, nobody important had visited the branch for about the last 3 years, but that didn't matter, this is LinkedIn, so as long as it looked good, that's all that mattered. 'We're super-proud to open our flagship new branch in Fulham Broadway' said the post but I was more impressed that they'd managed to get the staff to force a smile for the photo and I wondered how long, even this shiny new branch would survive in the current climate.

Sitting in my garden for 3 months (literally) allowed me to work on my tan, proving again that even if brown wasn't for town, it was for me. It was weird not having to get up at a stupid time in the morning (even if I did), strange not to spend hours on my laptop looking at data and even more odd that I didn't have to worry about how many accounts we'd opened or how much money we'd lent. I was still angry about the way my career had been ended, but fortunately, didn't spend too long feeling sorry for myself — shit happens and I was more than big enough and ugly enough to know that none of us are indispensable. Ultimately, we're just a number, in my case, 06770797. And despite what those of us who have worked in large organisations for a long time may occasionally think, there is no loyalty, and the world most definitely doesn't owe us a living. And that's fine, right? We live in the moments that we live in, then we do something else and those new moments become our new story. We're rightly forgotten by the organisation before we've even finished getting home on that last night, but so what? Even I had believed that I was important, I certainly wasn't now; I had gone from Graham Pannett, Market Director to (just) Graham Pannett. Regardless of whether or not I had been a role model for some aspiring young bucks, or an experienced bloke that could be helpful for a new project, it was irrelevant now — when the organisation eventually decides, as it did with me, that you're too old, or you're out of date, or your face doesn't fit anymore, then it's gone and when you're popping to the post office on a Tuesday morning, nobody needs a role model, and nobody gives a fuck; what you've achieved at work is irrelevant to the lovely lady in the chemist.

But the memories stay forever, well at least until we can no longer remember them, which in view of my family history of dementia, might not be that long. I'd stumbled into banking in 1981 and was lucky enough to hang in there for 42 years, despite a few 'near misses' along the way. I'd worked hard, mostly, but I'd been lucky along the way too. I was so fortunate to do so many different and varied roles, to learn loads about loads of things, and to get paid for the pleasure on 502 consecutive months. Along the way, I met so many wonderful people, the real heart of my story, the really important part, the really memorable part

Thank you so much to all of those who allowed me to part of their story, that has allowed me to tell mine.

Epilogue

If you've made it this far then I am so grateful to you for giving up your time and hanging in there; I hope you've enjoyed reading some of the stories. I'm conscious that I may have come across as bitter and twisted in some of my reflections, especially towards the end of my career, but truthfully, I'm not bitter at all. I've been fabulously lucky in my working (and personal) life and I honestly wouldn't change it — in hindsight I might have done some things differently, but I have no regrets. I am definitely twisted though, as confirmed by Richard, my Chiropractor, who reminds me twice a week that too many years spent at a desk, often slouched over a screen, isn't good for you.

It's a weird feeling when, in what seems like 'all of a sudden' (even if in reality the process of leaving was painfully protracted - not being allowed to tell anyone that I'd been displaced for the 'time-being' turned out to be 10 weeks), you realise that you aren't actually employed anymore. It hit me the most when on August 23, nothing exciting happened to my bank account, other than a direct debit to The Hampton Spinal Centre reminding me of what remarkable value for money healthcare is these days.

At the time of writing, it's been about 18 months since I left the bank and so work and gardening leave is now a distant memory and I'm well into fully fledged 'not really doing very much'. It's a little scary at times even if, a bit like the Queen passing away, everyone knew it was going to happen one day, but maybe just not quite yet. I told someone the other day that my redundancy was unexpected and they rightly replied 'Really, at your age?' Thanks Mum.

Being unemployed, or simply retired, can have tremendous financial repercussions for you and your family, but in truth, the hardest part is just not feeling like anybody sees value in you; employment is key to a sense of self, determining how you measure your social status and moral worth. Employment has important functions beyond income — it also provides a way to structure our time, provides a sense of purpose, and broadens our social contacts. From this perspective, unemployment not only takes away income, but damages a key organising element of our lives. And I've missed the obvious buzz of being around other people (albeit fortunately I've been able to stay connected with the majority of those that I care about) and also, to an extent, the rhythm and discipline of 'having' to do stuff.

Conversely, I've felt wonderfully unburdened by not being answerable to anybody called 'my boss', other than Mrs P of course who, thankfully, after many years of disappointment, doesn't demand or indeed expect much from me at all. The decisions I make every day are mine, so if I have a good day, it's my fault and if I have a bad day it's my fault too — it's liberating on a very basic level and it has made me somewhat envious of those people who took the brave decision to be self-employed early in their lives.

Strangely, every Friday still has that Friday feeling, Saturdays are still the best day of the week and Sundays have become more enjoyable as I worry less about Mondays! Writing has kept me busy, I've spent a lot of time travelling and I've also got involved with a local music venue which is fun, exciting, and certainly a bit more rock and roll than banking and lawn green bowls. I'm not sure what I'm going to do next, and I doubt that Mr. Neal is still around for any careers advice and I'm certainly not going to make the same mistake of asking Mum for her opinion again, so I'll have to make all my own choices this time. The great thing now is that even if they turn out to be the wrong choices, they'll at least be mine.

I've found the process of reflecting over my lifetime mildly cathartic — the process of reflection has made me think more about why *I am like I am*, especially how much I've been influenced by my dad - he was a talented man who received national awards for both model car-making and photography yet still chose not to use his double-barrelled surname because he believed that using a hyphen was only for people who had 'achieved something' and, in his own opinion, he hadn't. I now realise that his misplaced lack of confidence and bouts of imposter syndrome rubbed off on me far more than I'd previously been aware of.

Finally, although Brown's Not For Town is obviously about me (apart from Barbados, Chelsea FC, The Jam, Pale Ale and Thunderbirds it's the only thing I actually know anything about) I have also tried to share some of the lessons that I've learned over the years, so I hope that a few are of use in some way — it would give me great pleasure to know that even just a few people have benefited from my ramblings in some way. Also, for those of you who have worked in a bank, especially for a few years, it would be lovely to know that reading my book may have brought back some happy memories of your own.

And finally, I do apologise for the swearing. Those who know me will be aware that I do occasionally have a 'potty mouth'; my Mum read an early draft copy of the book whilst we were away in France recently and I winced every time she picked it up. I know it's neither clever nor funny, it's just one of the things that are 'me' and ultimately, that is what I wanted the book to be about — me trying to be me. Perhaps, back in the day, brown may not have been for town, but if you do want to wear brown shoes, or green ones or pink ones, then fucking well wear them. **Be You.**

Acknowledgements

Lisa — thank-you for putting up with me, for being there and for letting me disappear to the pub most days to write;

Jack, Charlie, Rosie and Evie — I love you very much, even if I don't say it very much. This book isn't really about you guys but you're more important to me than anything else, even Chelsea;

Mum — of course, for everything and I don't really blame you for bad career advice;

Dad — you taught me a lot, even if you didn't realise it;

Sue — we had fun, and despite the arguments, I know that you looked after me. And thanks for the proof-reading;

Paul Weller — for giving me a balance during my formative years, for the English 'O' level and for the lyrics for the chapter headings;

Steve The Cheese — for your help and your encouragement to go for it;

Kevin — for giving me that first chance, **Trev** for the fresh start, **Richard** for that last chance;

Turps and Michelle — for keeping me going when things were tough, **Steve** for sticking up for me when I needed it;

Knowlesey, Mo and **Jack** and the **East London team** — for the best three years;

Peter — for understanding me like nobody else has;

Brian — wherever you are, for the pies and the pints,:

Daz — for the fun times, **Dazzer** for the table tennis;

And to all the other great people (you know who you are) that I've been lucky to work with over the years and for letting me be part of *your* story.

References

Introduction: *Come in Smithers old boy, take a seat, take the weight off your feet, I've some news to tell you, there's no longer a position for you. Sorry Smithers Jones'*, The Jam, Smithers-Jones (B.Foxton)

Chapter 1: *Playground kids and creaking swings,* The Jam, A Town Called Malice (P. Weller)

Chapter 2: *Life is timeless days are long when you're young.,* The Jam, When You're Young (P. Weller)

Chapter 3: *And when I lie on my pillow at night, I dream I could fight like David Watts,* The Jam, David Watts (R. Davies)

Chapter 4: *Pin stripe suit, clean shirt and tie, stops off at the corner shop, to buy The Times,* The Jam, Smithers-Jones (B. Foxton)

Chapter 5: *You can't wait to be grown up, acceptance into the capital world,* The Jam, When You're Young (P. Weller)

Chapter 6: *We'll see kidney machines replaced by rockets and guns,* The Jam, Going Underground (P.Weller)

Chapter 7: *Sup up your beer and collect your fags,* The Jam, Eton Rifles (P. Weller)

Chapter 8: *Thick as thieves us, we'll stick together for all time,* The Jam, Thick as Thieves (P. Weller)

Chapter 9: *And I think of what you might have been, a man of such great promise, oh but you forgot the dream,* The Style Council, A Man of Great Promise (P. Weller)

Chapter 10: *Saturday's boys live life with insults, drink lots of beer and wait for half time results,* The Jam, Saturday's Kids (P. Weller)

Chapter 11: *The more we get, the more we lose, when all is more it's more we choose, there's always something else in store,* Paul Weller, The More (P. Weller)

Chapter 12: *The distant echo of faraway voices boarding faraway trains,* The Jam, Down in the Tube Station at Midnight (P. Weller)

Chapter 13: *What chance have you got against a tie and a crest,* The Jam, Eton Rifles (P. Weller)

Chapter 14: *To be someone must be a wonderful thing,* The Jam, To Be Someone (P. Weller)

Chapter 15: *And in my mind I saw the place, as each memory returned to trace, dear reminders of who I am, the very roots upon which I stand,* Uh Huh, Oh yeh, Paul Weller (P. Weller)

Chapter 16: *Anything that you wanna do, anyplace that you wanna go, don't need permission for everything that you want,* The Jam, Art School (P. Weller)

Chapter 17: *Lights going out and a kick in the balls,* The Jam, That's Entertainment (P. Weller)

Chapter 18: *Lights go out and the walls come tumbling down,* The Style Council, Walls Come Tumbling Down (P. Weller)

Chapter 19: *The wine will be flat and the curry's gone cold,* The Jam, Down in the Tube Station at Midnight (P. Weller)

Chapter 20: *Like a perfect stranger, you came into my life, then like the perfect lone ranger, you rode away,* The Jam, Thick as Thieves (P. Weller)

Chapter 21: *And you find out life isn't like that, it's so hard to understand, why the world is your oyster but your future's a clam,* The Jam, When You're Young (P. Weller)

Chapter 22: *Golden rain, will bring you riches, All the good things you deserve and now,* Paul Weller, Wild, Wild Wood (P. Weller)

Chapter 23: *Found myself in a strange town,* The Jam, Strange Town (P. Weller)

Chapter 24: *I don't know what I'm doing here, 'cos it's not my scene at all,* The Jam, A Bomb in Wardour Street (P. Weller)

Chapter 25: *Climbing, forever trying, to find your way out of the wild, wild wood,* Paul Weller, The Wild, Wild Wood (P. Weller)

Chapter 26: *They let you think you're king but you're really a pawn,* The Jam, Strange Town (P. Weller)

Chapter 27: *Stop apologising for the things you've never done,* The Jam, A Town Called Malice (P. Weller)

Chapter 28: *Some people might say that I should strive for more,* The Jam, Going Underground (P. Weller)

Chapter 29: *Daylight turns to moonlight, and I'm at my best,* The Style Council, My Ever Changing Moods (P. Weller)

Chapter 30: *'Cos time is short and life is cruel,* The Jam, A Town Called Malice (P. Weller)

Chapter 31: *See me walking around I'm the boy about town that you heard of, see me walking the streets I'm on top of the world that you heard of,* The Jam, Boy about Town (P. Weller)

Chapter 32: *We were so close and nothing came between us or the world,* The Jam, Thick as Thieves (P. Weller)

Chapter 33: *You better listen now you've said your bit,* The Jam, In the City (P. Weller)

Chapter 34: *Some people might say my life's in a rut,* The Jam, Going Underground (P. Weller)

Chapter 35: *Oh and it won't let you go, 'til you finally come to rest and someone picks you up, upstreet downstreet and puts you in the bin,* The Jam, Boy about Town (P. Weller)

Printed in Great Britain
by Amazon